"Ed Breslin's pleasant and useful book is like his definition of a good speech: "A good speech and a good book, like a bathing suit, should be long en___ *__ *_ _over the subject — and short eno__ __ _ __ __i____i__."

Toro

D0732595

"I found Ed Breslin's material interesting, both in its content and assemblage. His compilation, with its easy to use index, should be a useful tool for any public speaker."

ALEXANDER M. HAIG
Former U.S. Secretary of State

"Your book is indispensable to someone like me who wishes to appear instantly apt, informed, and wise."

DON HARRON
Performer, broadcaster, author

"I enjoyed reading your manuscript immensely. So did several people I showed it to. Your collection will lend a sparkle to anyone about to make a speech or write an article. It's guaranteed to improve your conversation — so much so you'll start wanting to talk to yourself.
"Quote Me" is both entertaining and useful. No politician, writer, or public speaker can afford to be without a copy."

IRVING LAYTON
Poet and Controversialist

"It has been said that men show their characters in nothing more clearly than what they think witty. Ed Breslin will charm you with the nitty gritty of what perhaps keeps us sane. He zeroes in, with flair, on the sages throughout the centuries."

JOHNNY LOMBARDI
President CHIN Radio-TV International

i

ii

"I think 'Quote Me' is terrific...in truth I've already stolen a few quotes and proverbs for speeches I've made since you sent me the manuscript...
I have several more speeches coming up. Please send me the complete book as soon as possible."

DINI PETTY
Host, Dini Petty Show, CFTO-TV

"The manuscript was fun....Turning the pages I encountered many old friends and a panoply of happy new acquaintances."

W. GUNTHER PLAUT
Senior scholar, Holy Blossom Temple

"A unique collection! It's clear that Ed Breslin has put an enormous amount of work into this book. I'm sure a lot of people will enjoy it and find it very useful, too!"

DAVID SCHATZKY
Former CBC host, Metro Morning, Radio Noon shows

"J. Edward Breslin's 'Quote Me!' is admirably researched, with an emphasis on what makes you laugh. A well-indexed reference book, it can be dipped into or read straight through."

SUSAN SMITH
Book Review Producer, Business World

"Need the apt quote, the pertinent quip, the appropriate 'bon mot'? Ed Breslin's compilation of the 'best' has it!"

CHARLES TEMPLETON
Author and Commentator

iv

"QUOTE ME"

HOW TO ADD
WIT AND WISDOM
TO YOUR CONVERSATION

Compiled by
J. Edward Breslin

HOUNSLOW

READ ME FIRST

This book has three purposes

1. To make you a more interesting conversationalist as well as a more entertaining personality by helping you to remember and use clever and colourful "quotes."

2. To present philosophic thoughts the way they were expressed by the great thinkers of the past and the present.

3. To entertain you with wit, humour, picturesque thoughts, and beautiful word images.

How this book is set up

Each entry appears in two columns. In most instances, the actual "quote" appears in the right-hand column with a "lead-in" thought on the left side. See below:

• OLD AGE •

Sign of old age —

▶ *"When you wake up in the morning tired and lustless."*

• ARGUING •

How I didn't win the fight!

▶ *"Thrusting my nose firmly between his teeth, I threw him heavily to the ground on top of me."*

— Mark Twain

> In other instances, a portion of the "quote" appears on the left and the remaining part on the right. See below:

• WORRY •

I've got so many worries that...

▶ *if another problem came up today, I wouldn't have time to worry about it for at least 2 weeks."*

• ANGER •

"I refuse to answer that question on the grounds...

▶ *that it may infuriate me!"*

> In other instances, the left column asks you a question, and the right column provides the answer. See below:

• SPEECHES •

How long should a speech be?

▶ *"A speech, like a bathing suit, should be long enough to cover the subject — and short enough to be interesting."*

• APPEARANCE •

Does your appearance really count?

▶ *"Never judge by appearances but remember that's how people will judge you!"*

> And finally, in other instances, the left column presents an interpretation of the "quote" that appears in the right column. See below:

Plan things so that the part you enjoy most is not at the beginning — but at the end.

▶ *"'Tis the dessert that graces all the feast, for an ill end disparages the rest."*

— William Shakespeare

Lend money to a friend and you'll often lose the friend! Borrow unduly and you'll be a poor conserver of your resources.

▶ *"Neither a borrower nor a lender be; For loan oft loses both itself and friend, And borrowing dulls the edge of husbandry."*

— William Shakespeare

HERE IS WHO CAN USE THIS BOOK

Are you one of the following?

- Are you somebody who every once in a while has to **speak** at a business meeting, a wedding, a birthday party, or an occasion of one kind or another?

- Are you ever called upon to act as a master of ceremonies or **toastmaster**?

- Are you ever asked to write a **product description**, a release for press or promotional purposes, or a marketing analysis?

- Are you employed by a company or are you a member of a business group or professional association and called upon to **fine-tune** your ideas and expressions?

- Are you often stuck for the **opening** — or **closing** — line of a presentation or address?

- Are you a person who likes beautiful **word images**?

- Are you an **attorney** or **trial lawyer** in need of a famous person's quotation to strengthen an otherwise flat case?

- Are you someone with a reasonably good I.Q., who never has the time to read books, who would like to appear **well-read**?

- Are you a **teacher** or **instructor** who now and then feels the need to pep up a presentation?

- Are you someone who can deliver a **sermon** but who needs some verbal fireworks to help keep the audience listening?

- Are you poor at telling stories and jokes and yet want to appear **witty** at times?

- Are you in danger of losing your side of the **argument** or discussion unless you can quote a high-profile source who shares your view?

- Are you a non-sparkling conversationalist who would like to add sparkle and lustre to your **conversation**?

Whoever you are, this book will help you!

HOW TO USE THIS BOOK

For those who want an easy way
to memorize selected quotes.

**Follow these guidelines
and you'll be able to recall a surprising number of "quotes"
for use in everyday conversation.**

1. First read the words in the left-hand column.

2. Visualize the situation or idea that these words convey.

3. Then read the related **quote** appearing in the right-hand column.

4. The best way to remember a **quote** is to fix an **association** between the idea or situation on the left side with that of the **quote** on the right side.

5. Any time you want to test yourself, cover up the right side. Read only the left side to see if you can recollect the **Quote**.

Repetition will be the key to remembering.

ACKNOWLEDGEMENTS

I with to thank Hannah, my lovely wife, for permitting me to ignore her for countless hours over an eternity of time. Thanks also to our four "kids", Stephen, Perry, Cindy and Blake — their spouses and their kids — for acting as sounding-boards in the selection of entries.

Thanks to Jerome Breslin who originally typeset the entire handwritten manuscript. Thanks to Lynda Wilson and the staff at Graphics 'R Us Inc. for guiding the book so beautifully through all stages of production.

Thanks to Gerard Williams for his aesthetic taste in designing the covers, and for collaborating with the layout of pages and the selection of type face, to John Robert Colombo whose help and guidance throughout was invaluable, and to Tony Hawke who published the book.

Thanks to the French aphorist Michel de Montaigne for composing one of my favourite quotations:

"I gather the flowers by the wayside, by the brooks and in the meadows, and only the string with which I bind them together is my own."

Finally, let me offer thanks to all those creative giants whose gems appear within the covers of this book.

J. Edward Breslin
Toronto, Ontario, Canada
1990

Dedicated to
The Memory of my Father and Mother
Hyman and Sarah Pearl Breslin
With Gratitude

"Quote Me"

How to Add Wit and Wisdom to Your Conversation

Copyright© 1990 by J. Edward Breslin

All Rights Reserved.

ISBN 0-88882-128-X

Publisher: Anthony Hawke
Designer: Gerard Williams
Compositor: Graphics 'R Us Inc.
Printer: Gagné Printing Ltd.

Hounslow Press
A Division of Anthony R. Hawke Limited
124 Parkview Avenue
Willowdale, Ontario, Canada
M2N 3Y5

Printed and bound in Canada

CONTENTS

PREFACE

How this book compares with all other books of quotations

Although there are many collections of quotations in libraries and book-stores, this is a book of quotations with a difference. **In fact, it's the first book of its kind.** It resembles no other collection anywhere in the world in its presentation of quotations and proverbs. Two factors make it different.

1. The two-column format.
2. The brevity of the entries.

This is not a formal scholarly work. It's geared to conversational use. It was put together with a sense of rhythm, surprise and animation. But here's where the **big difference** lies between this book and all previous books of its type.

People turn to the standard "quote books" for literary, academic or reference purposes — rarely for pleasure and personal use alone. The average interest-span is too short-lived. And as for other types of books in this category, they're jammed with an over-abundance of heavy reading, lengthy verse, and often inane and boring banalities.

But in a book like this one, with its two-column format, after you read the left-hand side, your curiosity compels you to read the completion of the idea on the right-hand side. **Reading thus becomes sheer pleasure.**

Open the book at any page and you'll find a juxtaposition of deep, philosophic expressions of thought alongside light, flippant one-liners. My aim is to induce you to pick up the book for diversion — for browsing. This is not the kind of book to read in a single sitting or in a series of single sittings. It's the kind of book you open from time to time and each time you find something new in it, something entertaining. As well, you'll find remarks that you can put to use to enrich your own life.

Compared with the standard reference book of quotations, this book has a three-way appeal:

1. It's a storehouse of aphorisms and proverbial expressions.

2. It has practical use in conversation, in writing, and especially in speech-making.

3. It offers sheer reading pleasure and stimulation of the intellect.

In praise of reading a book of quotations

"The study of proverbs may be more instructive and comprehensive than the most elaborate scheme of philosophy."
— *William Motherwell*

"The wisdom of the wise and the experience of the ages are perpetuated by quotations."
— *Benjamin Disraeli*

"It is a good thing for an uneducated man to read books of quotations."
— *Winston Churchill*

"When a thing has been said and said well, have no scruple. Take it and copy it."
— *Anatole France*

"I quote others only the better to express myself."
— *Michel de Montaigne*

What this book is not

Caution! This book is **not** intended to be a "study book." It's intended for **entertainment** and **pleasure** and **self-improvement**. For those readers who may wish to memorize selected entries, the two-column format is a unique and simple aid for memorization.

What this book is

This is essentially a **book of ideas**. As a tool, it's interesting to compare it with *Roget's Thesaurus*. It too is a tool. Writers generally develop ideas and then consult a thesaurus only to seek out the right single word or words to embellish their ideas.

But in a book of quotations, like this one, no thesaurus or mental gymnastics are required. Both the idea and the embellishment are already formed within the quotation itself, clothed in "the best words and in the best order."

Somerset Maugham said, "Money is the sixth sense without which you can't enjoy the other five."

But for exquisite and enduring delights of the mind, you don't need money! To have one's mind stored with many melodious expressions of the high thoughts, wit and beautiful imagery — **that too is wealth!**

The accuracy of "who said that?"

Is it possible to trace all original sources of quotations? No, it is not. But since the essence of a quotation is its thought, only a limited number of thought categories exist in life. And it's these very same thoughts that have occurred over and over to so many different minds throughout history.

But remember, writers who convey thoughts are always copying and borrowing from each other. And they knowingly ignore the common suspicion that "originality is undetected plagiarism." But perhaps that's not always a sin. This thought comes from James Russell Lowell and gives solace:

> *"though old the thought and oft expressed,*
> *'Tis his at last who says it best."*

Throughout the book, many entries omit the name of the author. I either did not know the name or was not sure of the accuracy of the ascription. Some entries are my own rewrites of others. Many are of my own composition. However, I intentionally omitted to credit them to myself. I do not claim their authorship because minds more erudite than my own might challenge some of my authorship!

(Nonetheless, to prove how brilliant and witty I am — some of the contents of this book have to rub off onto its compiler and onto its readers too! — I shall claim the authorship of two only **lonely quotations** in the book. I'll leave the conscientious reader the task of finding the two by-lines that read "J. Edward Breslin.")

What to do if you don't know "who said it?"

At one time or another, everybody has read or heard a good quote but failed to write it down. Later, when you go to retrieve it, you remember neither the line nor the author, and it's gone forever. My advice is start copying those quotes when you hear them!

But if you do remember it and want to use it — and you don't remember the name of the author — **here's a little trick** you can use. Just say, "Aristotle said that." Everybody will be impressed and few people will know the difference!

Entries come from people in all walks of life: journalists, authors, the theatre, the world of business, radio and television, historians, the movies, teachers, scientists, military leaders, statesmen and philosophers.

What about subjects and headings?

There are few abstract headings in this book. I prefer to avoid them. Often a **popular phrase** is the only really accurate way of conveying what is meant to be said.

For instance, I prefer the crisp heading of **Shut Up!** to the abstract heading of **Silence**. It is more fun to read and probably easier to find. Likewise, I opted for colloquial phrases like the following: **The Easy Way, How to Go, Live Now, Get Lost, Maybe, Your Mouth, Making Notes** and **So Ugly**. That explains some of the **unorthodox** headings in this book.

How this book evolved

Over the years, in my reading I came upon many philosophical and witty quotations that stimulated me and gave me much pleasure. My problem was simple: "How could I, with an average memory, recall even a handful of them for use in everyday conversation?" I set myself the task of devising systems that would assist me in recalling a few of them. I hit upon **four techniques**.

My first technique — was the idea of **dividing** the quotation into two parts and setting down each part in one of two adjacent columns.

My second technique — was to pose a **question** on the left-hand side of the page and to supply the **answer** on the right-hand side, using the entire quotation as the "answer."

My third technique — was to set down a **situation** or an **idea** on the left side and to provide the appropriate quotation as a response on the right side.

Finally, my fourth technique — was to enter on the left side a **translation** in everyday language of the deep or philosophical thought that appeared on the right side.

I found, upon reading the very same quotations again but this time arranged in the two-column format, that my enjoyment was greatly enhanced. It then occurred to me that people like myself who love quotations would share my enjoyment if I collected enough quotations for a full-length book arranged along these lines. Hence *"Quote Me"* It took me five years to bring everything together.

The ease and reward of writing a book

It's very easy to write a book. It really is! "The actor Michael Caine, playing the part of a writer in the movie *The Romantic Englishwoman*, says, *"I've found all the words in the dictionary; now all I have to do is put them in the right order."*

It requires some degree of persistence and a not small amount of perspiration. But what a pleasure it is when the job is done!

It's a distinct pleasure for me because, although I have a degree in Commerce and Finance, I feel I would like to have spent less time in the world of manufacturing and marketing and more in the world of ideas. From the age of thirteen, when my English teacher introduced me to the beautiful language of William Shakespeare's play *The Merchant of Venice*, I have loved words! This love like a flame has glowed for a long time. This book is being completed by the author in his eighty-first year! Such is the power of words and ideas.

The last word

The last word is really seven words in length. But what a profound effect these seven words can have on a person!

The words in question were spoken in Ancient Greece — by Socrates — but they are as valid today as they were more than two thousand years ago.

The words are:

"The unexamined life is not worth living."

J. Edward Breslin
Toronto, Ontario, Canada
1990

"QUOTE ME"

"Thinking is like living and dying.
Each of us must do it for himself."

—Josiah Royce

A

• ABILITY •

How many men made it!

▶ *"I got where I am through sheer ability (spelled i-n-h-e-r-i-t-a-n-c-e)."*
— Malcolm S. Forbes

The ability that others will appreciate in you.

▶ *"The greatest ability is dependability."*
— Curt Bergwall

Do I owe my advanced creative ability to all the creative geniuses who preceded me?

▶ *"If I have been able to see farther than others, it was because I stood on the shoulders of giants."*
— Sir Isaac Newton

Can you or can't you?

▶ *"The man who says I can't is usually right about it."*

The test of real ability.

▶ *"There is something that is much more scarce, something rarer than ability. It is the ability to recognize ability."*
— Robert Half

What is more important than knowing what things you have the ability to do?

▶ *"Sometimes it is more important to discover what one cannot do, than what one can do."*
— Lin Yutang

• ABORTION •

Observation about abortion.

▶ *"Have you ever observed that those in favour of abortion have already been born!"*

• ABSENCE •

What effect does absence make?

▶ *"Absence makes the heart go yonder."*

— Robert Byrne

• ABSENT-MINDED •

"He's so absent-minded that his mind and body...

▶ *rarely keep company with one another!"*

"You're so absent-minded. You're like...

▶ *the man searching for the horse he's riding."*

"He's so absent-minded. He's like...

▶ *the porcupine that backed into the cactus and said: 'Is that you, Mama'"?*

• ABSTAINING •

Definition of an "Abstainer" and what an abstainer doesn't abstain from.

▶ *"An abstainer is a weak person who yields to the temptation of denying a pleasure. A total abstainer is one who abstains from everything but abstention, and especially from inactivity in the affairs of others."*

— Ambrose Bierce

• ABSURDITY •

Definiton of "Absurdity" and its relationship to your own opinion.

▶ *"Absurdity is a statement or belief manifestly inconsistent with one's own opinion."*

— Ambrose Bierce

• ACCIDENTS •

Why unnecessary accidents happen.

▶ *"Constant exposure to dangers will breed contempt for them."*

— Seneca

Most accidents are symptoms of lack of caution!

▶ *"If you are going to thrust your hand among thorns, wear a leather glove."*

• ACCUMULATING •

Is it time to stop accumulating things?

▶ *"Everything you collect means just another thing for you to keep clean."*

• ACCUSATIONS! •

There's no accusation, no matter how false, that does not leave a blemish.

▶ *"Even doubtful accusations leave a stain behind them."*

• ACHIEVEMENT •

So you think you've got something going for you as an achiever.

▶ *"You can lead a horse to water, but if you can make him lie on his back and float, then you've really got something going!"*

In the world there are only two tragedies. What are they in relation to your wants?

▶ *"One is not to get your heart's desire. The other is to get it."*

— George Bernard Shaw

"When you catch what you're after...

▶ *it's gone!"*

— Malcolm S. Forbes

Underachievers have little right to resent those who achieve!

▶ *"Underachievers are not born, they are made."*

— Arthur Weider

• ACQUAINTANCES •

Definition of an
Acquaintance —

▸ *"Acquaintance, n: a person whom we know well enough to borrow from, but not well enough to lend to."*

— Ambrose Bierce

Why everybody needs two kinds of acquaintances.

▸ *"We need two kinds of acquaintances, one to complain to, while we boast to the others."*

— Logan Smith

• ACT NOW! •

"I must do something will always solve more problems than...

▸ *something must be done!"*

"When you want to do something, act first and ask later!

▸ *It's often easier to apologize than get permission."*

• ACTING! •

What's the key thing in acting?

▸ *"The key thing in acting is honesty. Once you know how to fake that, you've got it made!"*

The esteem in which some movie directors hold actors.

▸ *"I never said all actors are cattle, what I said was all actors should be treated like cattle."*

— Alfred Hitchcock

What effect on an audience represents the test of a good actor?

▸ *"Acting consists of the ability to keep an audience from coughing."*

— Jean-Louis Barrault

Do Academy Awards really determine the best actor?

▸ *Humphrey Bogart, who won an Oscar for his appearance in "The African Queen": "This doesn't prove I'm the best actor of the year. The only honest way to determine that would be for everybody to play Hamlet, and let the best man win."*

"The most magical moment in the theater is a silence so complete that ...

▶ *you can't even hear people breathe. It means that you've got them!"*

— Hume Cronyn

The credo of the consummate actor.

▶ *"Ask not what the role can do for you. Ask what you can do for the role!"*

How actors should react to applause.

▶ *"My advice to you concerning applause is this: enjoy it but never quite believe it."*

— Robert Montgomery

"I'm a great actor! When my director asks me to cry, I think of my Sex Life.

▶ *When he asks me to laugh, I think of my Sex Life."*

— George Burns

Is the world full of nothing but phony actors?

▶ *"All the world's a stage. And all the men and women merely players."*

— William Shakespeare

• THE ACTION! •

If you want the right kind of action, go where the right kind of action is!

▶ *When Willie Sutton, one-time bank robber, was asked why he robbed banks, he replied: "I rob banks because that's where the money is."*

• ADMIRATION •

What is "Admiration" and what do we look for in others to command this esteem?

▶ *"Admiration is our polite recognition of another's resemblance to ourselves."*

— Ambrose Bierce

"Admiration is a very short-lived passion, that immediately decays upon...

▶ *growing familiar with its object."*

— Joseph Addison

The difference between Loving and Admiring.

▶ *"To Love is to admire with the heart. To Admire is to love with the mind."*

— Théophile Gautier

• TAKING ADVANTAGE! •

He'll take advantage of you every time!

▶ *"He's the kind of guy that goes through a revolving door on your push!"*

How America took the land away from the Indians.

▶ *"We stole it fair and square."*

• ADVERSITY •

Does adversity strengthen the strong and weaken the weak?

▶ *"Hammering hardens steel but crumbles putty."*

Does an ill wind ever blow any good?

▶ *"It's an ill wind that shows no pretty knees!"*

Is anybody ever without a share of adversity?

▶ *"Thy fate is the common fate of all; Into each life some rain must fall."*
— Henry Wadsworth Longfellow

• ADVERTISING •

"Without advertising a terrible thing happens ...

▶ *nothing!"*

In favour of advertising.

▶ *"Nothing except the Mint can make money without advertising."*
— Thomas B. Macaulay

When should the business world advertise?

▶ *"When business is good it pays to advertise; when business is bad you've got to advertise."*

Advertising advice to shoe stores!

▶ *"To women, don't sell shoes — sell lovely feet!"*

How much should we allow advertisers to exaggerate?

▶ *"No one can deny that much of our modern advertising is essentially dishonest. The practical question is, how much lying for private profit is to be permitted by law?"*
— Carl Becker

No matter how
reasonably truthful an
"advertisement" is —
the customer too must
exercise responsibility!

▶ *"The simple believeth
every word:
But the prudent man
looketh well to his
going."*

Does advertising improve the
quality of products?

▶ *"Let advertisers spend the same
amount of money improving their
product that they do on advertising
and they wouldn't have to advertise
it."*

— Will Rogers

Advertising should appeal to
the customer's reason, instinct
and sentiment. It should give
facts proving the use, quality,
or superiority of the article
offered.

▶ *"Ignorance of the purpose of an
alarm clock makes it uesless to African
aborigines, except as an ornament."*

"The function of the
advertising industry is...

▶ *to make somebody think he needs
something that very possibly he
doesn't need, or to make him think one
version of something is better than
another version when the grounds for
such a belief really don't exist."*

— Marvin E. Frankel

Does advertising sell things to
people they don't need?

▶ *"Those who say advertising sells
people things they don't need remind
us of the saleman who once sold two
hats to a man with only one head."*

How T.V. commercials
would re-write
"Mary had a little
lamb."

▶ *"Mary had a little
lamb.
Its fleece was
enzyme white!"*

"The more facts you tell, the
more you sell.

▶ *An advertisement's chance for
success invariably increases as the
number of pertinent merchandise facts
included in the advertisement
increases."*

— Charles Edwards

"Doing business without advertising is like winking at a girl in the dark.

▶ *You know what you are doing but nobody else does."*

— Ed Howe

The seemingly impossible challenge to make an ordinary product seem extraordinary.

▶ *"No saleable product is so devoid of merit that by intelligent presentation it cannot be favourably distinguished from competitive products."*

— John L. Love

How advertising built William Wrigley an empire.

▶ *"Tell 'em quick and tell 'em often. Explain to folks plainly and sincerely what you have to sell. Keep everlastingly coming at them. Advertising and selling is pretty much like shovelling a furnace. Once you stop stoking, the fire goes out."*

— Wm. Wrigley Jr.

"When writing ads, the shorter the headline...

▶ *the longer it stays in somebody's head."*

— Tom Allen

Help wanted ad —

▶ *"Man to assemble nuclear fissionable isotopes, molecular reactivity counters, and three-phase cyclotronic uranium photosynthesizers. No experience necessary."*

What legal privilege is advertising given?

▶ *"Advertising is legalized lying."*

— H. G. Wells

"When someone stops advertising someone stops buying.

▶ *Less buying equals less selling. Less selling equals less making things. Less making equals less earning. When someone stops earning someone stops buying."*

— Edwin H. Stuart

• ADVICE •

When Ted Turner of Turner Broadcasting was asked — "What advice would you give your children?" he replied...

▶ *"Early to bed Early to rise Work like hell And advertise"!*

Advice on how to give advice!

▶ *"Whatever advice you give, be short!"*

— Horace

"Keep five yards from a carriage, ten yards from a horse, and a hundred yards from an elephant.

▶ *But the distance one should keep from a wicked man cannot be measured."*

— Indian proverb

"Don't run too far.

▶ *You will have to return the same distance."*

If you want to make people "throw up", tell them how happy you are!

▶ *"I can sympathize with people's pains, but not with their pleasures. There is something curiously boring about somebody else's happiness."*

— Margaret Hungerford

It takes one real scare to make you realize you should have listened to the good advice in the first place!

▶ *"A good scare is worth more to a man than good advice."*

To what extent do people in need of advice appreciate getting advice?

▶ *"Advice is seldom welcome; and those who want it the most always like it the least."*

"One of the lessons of history is...

▶ *that nothing is often a good thing to do and always a clever thing to say."*

"Never take any advice...

▶ *including this!"*

Caution when baiting a mouse-trap with cheese!

▶ *"Always leave room for the mouse!"*

— H. H Munro

Advice on how to await the outcome.

▶ *"Hope for the best. Prepare for the worst!"*

What kind of advice should you give people?

▶ *"When a man comes to me for advice I find out the kind of advice he wants — and I give it to him."*

— Josh Billings

"He who is always his own counsellor...

▶ *will often have a fool for his client."*

"Don't be too sweet, lest you be eaten up.

▶ *Don't be too bitter, lest you be spewed out!"*

— Jewish proverb

Is "Be Yourself" good advice?

▶ *"Be Yourself is the worst advice you can give to some people."*

— Tom Masson

"Minimize your triumphs ...

▶ *and your failures"!*

If someone gives you so-called good advice what should you do?

▶ *"Do the opposite; you can be sure it will be the right thing nine out of ten times!"*

— Anselm Feuerbach

"He who can take advice is sometimes superior to...

▶ *him who can give it."*

— Karl von Knebel

"A word of advice.

▶ *Don't give it"!*

Is "a word to the wise" sufficient?

▶ *"A word to the wise is not sufficient if it doesn't make sense."*

— James Thurber

Better straighten out your thinking or you'll be going nowhere!

▶ *"He who goes around in circles will not become a big wheel!"*

Don't cut your nose to spite your face!

▶ *"Heat not a furnace for your foe so hot that it do singe yourself."*

— William Shakespeare

Don't throw mud!

▶ *"He who slings mud, loses ground."*

"Seeking advice is...

▶ *what we ask when we seek approbation."*

"If you can tell the difference between good advice and bad advice...

▶ *you don't need advice."*

— Laurence J. Peter

Lay off too much advice to your friend!

▶ *"Friendship will not stand the strain of very much good advice for very long."*

— Robert Lynd

Some good advice!

▶ *"Get good advice!"*
— William Safire

When there's nothing you can do about an unsolveable problem.

▶ *"Swallow three times and then throw up!"*

Never give advice!

▶ *"Wise men don't need it. Fools won't heed it."*

"Left alone, things go from ...

▶ *bad to worse."*

• OLD AGE •

Three signs of old age.

▶ *"One is the loss of memory and I can't remember the other two!"*

Can anybody truly say old age is a desirable or enviable thing?

▶ *"Whatever poet, orator or sage may say of it, old age is still old age."*
— Sinclair Lewis

"He has reached the Age of Metal...

▶ *Silver in his hair. Gold in his teeth, and Lead in his Arse!"*

Relationship of restaurant food to old age.

▶ *"Old age is the period when men pay more attention to their food than they do to the waitress."*

Blessed are you who are kind to the aged and remember that —

▶ *"My ears strain to hear. My wits are slow. I spill food. I repeat my stories. And I breathe happiness when you visit."*

Formula for loss of memory in Old Age "ICR = FI".

▶ *I have discovered the secret formula for a carefree Old Age: ICR = FI — "If You Can't Recall It, Forget It."*
— Goodman Ace

"You know you're getting older when...

▶ *'scoring' has only to do with shuffleboard."*

Sign of old age —

▶ *"When you wake up in the morning tired and lustless."*

A man's reaction when he's told that he's an old man.

▶ *"A person is always startled when he hears himself seriously called an old man for the first time."*

— Oliver Wendell Holmes

How come so many people my age look so old?

▶ *"Of late I appear*
To have reached that stage
When people look old
Who are only my age."

— Richard Armour

A method by which we could all be younger.

▶ *"I'm sixty-five and I guess that puts me in with the geriatrics, but if there were fifteen months in every year, I'd only be forty-eight."*

— James Thurber

Making fun of yourself when you're approaching old age.

▶ *"I am in the prime of senility."*

— Joel Chandler Harris

Lament of an Octogenarian.

▶ *"If I don't die soon there will be nobody left to go to my funeral!"*

Maybe old age isn't as bad as it sounds!

▶ *"After all, as you lose your marbles, you don't know that you haven't still got a full complement."*

How old do you have to be for me to feel you've reached old age?

▶ *"To me, old age is always fifteen years older than I am."*

— Bernard Baruch

Casey Stengel on reaching age seventy!

▶ *"I'll never make the mistake of bein' seventy again!"*

— Casey Stengel

What makes a grandfather feel old?

▶ *"Grandchildren don't make a man feel old; it's the knowledge that he's married to a grandmother."*

— G. Norman Collie

Don't complain if fate allows you to join a minority!

▶ "Old Age is one minority who with luck we join."

He's so old...

▶ he knew the Dead Sea when it was sick!"

Is age a time of life?

▶ "Youth — or age — is not a time of life. It is a state of mind!"
— Samuel Ullman

Should you resent growing old?

▶ "Do not resent growing old — many are denied the privilege."

One good thing about getting older —

▶ "All the people you could have married now look like the one you married!"

Why worry about getting older?

▶ "When we stop getting older, we're dead."
— Burton Hillis

Why should you consider old age not so bad?

▶ "Old age is not so bad when you consider the alternatives."
— Maurice Chevalier

"She's so old...

▶ she counts in Roman numerals."

Upon what does age depend?

▶ "Age does not depend upon years, but upon temperament and health. Some men are born old, and some never grow so."
— Tryon Edwards

"Age is a matter of the mind.

▶ If you don't mind it doesn't matter!"

Is 70 years of age really old?

▶ "To be 70 years young is sometimes more cheerful than to be 40 years old!"
— Oliver Wendell Holmes

How old age affects your zipper!

▶ "First you forget names, then you forget faces, then you forget to pull your zipper up, then you forget to pull your zipper down."
— Leo Rosenberg

How to live to a ripe old age!

▶ *"If you drink a glass of water every day for 1,200 months, you will live to be a centenarian."*

How to tell you're getting old.

▶ *"Whenever a man's friends begin to compliment him about looking young he may be sure that they think he is growing old."*
— Washington Irving

Bob Hope at age 75 and the stage makeup his age required.

▶ *"My makeup kit weighs more than I do. My makeup man has to be flown in from Lourdes."*

To someone who can't believe his age.

▶ *"It takes about 10 years to get used to how old you are."*

How people up in years should interpret a compliment about their looks.

▶ *"You've heard of the three ages of man: youth, middle age, and 'you're looking wonderful'"!*
— Francis Joseph, Cardinal Spellman

A reminder to show empathy for the aged.

▶ *"I'm growing fonder of my staff;*
I'm growing dimmer in the eyes;
I'm growing fainter in my laugh;
I'm growing deeper in my sighs;
I'm growing careless of my dress;
I'm growing frugal of my gold;
I'm growing wise; I'm growing,
— yes —
I'm growing old."
— Marshal de Saxe

Be tolerant of the slow gait of the elderly!

▶ *"To a weary horse even his own tail is a burden."*
— Czech proverb

"He's at the age now...

▶ *that when a girl says NO, he says THANKS."*

"The only thing I don't like about old age is...

▶ *when you feel like the morning after the night before — and you haven't even been anywhere."*

• MIDDLE AGE •

Middle Age and a good time.

▶ *"Middle age is that period in a man's life when he'd rather not have a good time than have to get over it."*

Does life begin after age 40?

▶ *"He is living proof that life doesn't begin after 40!"*

Middle Age's hardest decision.

▶ *"The hardest decision in life: When to start middle age."*

"People who say you're just as old as you feel are all wrong ...

▶ *fortunately"!*

What's bad about middle age?

▶ *"The knowledge that you'll soon outgrow it!"*

"Middle age is...

▶ *when your wife tells you to pull in your stomach and you already have."*

— Jack Barry

One of the chief pleasures of middle age in terms of marriage is what?

▶ *"It is looking at the picture of the girl you didn't marry."*

• AGE (YOUTH) •

Socrates on Youth

▶ *"Our youth now loves luxury. They have bad manners, contempt for authority, disrespect for older people. Children nowadays are tyrants. They no longer rise when their elders enter the room. They contradict their parents, chatter before company, gobble their food, and tyrannize their teachers."*

— Socrates (429 B.C.)

Peter the Hermit on Youth.

▶ *"The world is passing through troubled times. The young people of today think of nothing but themselves. They have no reverence for parents or old people. They are impatient of all restraint. They talk as if they alone know anything, and what passes for wisdom with us is foolishness with them. As for girls, they are forward, immodest and unwomanly in speech, behaviour and dress."*

— Peter the Hermit (1247 A.D.)

The difference between young people and old people.

▶ *"Beautiful young people are accidents of nature. Beautiful old people are works of art."*

— Marjorie Barstow Greenbie

The dreams of youth are day dreams. The dreams of middle age are reality.

▶ *"The youth gets together his materials to build a bridge to the moon...and at length, the middle-aged man concludes to build a woodshed with them."*

— Henry David Thoreau

Youth lacks knowledge. Old age lacks strength.

▶ *"If youth but knew, if old age but could."*

— Henri Estienne

Will reason work with teenagers?

▶ *"There's nothing wrong with teenagers that reasoning with them won't aggravate."*

"Age and youth look upon life from the opposite ends of the telescope.

▶ *It is exceedingly long, — it is exceedingly short."*

— Henry Ward Beecher

Do the young ever achieve the impossible?

▶ *"The young do not know enough to be prudent and therefore they attempt the impossible — and achieve it generation after generation."*

— Pearl S. Buck

At what stage of life is Adolescence?

▶ *"The stage between puberty and adultery."*

I was too young to know what I ▶ *"My salad days.*
was doing. Those were — *When I was green in judgment."*
— William Shakespeare

Advice if you are ▶ *"Always give her the*
ever in doubt as to *benefit of the doubt."*
whether or not you — Thomas Carlyle
should kiss a pretty girl.

How the young and the old ▶ *"In youth the days are short and the*
differ in their reaction to the *years are long; in old age the years are*
passing of time. *short and the days long."*

A young person assumes ▶ *"Don't laugh at a youth for his*
affectations until he finds his *affectations; he's only trying on one*
own identity. *face after another till he finds his own."*
— Logan Pearsall Smith

At age 14, I rated my father ▶ *"When I was a boy of fourteen, my*
uninformed. At age 21 I found *father was so ignorant I could hardly*
him savvy. How come? *stand to have the old man around. But*
when I got to be twenty-one, I was
astonished at how much the old man
had learned in seven years."
— Mark Twain

Do youth's radical attitudes of ▶ *"Every generation revolts against its*
their present generation *fathers and makes friends with its*
generally swing back to the *grandfathers."*
patterns of the preceding — Lewis Mumford
generation?

"Youth would be more ▶ *it came later in life!"*
interesting if...

• THE AGNOSTIC •

Why many reasoning people ▶ *"Reason is the enemy of faith."*
are agnostic.
— Martin Luther

"The only thing an agnostic is ▶ *that he doesn't know."*
sure of is...

"The agnostic's prayer...

▶ *O God, if there is a god, save my soul, if I have a soul."*

— Ernest Renan

Why Charles Darwin was an agnostic.

▶ *"The mystery of the beginning of all things is insoluble by us; and I for one must be content to remain an agnostic."*

— Charles Darwin

Why Clarence Darrow was an agnostic.

▶ *"I am an agnostic. I do not pretend to know what many ignorant men are sure of."*

— Clarence Darrow

• BEING AGREEABLE •

"When you say that you agree to a thing in principle, you mean...

▶ *you have not the slightest intention of carrying it out."*

— Otto von Bismarck

Definition of an "Agreeable Person" —

▶ *"One who agrees with me."*

• ALIBIS! •

Don't give me that phony alibi!

▶ *"It's a poor workman who blames his tools!"*

"It takes less time to do a thing right than...

▶ *to explain why you did it wrong."*

— Henry Wadsworth Longfellow

• ALIMONY •

How to avoid alimony —

▶ *"Stay married or stay single!"*

Alimony and its effect on your living.

▶ *"Alimony is the high cost of leaving!"*

• MAKE ALLOWANCES! •

A memorable lesson to remember when you ask someone to do something that you find easy to do.

▶ *"If, in instructing a child, you are vexed with it for want of adroitness, try, if you have never tried before, to write with your left hand, and then remember that a child is all left hand."*

— J. F. Boyes

• ALLURING •

If a woman wants to be most alluring — hold out longer!

▶ *"She most attracts who longest can refuse."*

— Aaron Hill

• AMBASSADORS •

What an ambassador so often really is.

▶ *"An ambassador is an honest man, sent to lie abroad for the good of his country."*

— Sir Henry Wotton

• AMBIDEXTROUS •

An artful dodger's definition of "Ambidextrous" —

▶ *"Being ambidextrous is being able to pick with equal skill a right-hand pocket or a left."*

— Ambrose Bierce

• AMBITION •

"Ambition is...

▶ *the germ of achievement!"*

If Love were competing with Ambition, which would win?

▶ *"If love and ambition should be in equal balance, and come to jostle with equal force, I make no doubt but that the last would win the prize."*

— Michel de Montaigne

People who have ambition recognize the validity of the aphorism —

▶ *"What was, was; what is, is; what is to be will be what we make it."*

The secret impetus to ambition.

▶ *"Few enterprises of great labor or hazard would be undertaken if we had not the power of magnifying the advantages we expect from them."*
— Samuel Johnson

Why you should reach high.

▶ *"It keeps you on your toes!"*

• ANALYZING •

If it's working OK — stop analyzing it so much!

▶ *To the centipede!: "How do you coordinate all those legs?"*
"I never thought of it before" — as he left the room stumbling all over himself.

"Why is it that when you go to a meeting ...

▶ *an empty chair is the hardest thing to find empty?"*

• ANATOMY •

How anatomy looks —

▶ *"Always better on a girl!"*

Which part of your body creates most problems?

▶ *"Of all the organs in the human body the tongue is by far the most dangerous!"*
— Rabbi Heschel

• YOUR ANCESTORS •

Should people assume grandness because of illustrious ancestors?

▶ *"It is indeed a desirable thing to be well descended, but the glory belongs to our ancestors."*
— Plutarch

Do we endow our ancestors with more wisdom than they merit?

▶ *"Of all the authorities to which men can be called to submit, the wisdom of our ancestors is the most whimsically absurd."*
— Jeremy Taylor

"The man who has not anything to boast of but his illustrious ancestors is like a potato...

▶ *the only good belonging to him is underground."*
— Sir Thomas Overbury

• ANGER •

How to behave when you're angry or very angry!

▶ *"When angry, count four; when very angry, swear."*
— Mark Twain

"I refuse to answer that question on the grounds...

▶ *that it may infuriate me!"*

Control your temper!

▶ *"ANGER is one letter away from DANGER."*

How to handle your anger when you're going to write a letter.

▶ *"Never answer a letter while you are angry."*
— Chinese proverb

When he gets mad, he doesn't know if he's coming or going!

▶ *"He's like the bottom part of a double boiler — gets all worked up but doesn't know what's cooking."*

When you're angry, blow your top! Keeping anger inside only kindles it.

▶ *"Anger as soon as fed is dead — 'Tis starving makes it fat."*
— Emily Dickinson

Under what circumstances should you avoid giving or taking advice?

▶ *"Anger is a bad counselor."*
— French proverb

The greatest remedy for anger is —

▶ *"Delay!"*
— Seneca

What should you do when you get mad?

▶ *"Don't get mad, get even."*
— Robert F. Kennedy

When to pacify or not to pacify.

▶ *"Never try to pacify someone at the height of his rage!"*

Should you argue when you're angry?

▶ *"Speak when you're angry and you'll make the best speech you'll ever regret!"*

• ANGUISH AND ANXIETY •

Many many people submerge their anguish in silence.

▶ *"I do believe there is many a tear in the heart that never reaches the eyes."*
— Norman MacEwan

Anxiety uses tomorrow's storms with what negative result?

▸ *"To cloud today's sunshine."*

• THE ANIMAL WORLD •

Hooray to those people who protect our furry animal friends!

▸ *"Real people wear fake fur!"*

What's the trick of wearing a mink coat as against a cloth coat?

▸ *"The trick of wearing mink is to look as though you were wearing a cloth coat. The trick of wearing a cloth coat is to look as though you were wearing mink."*
— Pierre Balmain

Maxim of Animal Rights Conservationists —

▸ *"It takes 40 dumb animals to make a fur coat and only one to wear it."*

As the rabbit said —

▸ *"I don't care what people say — I can't multiply."*

How drinking and love making differentiate us from animals.

▸ *"We drink without thirst, and we make love any time, madame. Only this distinguishes us from the other animals."*
— Beaumarchais

Animals don't "pop pills" — and thereby differ from man.

▸ *"The desire to take medicine is perhaps the greatest feature which distinguishes man from animals."*
— William Osler

The way to stop a charging elephant —

▸ *"Take away his credit card!"*

Pun about the female deer and the male deer.

▸ *"A female deer was chasing a male deer. But it was actually a Doe trying to make a fast Buck!"*

"You can lead a horse to drink...

▸ *but you can't make him water!"*

Sign at zoo —

▶ *"You're now looking at the most dangerous animal in the world. Not only does it exterminate entire species — but it now has the power to wipe out all forms of life on earth."*
(The sign was posted on top of a mirror.)

What's the dumbest animal at the zoo?

▶ *"Of all the animals at the zoo, The one most curious is you."*

In defense of mink and all other furry animals.

▶ *"No one in this world needs a mink coat but a mink."*

Getting even!

▶ *"It cost me never a stab nor squirm*
To tread by chance upon a worm.
'Aha, my little dear' I say,
'Your clan will pay me back one day.'"

— Dorothy Parker

The profound but loveable difference between a cat and a dog.

▶ *"Dogs come when they're called; cats take a message and get back to you."*

• ANNOYING! •

Are you trying to annoy me?

▶ *"You certainly are trying. Very trying!"*

What to say after you've really annoyed somebody.

▶ *"Just be glad I'm not twins!"*

When somebody bugs you.

▶ *"I wish I were a frog. They can eat whatever bugs them."*

• ABOUT ANTS •

"If ants are so busy...

▶ *how come they have time to go on so many picnics?"*

As one ant said to the other —

▶ *"We can't go on like this. For you life is just one big picnic!"*

• ANTIQUES •

Sign in an antique shop —

▶ *"There will be a charge of 50¢ if I have to listen to what your mother had."*

• APATHY •

"The No. 1 problem in our country is apathy.

▶ *But who cares!"*

• APHRODISIACS •

"One of the most effective aphrodisiacs is...

▶ *prolonged abstinence!"*

• APOLOGIZE! •

Too many defend an error to their detriment.

▶ *"An error gracefully acknowledged is a victory won.*
— Caroline L. Gascoigne

The best way to handle an error.

▶ *"Admitting Error clears the Score And proves you Wiser than before."*
— Arthur Guiterman

Should you explain or apologize?

▶ *"An apology is better than an explanation — and quicker!"*
— William Feather

To merely apologize doesn't heal the damage done.

▶ *"To unstring the bow is not to heal the wound."*
— French proverb

When a husband or a wife is stubborn remember!

▶ *"An ounce of apology is worth a pound of loneliness."*

• APPEARANCE •

Be on guard against a seemingly empathetic appearance!

▶ *"Under that warm exterior often beats a heart of stone."*

Does your appearance really count?

▶ "Never judge by appearances but remember that's how people will judge you!"

From what two sources comes good appearance and to what degree?

▶ "Three-tenths of a good appearance are due to nature; seven-tenths to dress.

— Chinese proverb

Life is a constant evolution of of new schools of art, literature and fashion. Which of the three schools is a man of eighty most witness to?

▶ "A man of eighty has outlived probably three new schools of painting, two of architecture and poetry, and a hundred in dress."

— Joyce Carey

Never ever forget the "Iceberg Theorem".

▶ "7/8 of everything can't be seen!"

Opportunities aren't always as remote as they appear.

▶ "The greenest grass is under your feet!"

Don't under estimate him merely because of a quiet manner and soft voice.

▶ "Smooth runs the water where the brook is deep."

— William Shakespeare

"If the eye were so acute as to rival the finest microscope, and to discern the smallest hair upon the leg of a gnat, it would be a curse, and not a blessing to us.

▶ It would make all things appear rugged and deformed; the most finely polished crystal would be uneven and rough; the sight of our own selves would affright us; the smoothest skin would be beset all over with rugged scales and bristly hair."

— Richard Bentley

Appearances are deceptive.

▶ "Never mistake good tailoring for intelligence!"

Do people judge by appearance or reality?

▶ "Men in general judge more from appearance than from reality. All men have eyes, but few have the gift of penetration."

— Niccolò Machiavelli

How to become better looking.

▶ "A smile is an inexpensive way to improve your looks."

"Far off fields look green!"   ▶ " 'Tis distance lends enchantment
to the view."

— Thomas Campbell

• APPEASERS •

"An appeaser is one who   ▶ hoping it will eat him last."
feeds a crocodile ...

— Winston Churchill

• APPRECIATION •

How to appreciate all that you   ▶ "Just think how happy you would be if
possess.   you lost everything you have right
now, and then it got back again."

— Frances Rodman

There's no appreciation if it's   ▶ "They grumble the most who see the
free.   show on free passes."

"The deepest principle of.   ▶ the craving to be appreciated."
Human Nature is ...

— William James

"The most difficult thing in   ▶ until we lose it."
the world is to appreciate what
we have ...

Are things that come too   ▶ "What we obtain too cheaply, we
easily appreciated to the full?   esteem too lightly; it is dearness only
that gives everything its value."

— Thomas Paine

• APTITUDES •

Do experts ever make   ▶ "Ruth made a big mistake when he
mistakes in judging aptitudes?   gave up pitching."

— Tris Speaker

Vocational adviser's advice to   ▶ "Your vocational aptitude test
a student after an aptitude test!   indicates that your best opportunities
lie in a field where your father holds an
influential position."

• ARCHITECTURE •

How architecture should relate to nature.

▶ *"Good architecture lets nature in."*

— I.M. Pei

Definition of Architecture —

▶ *"Architecture in general is frozen music."*

— Friedrich von Schelling

Mies van der Rohe was the originator of rectangular high rise building architecture, free of ornament. (1920-1930)

▶ *Rohe's philosophy —*
"Less is More."
Today's new philosophy —
"Less is a bore."

— Robert Venturi

• ARDOUR •

Does ardour and passion wane too fast?

▶ *"Men are April when they woo, December when they wed."*

— William Shakespeare

• ARGUING •

What to say to appease an argument between a husband and wife.

▶ *"The only time husband and wife see eye to eye is when they're the same height!"*

How to bring delight into an argument.

▶ *"The sweetest words of pen or song*
Are these
You are right and I was wrong."

How do you fare when you argue with an ignorant person?

▶ *"It is impossible to defeat an ignorant man in argument."*

— William G. McAdoo

Should a high IQ argue with a fool?

▶ *"There is no sense in having an argument with a man so stupid he doesn't know you have the better of him."*

— John Raper

How I didn't win the fight!

▶ *"Thrusting my nose firmly between his teeth, I threw him heavily to the ground on top of me."*

— Mark Twain

What lack of ability causes ▶ *"People generally quarrel because*
people to quarrel? *they cannot argue."*

— Gilbert K. Chesterton

When husband and wife have ▶ *"When you see a married couple*
an argument, how do you know *coming down the street, the one who is*
which one is madder than the *two or three steps ahead is the one*
other? *that's mad."*

— Helen Rowland

Interposing to settle a quarrel. ▶ *"Those who in quarrels interpose,*
Should you? *Must often wipe a bloody nose!"*

— John Gay

When I argue, how come I ▶ *"I always get the better when I argue*
forget to say all those clever *alone."*
things?

— Oliver Goldsmith

Do the most savage ▶ *"The most savage controversies are*
controversies concern matters *those about matters as to which there*
that can be proven? *is no good evidence either way."*

— Bertrand Russell

"There are two sides to every ▶ *until you take one."*
argument...

— Laurence J. Peter

Against what opponent is it ▶ *"Silence is one of the hardest things to*
toughest to win an argument? *refute."*

— Josh Billings

"If you don't agree with me... ▶ *it means you haven't been listening."*

"If you want to argue... ▶ *join a debating society!"*

"There's only one thing worse ▶ *and that's the man who will argue over*
than the man who will argue *nothing."*
over anything...

Will arguing ever really ▶ *"No matter how right you are, no*
persuade? *matter how wrong the other fellow is,*
no matter how much evidence you
have to prove it, you will never get him
to agree with you by arguing him
down."

"Discussion is an exchange of knowledge."
What is argument?

▶ *"Argument is an exchange of ignorance."*

— Robert Quillen

With whom should you not argue?

▶ *"I never make the mistake of arguing with people for whose opinions I have no respect."*

— Edward Gibbon

"There are three sides to every question.

▶ *Your side.*
My side.
And the facts!"

How not to handle a customer —

▶ *"Win the argument and lose the customer!"*

Don't always win the argument!

▶ *"If I can prove I'm right, I make things worse."*

— Henry Close

How to argue so that you win more often.

▶ *"A soft answer turneth away wrath. But grievous words stir up anger."*

— Book of Proverbs

"A quarrel is like a crack in a pail.

▶ *It widens all the time!"*

— Talmud

"Be reasonable.

▶ *Do it my way!"*

When the argument has no solution!

▶ *"Myself when young did eagerly frequent Doctor and Saint, and heard great argument About it and about; but evermore Came out by the same door wherein I went."*

—Omar Khayyám

It's tough to win an argument with people who ignore facts.

▶ *"Facts do not cease to exist because they are ignored."*

— Aldous Huxley

To say "You're wrong" — won't win the argument.

▶ *"Assertion is not argument; to contradict the statement of an opponent is not proof that you are correct."*

— Samuel Johnson

How to make an enemy during a discussion.	▶ *"If you wish to make a man your enemy, tell him simply, 'You are wrong.' This method works every time."*
	— Henry C. Link

• THE ARMY •

The role you're expected to fill when you're in the army.	▶ *"Theirs not to make reply, Theirs not to reason why, Theirs but to do and die."*
	— Alfred Lord Tennyson

Army Axiom —	▶ *"An order that can be misunderstood will be!"*

• AROMA •

Does the nose smell an aroma or hear it?	▶ *"An aroma is a whisper heard by the nose!"*

• ARTIFICIALITY •

"As artificial as...	▶ *studio laughter."*

• THE ARTS •

The difference between a Painter and an Artist!	▶ *"A Painter is a man who paints what sells. An Artist is a man who sells what he paints!"*
	— Pablo Picasso

Where should you go to hear ridiculous opinions about art?	▶ *"A painting in a museum hears more ridiculous opinions than anything else in the world."*
	— Edmond de Goncourt

Does new untried art innovation generally meet with resistance?	▶ *"Most modern art is rubbish — but so was most classical art, for that matter.*
	— Elmer Rice

What most effective role should an "Art Model" fill for an art student?

▶ *"The duty of an art model is to try to closely resemble the work of the art student!"*

Which part of his body does an artist paint with?

▶ *"A man paints with his brains and not with his hands."*
— Michelangelo

Very few people know what abstract art really is all about!

▶ *"Abstract Art: A product of the untalented, sold by the unprincipled to the utterly bewildered."*
— Al Capp

Which form of art excels all others?

▶ *"Of all those arts in which the wise excel, Nature's chief masterpiece is writing well."*
— John Sheffield

"A picture painted by Audubon is worth...

▶ *a thousand birds!"*

How to be an artist —

▶ *"Take the palette from the box, squeeze some paint on it from the tubes, dip your brush into the paint and daub the canvas with it."* Rembrandt, Titian and all other great painters used this method.

"A man who works with his hands is a laborer. A man who works with his hands and his brain is a craftsman.

▶ *But a man who works with his hands and his brain and his heart is an artist."*

• ASK! •

"To know the road ahead...

▶ *ask those coming back!"*
— Chinese proverb

"Better ask twice than...

▶ *go wrong once!"*
— German proverb

You'll never find out if you don't ask.

▶ *"The fool wonders, the wise man asks.* ·
— Benjamin Disraeli

"Don't hesitate to ask me for anything...

▶ *for my way of refusing is very polite!"*

The effect of a critic
on a pretentious art snob.

▶ *"A snob is anybody who
thinks a childish daub
of paint is great because
a critic says it is!"*

Don't be so timid.
Ask!

▶ *"Why and how are words so
important that they cannot be
too often used."*

— Napoleon

Know how to ask.

▶ *There is nothing more difficult for some
people, nor for others, easier."*

— Baltasar Gracian

• ASTROLOGY •

If you believe in astrology —
imagine how you might have
been a different you!

▶ *"If you had been born two days later,
you would have been kind, generous
and witty."*

"99.5% know their
astrological sign but...

▶ *most don't know their blood type!"*

• ASTRONOMY •

"This is like astronomy.

▶ *It's way over my head!"*

• ATHEISM •

What's the worst moment for
an atheist?

▶ *"The worst moment for the atheist is
is when he is really thankful and has
nobody to thank."*

— Dante Gabriel Rossetti

"I used to be an atheist. But
I gave it up.

▶ *They don't have any holidays!"*

— Bob Hope

The atheism of George
Santayana.

▶ *"My atheism, like that of Spinoza, is
true piety towards the universe and
denies only gods fashioned by men in
their own image, to be servants of their
human interests."*

— George Santayana

Is intolerance of other's religions a major cause of world strife?

▶ *"The equal toleration of all religions is the same thing as atheism."*

— Pope Leo XIII

Voltaire, an atheist, rebelled against ecclesiastic tyranny.

▶ *The man who says to me, "Believe as I do or God will damn you," will presently say to me, "Believe as I do or I will kill you."*

— Voltaire

"I am an atheist...

▶ *thank God!"*

How an atheist believes he evolved.

▶ *"An atheist is a man who believes himself an accident."*

— Francis Thompson

Do atheists forget they're atheists when faced with major adversity?

▶ *"There are no atheists in the fox holes."*

— William Thomas Cummings

• THE ATOM BOMB •

Will man ever be able to tap the power of the atom?

▶ *"There is no likelihood man can ever tap the power of the atom."*

— Robert Milliken

Thomas Edison foresees the atom bomb.

▶ *"There will one day spring from the brain of science a machine or force so fearful in its potentialities, so absolutely terrifying that even man, the fighter, who will dare torture and death in order to inflict torture and death, will be appalled, and so abandon war forever. What man's mind can create, man's character can control."*

— Thomas Alva Edison

The moment when the first atomic bomb was dropped on Hiroshima, Aug. 6, 1945.

▶ *"My God, what have we done?"*

— Captain Robert Lewis, Co-Pilot of the Enola Gay

When the first atomic explosion shook the New Mexico desert three weeks before Hiroshima, 1945.

▶ *"I am become death, the shatterer of worlds."*

— J. Robert Oppenheimer,
quoting the Bhagavad-Gita

Russian humour on nuclear war.

▶ *"In the event of an atomic bomb, place a white sheet over your head and walk slowly to the cemetary."*
Q. "Why walk slowly?"
A. "Not to cause panic."

"The atom bomb has changed everything except...

▶ *our way of thinking."*

— Albert Einstein

"The atom bomb can now be the great equalizer.

▶ *We can all be equally dead!"*

What to expect
from the atom bomb!

▶ *"Where is everybody?"*

— Carl Sandburg
(replying to the question, "What was it the last man on earth said?")

• ATTAINMENT •

Attaining a goal is far less pleasure than you expected.

▶ *"Is there anything in life so disenchanting as attainment?"*

— Robert Louis Stevenson

What do you do when you reach the top?

▶ *"The only thing left for a man who reaches the top is to find another mountain."*

"Nothing except a battle lost can be half so melancholy...

▶ *as a battle won!"*

— Duke of Wellington

"Anticipation is greater than realization."

▶ *"Getting there is more enjoyable than arriving."*

• GETTING ATTENTION •

How to make people take notice —

▶ *"People will sit up and take notice of you if you will sit up and take notice of what makes them sit up and take notice."*

— Frank Romer

• BEING AUTHORITATIVE •

To the uninformed guy who tries to sound authoritative.

▶ *"He always speaks with authority on what he knows nothing about!"*

• THE AUTOMOBILE •

Safety sign on highway —

▶ *"He looked.*
  She didn't.
  He is.
  She isn't."

It has been established that many otherwise sane and sensible people do suffer a form of insanity when they get behind the steering wheel.

▶ *"Always drive as if everybody else is crazy."*
  — The old taxi driver's maxim

How to make a car last a lifetime.

▶ *"Any car will last a lifetime, if you're careless enough."*

Bumper sticker cautioning the driver behind me.

▶ *"I drive the same way as you do!"*

Bumper sticker to get rid of a "Tailgater".

▶ *"Don't follow me, I'm lost."*

When driving a car, the left side is —

▶ *the "sui-cide".*

Advice to husbands of women drivers!

▶ *"If your wife insists on driving the car, don't stand in her way!"*

"It is rapidly getting to the point where a person killed in an auto accident...

▶ *died a natural death!*

The Golden Rule on driving a car —

▶ *"Drive toward others as you would have them drive toward you."*

Note found under a windshield wiper —

▶ *"I have just smashed your car. The people who saw the accident are watching me. They think I am writing down my name and address. They are wrong. Good luck!"*

Sign on thruway —

▶ *"Share your plans with the driver directly behind you!"*

Definition of a "Tree" to a woman —

▶ *"A tree is a natural object that attacks the car of a woman driver."*

"You can dodge some of the drivers all of the time, and all of the drivers some of the time, but...

▶ *you can't dodge all of the drivers all of the time."*

"Two finishes for automobiles...

▶ *lacquer and liquor!"*

What a hand-signal from a woman motorist means —

▶ *"A hand-signal from a woman motorist prepares us to expect the unexpected."*

"Parking tags are not so easy to get these days.

▶ *First you have to find a spot to park!"*

A sign outside of a little town in Japan —

▶ *"Please drive carefully. Our children might be disobeying us."*

Warning about drinking and driving!

▶ *"If you drive a car, don't drink because you may spill some!"*

Sign near a School —

▶ *"School — Don't Kill a Child."* Beneath was a childish scrawl: *"Wait For a Teacher."*

Are crashes accidents or are they caused?

▶ *"Semantically it is time we stopped gracing them with the euphemism 'accident'. Then we could start an educational program to reduce the violence."*

— A. G. Wynne Field

Sign on highway construction site —

▶ *"Take care which rut you use. You'll be in it for the next eleven miles!"*

• AUTO-SUGGESTION •

Popular formula for a cure by auto-suggestion in the 1920's that worked for a lot of people.

▶ *"Everyday, in every way, I am getting better and better."*

— Emile Coué

• THE AVERAGES •

How an average man becomes a somebody.

▶ *"I'm only an average man but I work harder at it than the average man."*
— Oliver Wendell Holmes

One man earns $20,000.
The second man earns $2,000.
The average earnings of each would be $11,000.
Moral: "Beware of averages!"

▶ *"Then there is the man who drowned crossing a stream with an average depth of six inches."*
— W.I.E. Gates

The hazard of just being average.

▶ *"When you're average, you're as close to the bottom as you are to the top."*

"Remember to keep plugging! The Law of Averages functions as absolutely as...

▶ *the Law of Gravity."*

What keeps the averages down?

▶ *"Not doing more than the average is what keeps the average down."*

The error in averages.

▶ *"Put one foot in a bucket of cold water and the other in hot water — and on the average you should be comfortable."*

B

• THE B.A. •

The relative unimportance today of a B.A.

▶ *"A B.A. is a person who has mastered the first two letters of the alphabet."*

• BACHELORS •

Is a bachelor a Yes man or No man?

▶ *"A bachelor is a fellow who can't take Yes for an answer!"*

Why bachelors know more about women than married men.

▶ *"If they didn't they'd be married, too."*
— H.L. Mencken

To be or not to be a bachelor?

▶ *"The problem that bothers a bachelor
A lot
Is whether he ought to stay single or
KNOT*
— F.G. Kernan

• BALDNESS •

"Baldness is...

▶ *a crisis coming to a head."*

"The only thing that will really prevent baldness is...

▶ *hair!"*
— Drew Berkowitz

"There's one thing about baldness.

▶ *It's neat!"*
— Don Herold

What a bargain is relating to price.

▶ *"Anything that's the same price now that it was a week ago!"*

• THE BANKER •

When will a banker lend you money?

▶ *"A banker is a man who lends you an umbrella when the weather is fair and takes it away from you when it rains."*

"I could have been a banker but..."

▶ *I lost interest!"*

• BANKRUPTCY •

To the business man who just went bankrupt —

▶ *"Nobody ever paid more — or sold for less than me!"*

• THE BARGAIN •

"A bargain is...

▶ *usually something you can't use at a price you can't resist."*

"A thing you don't want...

▶ *is dear at any price!"*

"It takes two to make a bargain, but...

▶ *only one gets it!"*

Nothing is free!

▶ *"The common law of business balance prohibits paying a little and getting a lot — it can't be done. If you deal with the lowest bidder, it is well to add something for the risk you run. And if you do that, you will have enough to pay for something better."*
— John Ruskin

• BAROMETER •

Definition of a "Barometer" and what it tells you about the weather.

▶ *"A barometer is an ingenious instrument which indicates what kind of weather we are having."*
— Ambrose Bierce

• BASEBALL •

"Staying out all night with a woman won't hurt you but...

▶ *looking for a woman all night will do you in!"*

— Casey Stengel

Don't let your opposition know the panic they're causing you!

▶ *"Don't let your emotion show on your shirtsleeve!"*

— Major League baseball maxim

"Baseball is 80% mental.

▶ *The other half is physical."*

— Yogi Berra

• BEAUTY AND THE BEAUTIFUL •

Can a woman's features alone make her beautiful?

▶ *"No woman can be handsome by the force of features alone any more than she can be witty by only the help of speech."*

— Thomas Hughes

Beauty does truly lie in the eye of the beholder!

▶ *"In the eyes of a lover pockmarks are dimples."*

— Japanese proverb

Is a naked man a thing of beauty?

▶ *"I have seen three emperors in their nakedness, and the sight was not inspiring."*

— Otto von Bismarck

Does a thing of beauty have to have a use?

▶ *"Remember that the most beautiful things in the world are the most useless; peacocks and lilies for instance."*

— John Ruskin

The answer you get when you ask a toad "What is beauty?"

▶ *"A female with two great round eyes coming out of her little head, a large flat mouth, a yellow belly and a brown back."*

— Voltaire

"If I tell you you have a beautiful body...

▶ *Will you hold it against me?"*

"Beauty is skin deep but ugly...

▶ *"goes right through to the bones!"*

Can beauty be enhanced by adding to it or subtracting from it?

▶ *"Beauty is the adjustment of all parts proportionately so that one cannot add or subtract or change without impairing the harmony of the whole."*
— Leon Battista Alberti

What is the best part of Beauty?

▶ *"The best part of beauty is that which no picture can express."*
— Francis Bacon

"Too bad you're not beautiful.

▶ *Then you'd be beautiful and dumb!"*

When a man sees a beautiful woman — does anybody have to tell him she's beautiful?

▶ *"Beauty itself doth itself persuade the eyes of men without an orator."*

— William Shakespeare

Is Beauty in the eye of the beholder?

▶ *"The beetle is a beauty in the eyes of its mother."*
— Arabian proverb

What's more difficult? To be beautiful or to appear to be beautiful?

▶ *"It is easy to be beautiful; it is difficult to appear so."*

— Frank O'Hara

Beauty is that which derives from what pleases the eye and ear: design, colour, figure, smoothness, motion, smallness, delicacy — the abstract terms of science and mathematics, and the many graces of writing.

▶ *"That pleasure which is at once the most pure, the most elevating and the most intense, is derived, I maintain from the contemplation of the beautiful."*
— Edgar Allan Poe

"Beauty and ugliness disappear equally under the wrinkles of age.

▶ *One is lost in them; the other hidden."*

Does that which is beautiful remain eternally beautiful?

▶ *"A thing of beauty is a joy forever, Its loveliness increases. It will never pass into nothingness."*
— John Keats

• BEHAVIOUR •

Respected rules of conduct.

▶ *"Do all the good you can,*
In all the ways you can,
In all the places you can,
At all the times you can,
To all the people you can,
As long as ever you can."

— John Wesley

As the mother hen said to her misbehaved baby chick —

▶ *"If your father could see you now, he'd turn over in his gravy!"*

"Never try to make anyone like yourself.

▶ *You know, and God knows, that one of you is enough!"*

— Ralph Waldo Emerson

"If you always live with those who limp...

▶ *you will yourself learn to limp."*

— Latin proverb

How sincere are most people?

▶ *"Half the people in America are faking it."*

— Robert Mitchum

When shouldn't you jump on a man?

▶ *"Don't jump on a man unless he's down."*

— Finley Peter Dunne

Should we turn the other cheek?

▶ *"He who turns the other cheek too far gets it in the neck!"*

Why the Japanese people are so homogeneous.

▶ *"The nail that sticks up gets pounded down."*

— Japanese proverb

How must men behave in the face of the world's unexplainable injustices?

▶ *"We must be greater than God, for we have to undo His injustice."*

— Jules Renard

Too often, we are unwillingly obliged to appease the other person.

▶ *"The art of pleasing is the art of deceiving."*

— French proverb

"He that lies with dogs...

▶ *shall rise with fleas!"*

"Give crabgrass an inch...

▶ *and it will take a yard!"*

How do people often behave towards those who show you kindness and towards those who show you scorn?

▶ *"People who bite the hand that feeds them usually lick the boot that kicks them."*

— Eric Hoffer

How to use your tongue and your eye.

▶ *"Be slow of tongue and quick of eye."*

— Miguel de Cervantes

"Blessed are they who believe in something...

▶ *even if it's nothing!"*

"The Middle East today is to ranting and cursing what...

▶ *Elizabethan England was to theater: the cradle of geniuses."*

— Lance Morrow

• TO BE OR NOT TO BE! •

Question!
"Where will you be?"

▶ *"I'm usually here or somewhere else!"*

— Yogi Berra

• BELLIGERENCE •

If your state of mind is belligerence you won't find it hard to provoke conflict.

▶ *"If the only tool you have is a hammer, you tend to see every problem as a nail."*

— Abraham Maslow

• BEREAVEMENT •

When there's a death, should we immediately try to assuage the grief of the bereaved?

▶ *"While grief is fresh, every attempt to divert it only irritates."*

— Samuel Johnson

Guide to visiting the
bereaved —

▶ *If the death was recent, it's more likely that the person will want to talk of nothing else, will need to talk of nothing else. There's a Hebrew proverb about "wearing out" grief — if you bottle it up, you'll never soften it. "Give sorrow words," said Shakespeare. "The grief that does not speak whispers the o'er-fraught heart and bids it break."*

— Barbara Walters

• BEWARE! •

To the fellow who won
the $10,000,000 reward for
proving he was kidnapped
by a U.F.O. but...

▶ *failed to read the small print which read — "Payable one dollar a year for ten million years."*

When things are going well,
it's time to expect the
unexpected!

▶ *"Beware when all things are safe."*

Beware of the sugary
tongue!

▶ *"The honey on her tongue Conceals the dagger in her belly!"*

— Chinese proverb

How to buy.

▶ *Always remember "CAVEAT EMPTOR!" Buyer Beware!*

• BIAS •

You're biased!

▶ *"You're like the Tower of Pisa — always leaning in one direction!"*

If you know a person is biased,
should you pay any attention to
his judgment of a situation?

▶ *"If Jack's in love, he's no judge of Jill's beauty."*

— Benjamin Franklin

To the guy who jumps to
conclusions!

▶ *"You should be in the Olympics, the way you jump to conclusions!"*

"For the other fellow to be
unbiased is...

▶ *to have the same bias you have!"*

All looks warped to a biased view.

▶ *"All looks yellow to a jaundiced eye."*

— Alexander Pope

• THE BIBLE •

Is there proof of the infallibility of the Bible?

▶ *"The dogma of the infallibility of the Bible is no more self-evident than is that of the infallibility of the popes."*

— Thomas Henry Huxley

In the Bible, did Christ ever predict his own resurrection?

▶ *"Never once did Christ utter a single word attesting to a personal resurrection and a life beyond the grave."*

— Leo Tolstoy

Can the Bible produce evidence for every situation?

▶ *"The devil can cite Scripture for his purpose."*

— William Shakespeare

The Bible contains every nuance of man's thoughts and behaviour except one. Name it!

▶ *"The total absence of humour from the Bible is one of the most singular things in all literature."*

— Alfred North Whitehead

And the Bible says "The meek shall inherit the earth."

▶ *"Meanwhile, the meek are a long time inheriting the earth."*

— Bob Edwards

The "Ten Commandments" — a re-write to fit the 20th century.

▶ *"The condition of the world today is such that if Moses were to descend from Mount Sinai today, the two tablets he would be carrying would be aspirin and valium!"*

The narration of evils residing in the Bible.

▶ *"Whenever we read the obscene stories, the voluptuous debaucheries, the cruel and tortuous executions, the unrelenting vindictiveness with which more than half the Bible is filled, it would be more consistent that we call it the word of a demon than the word of God. It is a history of wickedness that has served to corrupt and brutalize mankind."*

— Thomas Paine

The 12th Commandment — ▶ *"Thou shalt not hassle!"*

• BIGNESS •

Is size everything? ▶ *"The whale is endangered but you'll never get rid of ants!"*

• BIOGRAPHY •

"Biography is... ▶ *the most universally pleasant and profitable of all reading."*

— Thomas Carlyle

• BIRTHDAYS •

How behaviour of a man differs from a woman on Birthdays — ▶ *"When a man has a birthday he takes a day off, but when a woman has a birthday she takes a year off."*

• BLACKMAIL •

Pay off a blackmailer once and you're in for real blackmail! ▶ *"If the camel gets his nose in the tent, his body will soon follow."*

— Arabian proverb

• THE BLAME •

If you want to know who to blame, look in the mirror! ▶ *"The fault, dear Brutus, is not in our stars, but in ourselves that we are underlings."*

— William Shakespeare

• THE BLIND •

What happens if "the blind lead the blind"? ▶ *"Both shall fall into the ditch."*

— The Bible

• BOASTING •

"The man who says he never boasts... ▶ *is boasting."*

• BOOKS •

That which a collection of books does to a home —

▸ *"To add a library to a house is to give that house a soul."*
— Cicero

"There are many little ways to enlarge your child's world.

▸ *Love of books is the best of all.*
— Jacqueline Kennedy Onassis

The impression you make on people by owning a good library of books.

▸ *"No furniture so charming as books, even if you never open them, or read a single word."*
— Sydney Smith

The joy that some people have never experienced.

▸ *"I do pity unlearned gentlemen on a rainy day."*
— Lord Falkland

"Writing a book is the most intensive exercise anyone can give his brain.

▸ *It provided the therapy needed for a full spiritual recovery by enabling me to put Watergate behind me."*
— Richard M. Nixon

"It is not necessary to read all books: It is not necessary to read all of any book ravenously.

▸ *Some books are to be tasted, others to be swallowed, and some few to be chewed and digested."*
— Francis Bacon

When should a good book be read a second time?

▸ *"Any book which is at all important should be re-read immediately."*
— Arthur Schopenhauer

Advice on when to quit reading a book.

▸ *"Never read a book through merely because you have begun it."*
— John Witherspoon

"Read the best books first, or...

▸ *you may not have a chance to read them at all."*
— Thoreau

One way of criticizing a book —

▸ *"The covers of this book are too far apart."*
— Ambrose Bierce

"The great objection to new books is...

▸ *that they prevent our reading old ones."*

The miracle of books and their magnificent meaning for man!

▶ *"These are not books, lumps of lifeless paper, but minds alive on the shelves. One can call into range the voice of a man far distant in time and space, and hear him speaking to us, mind to mind, heart to heart."*

— Gilbert Highet

"A classic is a book which people praise but...

▶ *don't read!"*

Though often inferior in intellect, the publisher is boss!

▶ *"No author is a man of genius to his publisher."*

— Heinrich Heine

"Books are the legacies that a great genius leaves to mankind, which are delivered down from generation to generation, as presents to...

▶ *the posterity of those who are yet unborn."*

— Joseph Addison

"Do not consider a thing as proof because you find it written in books.

▶ *For just as a liar will deceive with his tongue, he will not be deterred from doing the same thing with his pen."*

— Moses Maimonides

"Never lend books, for no one ever returns them.

▶ *The only books I have in my library are books that other folks have lent me."*

— Anatole France

"To read junk novels in a world that holds Dickens, Tolstoy, Hugo, Shelley and Shakespeare is like...

▶ *being told you have the choice of all the diamonds in Tiffany's and then walking out with a bit of colored glass."*

• BOOZE •

Five reasons to drink.

▶ *"If all be true that I do think There are 5 reasons why we should drink. Good wine — a friend — or being dry Or lest we should be dry — by and by. Or any other reason why."*

The difference between a Drunk and an Alcoholic.

▶ *"The drunk doesn't have to attend all those damn meetings!"*

The effects of three shots of liquor.

▶ *"After the first glass — a lamb; after the second glass — a lion; after the third glass — a pig."*
— Talmud

"One reason I don't drink is...

▶ *that I want to know when I am having a good time."*
— Tallulah Bankhead

Why will drinking not drown your sorrow?

▶ *"People who drink to drown their sorrow should be told that sorrow knows how to swim."*
— Ann Landers

The drink that's been adopted by two out of three marriages.

▶ *"Marriage on the rocks!"*

How you know when you're drunk!

▶ *"He is not drunk who, from the floor, Can rise again and drink some more; But he is drunk who prostrate lies, And cannot drink and cannot rise."*

What has caused more drownings — Bacchus or Neptune?

▶ *"Bacchus (Greek God of Wine) has drowned more men than Neptune."* *(Greek God of the Sea)*

What happens when you mix brandy and water?

▶ *"A mixture of brandy and water spoils two good things."*
— Charles Lamb

Sign at cocktail bar —

▶ *"If you're driving your husband to drink, drive him here."*

Hope for alcoholics.

▶ *"I'm living proof you don't have to die for a drink."*
— Jason Robards

"Don't be fooled into believing alcohol is an effective turn-on.

▶ *A moderate amount reduces the inhibition — but as Shakespeare said, it increases the desire but damages the performance."*
— Ann Landers

Sign in English pub —

▶ *"Close Door — Wonderful Draught Inside."*

An invitation you can send to your party guest that will cut down on your liquor costs.

▶ *"Rather than presume your taste in liquor, I want you to feel free to bring your own choice."*

Why a lady should drink in moderation.

▶ *"Martinis, my dear, are befuddling; Take two, and no more, at the most; Take three, and you're under the table; Take four, and you're under the host."*

"If you drink, it's your business.

▶ *If you drink and drive, it's everybody's business!"*

Why I drink when I go out with other people.

▶ *"I drink to make other people more interesting."*

— George J. Nathan

Would you care to have a drink?

▶ *"No thank you. I'm just walking."*

A comment about wines that has more merit than meets the eye.

▶ *Wine produced in California under the name of champagne bears a label which says: "Beware of French imitations."*

Why W.C. Fields always kept a supply of booze on hand.

▶ *"I always keep a supply of stimulant handy in case I can see a snake — which I also keep handy."*

— W.C. Fields

Sign in cocktail lounge —

▶ *"If you drink to forget, please pay in advance!"*

"I could have been a bartender but...

▶ *I got all mixed up!"*

The Mona Lisa Cocktail —

▶ *"Two drinks, and you can't get the silly grin off your face!"*

Two reasons for drinking booze!

▸ *"There are two reasons for drinking; one is, when you are thirsty, to cure it; the other, when you are not thirsty, to prevent it... Prevention is better than cure."*

— Thomas Love Peacock

• THE BORE! •

How you can become a bore when I'm talking.

▸ *"A bore is a person who monopolizes the conversation when I have something brilliant to say."*

"We are always bored by...

▸ *those whom we bore."*

— French proverb

"Some people can stay longer in an hour than...

▸ *others can in a week!"*

"Somebody's boring me. Who?

▸ *I think it's me!"*

— Dylan Thomas

When someone bores you acutely.

▸ *"I like watching and listening to him I'm a masochist!"*

We often pardon those who bore us but...

▸ *we cannot pardon those whom we bore."*

— La Rochefoucauld

What one thing is it impossible to teach a bore?

▸ *"Bores bore each other too; but it never seems to teach them anything."*

— Don Marquis

Definition of a "Bore" during conversation.

▸ *"A bore is a person who talks when you wish him to listen."*

— Ambrose Bierce

What's a sure formula for boring people?

▸ *"The secret of boring people lies in telling them everything."*

— Voltaire

"A bore is a man who...

▸ *when you ask him how he is, tells you."*

— Bert Leston Taylor

"A bore is a person who deprives you of solitude...

▶ *without providing you with company."*

— Gian Vincenzo Lavina

Does a bore ever know he's a bore?

▶ *"A bore is the last one to find himself out."*

— Oliver Wendell Holmes

"I quit going with my girl because of illness and fatigue.

▶ *I got sick and tired of her!"*

• BOREDOM •

Don't ever go to that place for entertainment unless you like boredom!

▶ *"That place is great for people who like to watch paint dry."*

Is Boredom avoidable?

▶ *"Boredom is a choice!"*

Should there be any empathy for those people who find life monotonous?

▶ *"Monotony is the law of nature. Look at the monotonous manner in which the sun rises."*

— Mahatma Gandhi

How to cure boredom —

▶ *"Extreme boredom serves to cure boredom."*

— La Rochefoucauld

"It was so quiet there...

▶ *you could hear the grass grow."*

"I was bored...

▶ *right down to my cuticles."*

• BORROWING •

Lend money to a friend and you'll often lose the friend! Borrow unduly and you'll be a poor conserver of your resources.

▶ *"Neither a borrower nor a lender be; For loan oft loses both itself and friend, And borrowing dulls the edge of husbandry."*

— William Shakespeare

Shakespeare said — "Neither a borrower nor lender be!"

▶ *"Who goes a borrowing goes a sorrowing!"*

"Borrowing is... ▶ *not much better than begging."*

— G.E. Lessing

Be not a borrower! ▶ *"Better go hungry to bed, than rise a debtor."*

— Turkish proverb

• THE BOSS •

Is working your way up to become boss all it's cracked up to be? ▶ *"By working faithfully eight hours a day, you may eventually get to be a boss and work twelve hours a day."*

— Robert Frost

There can only be one boss! ▶ *"A ship, to run a straight course, can have but one pilot and one steering wheel. The same applies to the successful operation of a business. There cannot be a steering wheel at every seat in an organization."*

— Jules Ormont

"He called his wife ECHO because... ▶ *she always had the last word."*

"Don't regard me as being bossy... ▶ *but as your friend who is always right."*

The question "Who ought to be boss?" is like asking... ▶ *"Who ought to be the tenor in the quartet?" Obviously, the man who can sing tenor.*

— Henry Ford

Proof that the boss is smart! ▶ *"When you hire people who are smarter than you are — you prove you are smarter than they are."*

The How and Why to be a boss. ▶ *"The man who knows how will always have a job. The man who knows why will be his boss!"*

The advantage of having a stupid boss. ▶ *"Many who say their boss is stupid would be out of a job if he were smarter!"*

How to be a better boss —

▶ *"Dear Lord, please help me —*
To accept human beings as they are—
not yearn for perfect creatures;
To recognize ability — and encourage
it;
To understand shortcomings — and
make allowance for them;
To work patiently for improvement —
and not expect too much too quickly;
To appreciate what people do right —
not just criticize what they do wrong;
To be slow to anger and hard to
discourage;
To have the hide of an elephant and
the patience of Job;
In short, Lord, please help me be a
better boss!"

— John Luther

Guidelines to becoming boss.

▶ *"I Won't is a tramp,*
I Can't is a quitter,
I Don't Know is lazy,
I Wish I Could is a wisher,
I Might is waking up,
I Will Try is on his feet,
I Can is on his way,
I Will is at work,
I Did is now the boss."

— Earl Cassel

The kind of boss a baby is!

▶ *"A perfect example of minority rule!"*

The motto of my boss —

▶ *"If at first you don't succeed*
you're fired!"

There's got to be one boss
even if he's mediocre.

▶ *"One bad general is better than two*
good ones!"

— French proverb

Boasting about your worth to
the boss.

▶ *"Telling the boss what a good worker*
you are is worth one percent; showing
him is worth 99!"

Who your boss is at the
office

▶ *"He's the man who is early when*
you're late and late when you're
early."

"When the boss called me an idiot...

▶ *I agreed. After all I'm no fool!"*

"It's strange that so many smart people work for...

▶ *such ignorant bosses!"*

• THE BRAIN •

"The chain is as strong as its weakest link." How does the brain compare?

▶ *"The brain is as strong as its weakest think!"*

How much do you like your own brain?

▶ *"The brain is my 2nd favourite organ!"*

— Woody Allen

"The brain is a wonderful organ but unkind.

▶ *It starts working the moment you get up in the morning, and does not stop until you get into the office."*

— Robert Frost

"Don't worry about senility because...

▶ *if you become senile, you won't know it!"*

• THE BREAKFAST •

Are spouses intended to have breakfast together?

▶ *"My wife and I tried two or three times in the last forty years to have breakfast together, but it was so disagreeable we had to stop."*

— Winston Churchill

• LOW-BRED •

Definition of "Low-Bred" —

▶ *"Low-bred is raised instead of brought up."*

— Ambrose Bierce

• BREVITY •

Brevity is the soul of —   ▶ *"Lingerie."*

• YOUR BUDGET •

How to stay within a budget.   ▶ *"A small house is better than a large mortgage."*

Where do you rate when you ask "How much does it cost?"   ▶ *"If you have to ask how much it costs, you can't afford it."*
— J.P. Morgan

"I'm living so far beyond my income that...   ▶ *we may almost be said to be living apart."*
— E.E. Cummings

"If you don't want to lose your shirt...   ▶ *don't put so much on the cuff!"*

"A budget is what you stay within if...   ▶ *you go without!"*

"In spite of the cost of living...   ▶ *it's still popular."*
— Laurence J. Peter

What effect has inflation on how hard you have to work?   ▶ *"With inflation being so high these days, you've got to work like a dog — just to live like a dog!"*

"A fool and his money are soon parted.   ▶ *Now it happens to everybody!"*

If this statement be true that "Two can live as cheap as one" then —   ▶ *"This statement I concede, but weep: Where and how can one live cheap?"*

Trying to make both ends meet.   ▶ *"At today's high prices — you're lucky if you can make one end meet!"*

"Earn a little...   ▶ *and spend a little — less!"*
— John Stevenson

How to Budget —   ▶ *"Live within your income even if you have to borrow to do so!"*

"The easiest way to make ends meet... ▶ *is to get off your own!"*

"The reason many people don't live within their incomes is... ▶ *that they don't consider that living."*

"When prosperity comes... ▶ *do not use all of it!"*
— Confucius

"I hope they don't raise the standard of living! ▶ *I can't afford it."*

What a budget is and how it affects your debts. ▶ *"A budget is a schedule for going into debt systematically."*

"Eat before shopping. ▶ *If you go to the store hungry, you are likely to make unnecessary purchases."*

Warning when you spend more than you earn! ▶ *"When your outgo exceeds your income, your upkeep is your downfall."*

"If you save something when you have something... ▶ *you'll have something when you have nothing."*

"The only two that can live as cheap as one is... ▶ *a horse and a sparrow!"*

• BUREAUCRATS •

What kind of people run our giant bureaucracies? ▶ *"Bureaucracy is a giant mechanism operated by pygmies."*
— Honoré de Balzac

Advice to bureaucrats on how to say something. ▶ *"A mumble can never be quoted."*
— James H. Boren

"Bureaucrats are the only people in the world who can say absolutely nothing... ▶ *and mean it!"*
— James H. Boren

Speak no evil, see no evil, and hear no evil!"

▶ *How the bureaucrat says it —*
"Communicate no wickedness,
scrutinize no depravity,
auscultate no immorality!"

Boren's Laws for Bureaucrats!

▶ *"(1) When in charge ponder.*
(2) When in trouble delegate.
(3) When in doubt mumble."
— James H. Boren

The jargon of bureaucrats using phrases like "Integrated Criteria" and "Interactive Parameters", is nothing but disguised claptrap!

▶ *"Sour notes in music don't become*
sweet because the musician is
wearing a top hat and tails."
— John Heron

"Haste makes waste."

▶ *How the bureaucrat says it —*
"Precipitance entails negation of
economy."

• THE BUSINESS WORLD •

The ingredient that should not be overlooked by the man aspiring to go into business.

▶ *"The mechanics of running a business*
are really not very complicated when
you get down to essentials. You have
to make some stuff and sell it to
somebody for more than it cost you.
That's about all there is to it, except for
a few million details."
— John L. McCaffrey

"Business is like a wheelbarrow.

▶ *It stands still unless someone*
pushes it."

Not "How's Business" but...

▶ *"Where's Business?"*

There actually are times when Business and Pleasure can mix!

▶ *"A massage parlour is a business*
to do pleasure with."

"He knows as much about business as...

▶ *a cat knows about music!"*

Why trade unions should not push companies too far in their money demands.

▶ *"The worst crime against working*
people is a company which fails to
operate at a profit."
— Samuel Gompers

The tender-hearted
employer is the one
who is too tender-hearted
to fire the weakling.

▶ *The employer generally gets the employees he deserves.*
— Sir Walter Bilbey

Sign on office door —

▶ *"Enter without knocking. Please leave the same way!"*

"An unprofitable business is a loser for everyone.

▶ *The basic need of every company is to make a profit. Only then can it provide jobs and earnings for employees."*
— I.W. Abel

Every business organization can go sour.

▶ *"This is a Non-Profit Organization, We didn't plan it that way, but it is!"*

What business is all about!

▶ *"Business is the art of extracting money from another man's pocket without resorting to violence."*
— Max Amsterdam

"No matter how able, any employer or executive who insists on running a one-man enterprise...

▶ *courts unhappy circumstances when his powers dwindle."*
— B.C. Forbes

So why don't you ask me "How's business?"

▶ *Q. "So — how's business?"*
A. "Don't ask!"

"Business is so bad that...

▶ *even the accounts that don't intend to pay ain't buying."*
— Garment Center Adage

When to buy and sell.

▶ *"Buy when it rains. Sell when the sun is shining!"*

A business prayer —

▶ *"O Lord, help me to remember that no one ever lost a customer because the quality was too high, or the service too good!"*

Definition of Business —

▶ *"The game of transferring money from other people's pockets to mine."*

As the scissors grinder said when asked "How's business?"

▶ *"Fine, I never saw things so dull."*

Office Rules —

▶ *Rule No. 1*
   The boss is always right.
Rule No. 2
   If the boss is wrong refer to rule
   No. 1

"It is a socialist idea that making profits is a vice.

▶ *I consider the real vice is making losses."*

— Sir Winston Churchill

If you want to deal in business will you have to deal with everybody including the dishonest?

▶ *"He that resolves to deal with none but honest men, must leave off dealing."*

— Thomas Fuller

"The cost of doing business is as nothing compared with...

▶ *the cost of not doing business."*

"The best check-writing machine was made from...

▶ *Adam's rib."*

"Business is that which...

▶ *if you don't have any of, you go out of!"*

— Earl Wilson

Too many men, to their detriment, ignore intuition and suffer from —

▶ *"Analysis Paralysis."*

— Roy Rowen

Don't merely buy because of low price. Remember — wormy apples are cheaper!

▶ *"There is hardly anything in the world that some man cannot make a little worse and sell a little cheaper, and the people who consider price only are this man's lawful prey."*

— John Ruskin

When is the best time to buy things?

▶ *"A study of economics usually reveals that the best time to buy anything is last year."*

— Marty Allen

"How to get people to buy —

▶ *"People will buy anything that's one to a customer."*

— Sinclair Lewis

• BUSY! •

Why I'm so busy.

▶ *"My laziness leaves me no free time."*

"How busy is not so important as...

▶ *why busy. The bee is praised; the mosquito is swatted."*

"As busy as...

▶ *a mouse in a cheese factory!"*

C

• CALMNESS •

Calmness during
misfortune —

▸ *"The ability to bear with calmness the
misfortunes of others."*

• CANADA •

The questionable renown of
Canada in world fame!

▸ *"I don't even know what street
Canada is on."*

— Al Capone

• CANCER •

Every day, something new
causes cancer.

▸ *"We've reached the stage now where
even living is dangerous to your
health."*

• CAPITALISM •

"Under capitalism man
exploits man."
What about socialism?

▸ *"Under socialism the reverse is true."*

— Polish proverb

• CAUTION •

Before acting on an
irretrievable act, think — and
then think again!

▸ *Advice from an old carpenter:
"Measure twice and saw once."*

"Don't ever slam a door."
Why?

"You might want to go back!"
— Don Herold

'We can't cross a bridge until
we come to it.

▶ *I always like to lay down a pontoon
ahead of time."*
— Bernard M. Baruch

Don't be overly cautious!

▶ *"Show me a man who keeps his two
feet on the ground and I'll show you a
man who can't get his pants off!"*

Make sure you
have a backup
to fall back on.

▶ *"Never leave hold of what you've
got until you've got hold of
something else!*

Safety Hint —

▶ *"The moment you forget for a
moment, you may remember for a
lifetime."*

"If you must rise
early...

▶ *be sure you're a bird
and not a worm!"*

• CAVEMEN •

"All men are cavemen at first
but...

▶ *some cave in faster than others!"*

• THE CELEBRITY •

The frustration of a
Hollywood celebrity aspiring to
sponsor a fund-raising
program to aid medical
research.

▶ *"The trouble is all the good diseases
have already been taken by somebody
else."*

"A Celebrity is a man who
works all his life to become
famous enough to be
recognized...

▶ *then goes around in dark glasses so no
one will know who he is."*
— Earl Wilson

People generally endow their
celebrities with qualities that
don't exist.

▶ *"Now when I bore people at a party,
they think it's their fault."*

— Henry Kissinger

Why so many celebrities are annoyed being called an "Overnight Success".

▶ *"It takes twenty years to make an overnight success."*

— Eddie Cantor

The most exalted celebrity is only a plain ordinary human being who puts on his underwear one leg at a time.

▶ *"The greatest monarch on the proudest throne is obliged to sit up on his own arse."*

— Benjamin Franklin

Michael Jackson wore only one glove.
How about Vincent van Gogh?

"Van Gogh was the Michael Jackson of his day. He only wore one ear muff."

• CELIBACY •

Which is better — marriage or celibacy?

▶ *"As to marriage or celibacy, let a man take which he will, he is sure to repent."*

— Socrates

What some people think celibacy is —

▶ *"A disease of the brain."*

• CENSORSHIP •

The logic in concluding that a film censor must be a corrupt man.

▶ *"I wouldn't want my daughter to marry a film censor because if dirty films corrupt, he must be, by virtue of his total exposure to them, the most corrupt man in the country."*

— Pierre Berton

That which Censorship is.

▶ *"1 per cent thinking above the neck, and 99 per cent thinking below the belt."*

• CERTAINTY •

"The only sure thing is...

▶ *there's no sure thing!"*

• CHARACTER •

"No man is so exquisitely honest or upright in living but...

▶ *that ten times in his life he might not lawfully be hanged."*

— Michel de Montaigne

What's better than being a character?

▶ "Better to have character than be one!"

"A man's treatment of money is...

▶ the most decisive test of his character — how he makes it and how he spends it."
— James Moffatt

When your life is in mortal danger, most people promise to turn over a new leaf if they come out alive — but do they?

▶ "The wolf was sick, he vowed a monk to be;
But when he got well, a wolf once more was he."
— Walter Bower

"The measure of a man's real character is what he would do if...

▶ he knew he never would be found out."
— Thomas Babington Macaulay

Under what condition is character displayed?

▶ "Character is what you are in the dark."
— Dwight L. Mood

Here is a man of such flawless character that his legacy will light up the heavens.

▶ "When he shall die,
Take him and cut him out in little stars,
And he will make the face of heaven so fine,
That all the world will be in love with night,
And pay no worship to the garish sun."
— William Shakespeare

"Character is not made in crisis.

It is only exhibited!"

"You may not always be better than others but...

▶ you can always be better than yourself."
— Ivan Panin

What reveals a person's character more effectively than mere conversation?

▶ "You can discover more about a person in an hour of play than in a year of conversation."
— Plato

"Many a man would have turned rogue...

▶ if he knew how."
— William Hazlitt

Seven national crimes.

▶ *1. I don't think.*
2. I don't know.
3. I don't care.
4. I am too busy.
5. I "leave well enough
   alone."
6. I have no time to
   read and find out.
7. I am not interested.
— William J.H. Boetcker

"The size of a man can be measured by...

▶ *the size of the thing that makes him angry."*
— J. Kenfield Morley

"He has as much charisma as...

▶ *a dead catfish!"*

"I'm not the man I used to be...

▶ *and I never was!"*
— George Ade

"He's so 'small' that...

▶ *he could walk erect in a silk topper under the tummy of a worm and not scuff the hat or disturb the worm."*

• CHARITY AND BEING CHARITABLE •

Seven classes of Givers of Charity.

▶ *"First, those who give spontaneously and generously, but only to themselves — autogivers they might be called.*

Second, those who give thoughtlessly, without any real or high motive — givers of the occasion, as it were.

Third, those who give as a sop to conscience and self-esteem; in a species of atonement for the evil they do — penitential givers.

Fourth, those who give as a matter of display, to win public applause for their generosity — theatrical givers.

Fifth, those who give because others give, because they are expected to give, and are ashamed not to give, and therefore give grudgingly —
conventional givers.

Sixth, those who give because they feel they ought to give; who give through a sense of duty and not through love
— moral givers.

Seventh, those who give in the spirit of God who give because they love their neighbor as themselves, and above all things desire to help him — spiritual givers."

When being generous to others, what hidden defect lies behind the good act of the giver?

▶ *"Generosity is the vanity of giving."*
— La Rochefoucauld

"He who is not charitable with what he has, does but deceive himself when...

▶ *he thinks he would be charitable if he had more."*
— W. S. Plummer

Church sign —

▶ *"Since you can't take it with you why not leave it here?"*

Is it better to give or to receive?

▶ *"It's better to give than to receive — especially when it comes to aggravation."*

Is there true pure unselfishness?

▶ *"No one on earth ever aided another out of pure altruism. Everyone expected something back — as love or respect or gratitude."*

Doctrine of who should give and who should receive.

▶ *"From each according to his abilities, to each according to his needs."*
— Karl Marx

How a frown or a smile affects Giving.

▶ *"He gives little who gives much with a frown; he gives much who gives a little with a smile."*

"A bone to the dog is not charity.

▶ *Charity is the bone shared with the dog, when you are just as hungry as the dog."*

— Jack London

"When a poor man refuses to accept a gift...

▶ *call it a loan and hand it to him again!"*

— Talmud

"Blessed are those who can give without remembering...

▶ *and take without forgetting."*

— Elizabeth Bibesco

Where should charity begin and end?

▶ *"Charity begins at home, but should not end there."*

"Shall we call ourselves benevolent...

▶ *when the gifts we bestow do not cost us a single privation?*

Every little bit really does count!

▶ *"Nobody made a greater mistake than he who did nothing; because he could only do a little."*

— Edmund Burke

• CHARM •

"If you have charm you don't need to have anything else.

▶ *And if you don't have it, it doesn't much matter what else you have."*

— James M. Barrie

"Charm is a way of getting the answer yes without...

▶ *having asked any clear question."*

— Albert Camus

Throughout history why have Forbidden Charms always had their appeal?

▶ *"Things forbidden have a secret charm."*

— Tacitus

Definition of Charm —

▶ *"Money in the bank."*

— Josephine Gable

• CHASTE! •

Does chaste make virtue?

▶ *"Chaste makes waste!"*

• CHEATING •

"The ingenious phrase that deceives the public about our Watergates and our Irangates is called 'Plausible Deniability'...

▶ whereby a President's lieutenants arrange things so that he can always deny knowing what they have done on his behalf."

Speech to British businessmen telling them how to skin a customer!

▶ "When you are skinning your customers, you should leave some skin on to grow so that you can skin them again."
— Nikita Krushchev

Caution to the husband who cheats!

▶ "Here's to the man who takes wife,
Let him make no mistakes;
For there is a world of difference
Whose wife it is he takes."

How I learned not to trust so much!

▶ "He got the elevator and I got the shaft!"

• CHILDREN •

At what age can a child's character be more or less established for life?

▶ "Give me the children until they are seven and anyone may have them afterwards."
— St. Francis Xavier

"The best thing you can do for your children is...

▶ give them roots and give them wings."

"Insanity is hereditary.

▶ You can get it from your children!"
— Sam Levinson

"If you strike a child...

▶ strike him only with a shoelace!"
— Talmud

"When it comes to children, the have-nots have...

▶ and the haves have not!"

"If a child lives with...

▶ *Fairness —*
he learns justice,
with Hostility —
he learns to fight.
with Criticism —
he learns to condemn.
with Approval —
he learns to like himself."

Why do children tend to enjoy each day of life more than adults do?

▶ *"Children have neither a past nor a future. Thus they enjoy the present — which seldom happens to us."*
— Jean de la Bruyère

Cure for children's Reading Disability.

▶ *"Make reading illegal for all kids under 14!"*

What children really are to parents.

▶ *"Children are a torment and nothing else."*
— Leo Tolstoy

"He that spareth his rod...

▶ *hateth his son."*
— Book of Proverbs

The role that grandchildren fill.

▶ *"Grandchildren are God's way of compensating us for growing old."*
— Mary H. Waldrip

Should bright children be applauded?

▶ *"Bright children should be applauded — many with one hand!"*

Why do children have such endurance?

▶ *"Children's talent to endure stems from their ignorance of alternatives."*
— May Angelou

"He who teaches his child to live on small means leaves him...

▶ *a fortune!"*
— Elsie Lincoln Benedict

Idea on how to raise your young.

▶ *"Alligators have the right idea. They eat their young."*
— Eve Arden

"He who has no children has one sorrow.

▶ *He who has children has a thousand sorrows."*
— Turkish proverb

"Children are a great comfort in your old age... ▶ *and they help you reach it faster, too."*
— Lionel Kauffman

"You can learn many things from children. ▶ *How much patience you have, for instance."*
— Franklin P. Jones

"We can't give our children the future, strive though we may to make it secure but... ▶ *we can give them the present."*
— Kathleen Norris

Perspective of a child out shopping. ▶ *"Let's go home, Mommy. I'm tired of looking at elbows."*

Why you should respect every child. ▶ *"When I approach a child, he inspires in me two sentiments: tenderness for what he is, and respect for what he may become."*
— Louis Pasteur

"A child...should be pushed aside with the left hand... ▶ *and drawn closer with the right hand."*
— Talmud

Child Psychology — ▶ *"What children manage parents with!"*

A constructive way to compliment a child. ▶ *"If you want children to improve, let them hear the nice things you say about them to others."*
— Haim Ginott

• CHOICE •

When you offer a person a choice of two Evils — ▶ *"It's like asking the guy in the electric chair if he wants AC or DC electrical current."*

When a man is about to strike me, I have three choices. ▶ *1. "I can stand still and be injured.
2. I can strike back.
3. Or I can walk away."*

When you have two choices of remedy, don't take the drastic step first! ▶ *"Never cut what you can untie!"*
— Joseph Joubert

You're giving me damned little CHOICE! ▶ *"There's small choice in rotten apples!"*
— William Shakespeare

Everyone has Options on which path to take!

▶ *"Of all paths a man could strike into, there is, at any given moment, a best path for every man. This path, to find this path, and walk in it, is the one thing needful for him."*

— Thomas Carlyle

When choosing between two evils —

▶ *"I always like to try the one I've never tried before."*

— Mae West

Do you possess the hidden power to choose how you can live your life?

▶ *"I have the power to choose how I will live and think today."*

The choice you're giving me is like...

▶ *choosing between cholera and leprosy."*

Choice is one of the most important words in the dictionary.

▶ *"Remember. What you can do, you can NOT do!"*

— Aristotle

Why you selected what you did in a choice of evils.

▶ *"That choice did less to depress me than all the others!"*

• CHRISTMAS •

"If Christmas means anything...

▶ *it must mean that there are very few Christmas trees in Soviet Russia on Christmas Eve!"*

• THE CITIZEN •

What is it to be a good citizen?

▶ *"It is to acknowledge the other person's rights before asserting your own, but always to be conscious of your own. It is to be free in word and deed, but it is also to know that your freedom is subject to the other person's freedom."*

— Kahlil Gibran, the Lebanese poet

• CIVIL DISOBEDIENCE •

The origin of Civil Disobedience on how to handle unjust laws.

▶ *"Shall we be content to obey them, or shall we transgress them at once?... If unjust laws exist, civil disobedience is an effective way to oppose and change them."*
— Henry David Thoreau

"The teachings of Thoreau on Civil Disobedience are more alive today than ever before.

▶ *A sit-in at lunch counters, a freedom ride... a peaceful protest... all are outgrowths of Thoreau's insistence that evil must be resisted and no moral man can patiently adjust to injustice."*
— Martin Luther King Jr.

• CIVILIZATION •

Today progress suffers from far too much civilization.

▶ *"Progress might have been all right once, but it's gone on too long now."*
— Ogden Nash

Has our computerized civilization become too complex?

▶ *'If the safety pin had been invented this year instead of long ago, it would probably have six moving parts, two transistors and require a service man twice a year."*

Which four small nation states have contributed most to mankind?

▶ *"The nations which have put mankind and posterity most in their debt have been small states — Israel, Athens, Florence, Elizabethan England."*
— Dean Inge

Is mankind getting too much civilization?

▶ *"The end of the human race will be that it will eventually die of civilization."*
— Ralph Waldo Emerson

The more jobs we can perform without thinking affects civilization in what manner?

▶ *"Civilization advances by extending the number of important operations which we can perform without thinking."*
— Alfred North Whitehead

The most important equation in history leading to the atomic bomb, that can destroy civilization!

▶ $E = MC^2$
"Energy equals mass times the speed of light squared."
— Albert Einstein

• CLAIRVOYANCY •

"Vision is...

▶ *what people think clairvoyants have when they guess right!"*

"He who goes to the clairvoyant and lives by the crystal ball...

▶ *will eat ground glass!"*

• CLEVERNESS •

"The desire to appear clever often prevents...

▶ *our being so."*
— French proverb

• THE CLICHÉ •

Slang and the cliché are generally the language of the inarticulate.

▶ *"The cliché is the greatest labour-saving device ever invented by man; it eliminates the necessity of thought."*
— Richard Tobin

"Avoid Clichés...

▶ *like the Plague!"*

• THE CLOCK •

"The kind of alarm clock I want...

▶ *is one that rings when I'm ready to get up."*

How to set the clock for daylight saving time —

▶ *"Man springs forward and falls back."*

A nice feature of electric clocks.

▶ *"Electric clocks reveal to you Precisely when your fuses blew."*
— Leonard Schiff

"You can't turn back the clock.

▶ *But you can wind it up again!"*
— Bonnie Prudden

• YOUR CLOTHES •

When Marilyn Monroe was asked what she wore when she went to bed, her reply was —

▶ *"Chanel No. 5"*

"Judge not a man by his clothes, but...

▶ *by his wife's clothes."*
— Thomas R. Dewar

What most causes your clothes to wear out?

▶ *"Fashion wears out more apparel than the man."*
— William Shakespeare

"Put even the plainest woman into a beautiful dress...

▶ *and unconsciously she will try to live up to it."*
— Lady Duff-Gordon

The short skirt.

▶ *"As she shows, so shall we peep!"*

To what length wouldn't women go to show off a new dress?

▶ *"And by my grave you'd pray to have me back*
So I could see how well you look in black."
— Marco Carson

Know "How to Dress" to fit the occasion.

▶ *"If your clothes are seen by the other person before they see you, your chances of being a success are nil!"*
— Elmer Wheeler

Can we judge women by their clothes?

▶ *"You can't judge women by their clothes these days — there isn't enough evidence."*

Do your clothes make a difference?

▶ *"An emperor in his nightcap would not meet with half the respect of an emperor with a crown."*
— Oliver Goldsmith

"When she was poured into her clothes...

▶ *they forgot to say when!"*

How a person of taste will select his clothes.

▶ *"Costly thy habit as thy purse can buy,*
But not expressed in fancy; rich, not gaudy;
For the apparel oft proclaims the man."
— William Shakespeare

• CLUMSY! •

"He's as clumsy as... ▶ *a bull in a china shop!"*

• COFFIN •

Coffin — ▶ *The one article about which no one says, "I can get it for you wholesale."*

• COLD!! •

"It was so cold out that... ▶ *if the thermometer had been an inch longer, we'd all have frozen to death!"*

• COMEDIANS •

"With the collapse of vaudeville... ▶ *new talent has no place to stink!"*
— George Burns

How he got started in the entertainment world. ▶ *"I got started in radio. I used to fix them."*
— Soupy Sales

• THE COMMITTEE •

How a committee would end up as designers. ▶ *"A camel would be a racehorse designed by a committee."*

Comparing the effectiveness of a committee as against a single person of authority. ▶ *"Many an army has prospered under a bad commander, but no army has ever prospered under a debating society."*
— T. B. Macaulay

Should advisory committees always be listened to? ▶ *"If Columbus had had an advisory committee he would probably still be at the dock."*
— Justice Arthur Goldberg

Definition of a Committee — ▶ *"A group of men who keep minutes and waste hours."*
— Milton Berle

• COMMUNICATION •

The ambiguity of
Communication.

▶ *"I know you think you understood
what I said but what you heard was
not what I meant."*

The stupid listener and the
even dumber communicator.

▶ *"Communication is impossible when
he who hears doesn't know what he
who speaks means — and when he
who speaks doesn't know what he
himself means!"*

Advice on how to compose
written orders —

▶ *"Write your order not only so they can
be understood, but so they can not be
misunderstood."*

— Col. A. S. Newman

When you can't
understand somebody
who is explaining
something poorly.

▶ *"I think I understand
that incorrectly, right?"*

Why two people who
communicate misunderstand
each other so often.

▶ *"The spoken word belongs half to him
who speaks, and half to him who
hears."*

— French proverb

Learn to keep it simple. Don't
say what the Duchess in "Alice
in Wonderland" said to Alice —

▶ *"Be what you would seem to be — or,
if you'd like it put more simply — never
imagine yourself not to be otherwise
than what it might appear to others
that what you were or might have
been was not otherwise than what you
had been would have appeared to
them to be otherwise."*

• COMMUNISM •

"The theory of communism
may be summed up in one
sentence.

▶ *Abolish all private property."*

— Karl Marx and Friedrich Engels

"Russia has only one
opponent.

▶ *The explosive power of democratic
ideas and the inherent urge of the
human race in the direction of
freedom."*

— Karl Marx

Let's patch up our differences before it's too late! ▸ *"Time is passing, and it might be too late. The train might have already left the station."*

— Mikhail Gorbachev

The philosophy of Communism. ▸ *"Mad dogma."*

Karl Marx, profoundly affected by the philosophy of Hagel, theorized that capitalism would historically evolve into Communism. ▸ *1. "Thesis" —*
A movement from a
given situation.
2. "Antithesis" —
A movement from thesis
to its opposite.
3. "Synthesis" —
which conserves and
elevates the essential
characteristics and values
of the other two in a new
form. Each synthesis has its
own negation, and the process
goes on as before, always
producing richer and higher
syntheses.

— Friedrich Hegel

If religion is the opiate of the masses, what is communism? ▸ *"Communism is the opiate of the asses!"*

The Law of Communism on equality. ▸ *"Shortages will be divided equally among the peasants."*

"What is the one beneficial effect of going to Moscow? ▸ *You come home waving the American flag with all your might!"*

— Mary Tyler Moore

• COMMUTER •

Commuter — ▸ *"One who spends his life riding to and from his wife."*

• COMPASSION •

The awakening compassion of wealthy nations for the poor of other countries.

▶ *"Our age will be remembered not for its horrifying crimes or its astonishing inventions, but because it is the first generation in history in which mankind dared to believe it practical to make the benefits of civilization available to the whole human race."*

— Arnold J. Toynbee

• YOUR COMPETENCE •

"The Peter Principle"
In climbing the ladder of any organization, to what level of competence can an employee rise?

▶ *"In a hierarchy every employee tends to rise to his level of incompetence."*

— Lawrence J. Peter

• COMPETITION •

"The problem with competition is...

▶ *that it brings out the best in products and the worst in men!"*

— David Sarnoff

How competition motivates us.

▶ *"Our competition is always so damned good! We've got to be bettter!"*

How does competition guard and regulate our economy?

▶ *"Competition is the policeman of our economy."*

— E. C. Sammons

Can two people competing in the same business avoid being enemies?

▶ *"Two vinegar salesmen can't be friends."*

— Ancient proverb

An effective way to meet competition.

▶ *"I don't meet competition, I crush it!"*

— Charles Revson

"The only competition we need is...

▶ *to be better than we are!"*

"Never worry because a rival imitates you.

▶ *So long as he follows your tracks he can't pass you."*

• COMPLAINING! •

When you've got a Complaint, always go to the top dog!

▶ *"Why speak to the monkey when you can speak to the organ grinder. He's the boss."*

The eternal complainer!

▶ *"If he died and went to heaven, he'd find something to complain about!"*

Don't always be a grouch!

▶ *"It is the growing man who lives a dog's life."*

— Coleman Cox

Where should every kind of Knocker be?

▶ *"Always outside the door!"*

Complaint Form —

▶ *"Please write your complaint in the square below. Write legibly."*

• THE COMPLIMENT •

Beware of a compliment!

▶ *"It's only 18 inches between a pat on the back and a kick in the pants."*

About a really nice guy.

▶ *"God could have made a nicer guy — but he never did!"*

Should a compliment by any other than your equal be taken with a slight grain of salt?

▶ *"It is a matter of the simplest demonstration, that no man can be really appreciated but by his equal or superior.*

— John Ruskin

Is there any compliment greater than being loved?

▶ *"To be trusted is a greater compliment than to be loved."*

— George Macdonald

Hand out a deserved compliment!

▶ *"Make other people like themselves a little better, my son, and I promise you they will like you very well."*
— Lord Chesterfield

"The surest way to knock the chip off a fellow's shoulder is...

▶ *to pat him on the back."*
— Brewer Stork

How to react to a compliment to yourself and to a disparagement of others.

▶ *"Let us believe neither half of the good people tell us of ourselves, nor half the evil they say of others."*
— J. Pettit-Senn

Is a compliment truly a compliment or an act of superiority by the complimenter?

▶ *"Compliments and flattery oftenest excite my contempt by the pretension they imply; for who is he that assumes to flatter me? To compliment often implies an assumption of superiority in the complimenter. It is, in fact, a subtle detraction."*
— Henry David Thoreau

Start complimenting somebody if he does a good deed!

▶ *"When I did well, I heard it never. When I did ill, I heard it ever!"*

To bestow a compliment or to provoke anger. Which?

▶ *"One is more delightful for being told one is delightful — just as one is more angry for being told one is angry."*
— Katherine F. Gerould

Say and do the nice thing now!

▶ *"The bitterest tears shed over graves are for words left unsaid and deeds left undone."*
— Harriet Beecher Stowe

"He's one in a million but...

▶ *I forget which one."*

• COMPROMISE •

"To compromise is...

▶ *to slice a piece of cake in such a way that everyone believes he received the biggest piece."*
— Jan Peerce

"Let's compromise.　　　　▶ *Do it my way!*"

• THE COMPUTER •

Sign on Digital Computer. Needs careful reading!

▶ *"Das cumputen machine is nicht fur gerfingerpoken und mittengraben, is easy schnappen der springenwork, blowenfusen und poppencorken mit spitzensparken, ist nicht fur gewerken by das dummkptfen. Das rubbernecken sightseeren, keepen hands in das pockets. Relaxen und watch das blinkenlights!"*

Motto of COMPUTER haters!

▶ *"Strive at all times to bend, fold spindle & mutilate!"*

• CONCILIATING •

When conciliating with a stronger adversary, don't give away too much or you'll get chewed up!

▶ *"An infallible method of conciliating a tiger is to allow oneself to be devoured."*

— Konrad Adenauer

• CONFIDENCE •

"Confidence is a plant of...

▶ *slow growth."*

— William Pitt

The right philosophy for building self esteem.

▶ *"I can't wait till tomorrow because I get better looking everyday".*

— Joe Namath

• YOUR CONSCIENCE •

Why is a bad conscience a good conscience?

▶ *"A bad conscience is a conscience doing its duty."*

The voice of conscience says what?

▶ *"Conscience is the voice that says you shouldn't have done something after you did it."*

"Conscience takes up more room than...

▶ *all the rest of a person's insides."*
— Mark Twain

"Conscience is the inner voice that warns us...

▶ *that someone may be looking."*
— H. L. Mencken

How does the voice of conscience make you feel?

▶ *"Conscience is the still small voice that makes you feel still smaller."*
— James Sanaker

How you often feel when your sense of remorse is inadequate.

▶ *"I feel bad that I don't feel worse!"*
— Michael Frayne

• CONSERVATION •

In praise of conservationists!

▶ *"The sun, moon and stars would have disappeared long ago if they had happened to be within reach of predatory human hands."*
— Havelock Ellis

• THE CONSERVATIVE •

What is a real conservative?

▶ *"One who wants to conserve what he has."*

• BEING CONSIDERATE •

"He's so kind and considerate. He's like...

▶ *the guy who warms up the water when he drowns the kittens!"*

"The real art of conversation is not only to say the right thing in the right place but...

▶ *to leave unsaid the wrong thing at the tempting moment."* moment."
— Dorothy Nevill

Don't add burdens to the man who's already on the way down!

▶ *" 'Tis a cruelty to load a falling man."*
— William Shakespeare

Guidelines on considerate behaviour!

▶ *"Among those who stand, do not sit; among those who sit, do not stand. Among those who laugh, do not weep; among those who weep, do not laugh."*
— Jewish proverb

• BEING CONSISTENT •

Should you be afraid to
change your mind?

▶ *"When you're through changing you're
through!"*

— Bruce Barton

"Spurts don't count.

▶ *The final score makes no
mention of a splendid start
if the finish proves that
you were an 'also ran.'"*

— Herbert Kaufman

In what are men consistent?

▶ *"Inconsistency is the only thing in
which men are consistent."*

— Horace Smith

What kind of people generally
remain consistent?

▶ *"Consistency is the last refuge of the
unimaginative."*

— Oscar Wilde

It's a small mind that forever
remains consistent.

▶ *"The only man who can change his
mind is a man that's got one."*

— Edward Noyes Westcott

• CONQUEST •

When you're out for conquest,
what's the best thing you can
conquer?

▶ *"A man's conquest of himself dwarfs
the ascent of Everest."*

• CONTENTMENT •

Defintion of Contentment —

▶ *"Being satisfied with what you haven't
got!"*

— Ethel Watts Mumford

How to be content with your
lot —

▶ *"Since we cannot get what we like, let
us like what we can get!"*

— Spanish proverb

Instructions from a piece
of jade to people
of the Far East... and
for many, it works!

▶ *"To banish troubles, rub*
    this jade.
 I'll calm you down when
    nerves feel frayed.
 Thumb my groove to
    ease depression.
 Squeeze me hard, release
    aggression!"

• CONVERSATION •

Distinguish the difference
between a Gossip — a Bore and
a good Conversationalist.

▶ *"A gossip is one who talks to you*
about others; a bore is one who talks
to you about himself, and a brilliant
conversationalist is one who talks to
you about yourself."
— Lisa Kirk

Next time somebody's
listening to you — bear
this in mind!

▶ *"Most good listeners are usually*
thinking about something else."

You couldn't get a word in
edgewise!

▶ *"You couldn't keep a conversation*
going at all. Everybody was talking too
much."
— Yogi Berra

"How come we like telling
a story two or three times
but...

▶ *hate to hear it more*
than once!"

What is the secret ingredient
for good conversation?

▶ *"The great charm of conversation*
consists less in the display of one's
own wit and intelligence than in the
power to draw forth the resources of
others."
— Jean de la Bruyère

How to have a dull
uninteresting conversation.

▶ *"There is no conversation more boring*
than one where everybody agrees."
— Michel de Montaigne

They started to run out of
conversation.

▶ *"Conversational rigor mortis started*
setting in!"

"How do you feel in the presence of a more brilliant conversationalist than you?

▶ *"There is nothing by which a man exasperates most people more than by displaying a superior ability or brilliancy in conversation. They seem pleased at the time, but their envy makes them curse him at their hearts."*

— Samuel Johnson

What to say when you forget or run out of conversation.

▶ *"This brief silence is being brought to you by —"*

• COOPERATION •

Co-operation is spelled with two letters:

▶ *"WE."*

— George M. Verity

• CORRUPTION •

What works best for corruption?

▶ *"When it comes to corruption, nothing succeeds like money."*

— American proverb

• THE COTTAGE •

"The ideal summer cottage is...

▶ *one that visits twelve and sleeps two."*

• THE COUNTRYSIDE •

How come city folks think the countryside is so charming?

▶ *"The country has charms only for those not obliged to stay there."*

— Edouard Manet

• COURAGE •

"Courage is the art of being frightened without...

▶ *letting it show."*

"Courage is fear holding on...

▶ *a minute longer."*

— George S. Patton

"Too few have the courage... ▶ *of my convictions."*
— Robert M. Hutchins

Who has not courage should ▶ *"Legs."*
have

"True courage is not only a ▶ *also a parachute for falling!"*
balloon for rising but...

"Courage in people is like a ▶ *You never know their strength until*
tea bag. *they're in hot water."*

When does fear become ▶ *"Courage is fear that has said its*
courage? *prayers."*

How eating peanuts can serve ▶ *"No man in the world has more*
as a test of courage. *courage than the man who can stop*
after eating one peanut."
— Channing Pollock

• COWARDICE •

What is a Coward and how ▶ *"A coward is one who in a perilous*
does he think? *emergency thinks with his legs."*
— Ambrose Bierce

What you can facetiously say ▶ *"They tell me I'm the most colorful*
when you're afraid. *boxer in the West. I'm yellow!"*

A religious defense on being a ▶ *"I quit my boxing career because of*
coward. *religion. I'm a devout coward!"*

• THE CREDITOR •

"A creditor is worse than a ▶ *For a master owns only your person, a*
master. *creditor owns your dignity, and can*
belabour that."
— Victor Hugo

• CRIME •

Is there no crime that man can ▶ *"There is no crime of which one*
not fall prey to? *cannot image oneself to be the*
author."
— Johann Wolfgang von Goethe

"Starvation, and not sin, is the parent of...

▶ *modern crime!"*
— Oscar Wilde

How to deter crime —

▶ *"To make certain that crime does not pay, the government should take it over and try to run it."*
— G. Norman Collie

Where lies the source of most crime?

▶ *"Poverty is the mother of crime."*
— Marcus Aurelius

"Stop crime at its source.

▶ *Support planned parenthood!"*
— Robert Byrne

Is the penalty for a crime intended as punishment — or as a deterrent?

▶ *"Men are not hanged for stealing horses, but that horses may not be stolen."*
— Lord Halifax

A saying of people in jail.

▶ *"Don't do the crime if you can't stand the time!"*

He's such a crook!

▶ *"He'd steal a hot stove if he could lift it."*

You might as well perpetrate a big crime as a little one!

▶ *"As well be hanged for a sheep as for a lamb!"*
— English proverb

"It's strange that men should take up crime...

▶ *when there are so many legal ways to be dishonest."*

Attitude toward capital punishment in the Far East.

▶ *"It is no sin to kill a killer."*
— Hindu proverb

• CRISIS •

A Crisis is a turning point where things either get better or worse.

▶ *Sociologist Saul Alinksy observed: "The Chinese write the word 'crisis' with two characters. One means danger and the other means opportunity."*

• THE CRITICS! •

The esteem in which the Paderewski held critics.

▶ *"If I miss practice for one day, I know it. If I miss for two days, the public knows it. If I don't do any practicing for a month, the critics find it out."*

Defending the right of a critic to be a critic.

▶ *"Can't a critic give his opinion of an omelette without being asked to lay an egg?"*

— Clayton Rawson

"A drama critic is...

▶ *a person who surprises the playwright by informing him what he meant."*

— Wilson Mizner

"A critic is a man who knows the way but...

▶ *can't drive the car!"*

— Kenneth Tynan

That which critics cannot do.

▶ *"Critics are like eunuchs in a harem: they know how it's done, they've seen it done everyday, but they're unable to do it themselves."*

— Brendan Behan

The questionable tact of Abraham Lincoln as a book reviewer.

▶ *"People who like this sort of thing will find this the sort of thing they like."*

— Book review by Abraham Lincoln

Why don't critics focus more on the good than on the bad?

▶ *"A true critic ought rather to dwell upon excellences than imperfections, to discern the concealed beauties of a writer, and communicate to the world such things as are worth their observation.*

— Joseph Addison

• CRITICIZING •

Should any of us criticize the good and bad in others?

▶ *"There is so much good in the worst of us, and so much bad in the best of us, that it behooves all of us not to talk about the rest of us."*

— Robert Louis Stevenson

How big are you when you constantly detract and disparage?

▶ *"You have to be little to belittle!"*

Nothing on how to avoid criticism.

▶ *"To avoid criticism — do nothing, say nothing, be nothing!"*

Always criticize the other guy in private!

▶ *"Advice given in the midst of a crowd is loathsome."*

— Arabian proverb

"They should call you 'Opportunity' because...

▶ *you're always knocking."*

People will take criticism in many sectors of their lives but everybody has his own tender spot.

▶ *"Goering, number two Nazi, could accept calmly criticism of the murder of millions as a military or political expedient, but broke into anger when accused of lying."*

— John Heron

"I can stand any amount of criticism as long as...

▶ *it is unqualified praise."*

— Noel Coward

When somebody heartlessly and unfairly criticizes you.

▶ *"It's a lot easier to throw spears than to catch them!"*

— Chinese proverb

"Don't tell your friends their social faults.

▶ *They will cure the fault and never forgive you!"*

— Logan Pearsall Smith

"Honest criticism is hard to take...

▶ *particularly from a relative, a friend, an acquaintance, or a stranger."*

— Franklin Jones

It's so easy to criticize after the event.

▶ *"Everybody has 20/20 hindsight."*

He's always berating people.

▶ *"If he saw you walking on water he'd say you can't swim!"*

• CRYING •

When disaster hits here's why I can't cry or laugh.

▶ *"I'm too old to cry and it hurts too much to laugh."*

Guide to making people weep or laugh —

▶ *"If you want to make people weep, you must weep yourself. If you want to make people laugh, your face must remain serious."*

— Giovanni Casanova

"You should never cry over anything unless...

▶ *it can cry over you!"*

"You may forget who you laughed with but...

▶ *you'll never forget who you cried with!"*

Why the world will laugh with you but not cry.

▶ *"Laugh, and the world laughs with you,*
   Weep, and you weep alone;
   For this brave old earth must borrow its mirth,
   It has trouble enough of its own."

— Ella Wheeler Wilcox

"Instead of crying over spilt milk...

▶ *go milk another cow!"*

• CULTURE •

Culture is to know what?

▶ *"Culture is to know the best that has been said and thought in the world."*

— Matthew Arnold

• CURIOSITY •

Curiosity killed the cat!

▶ *"Some of us have to put our finger on the burner to find out if it's hot."*

"The man who does not habitually wonder is but...

▶ *a pair of spectacles behind which there is no eye."*

— Thomas Carlyle

• THE CYNIC! •

The original Greek word for "Cynic" was derived from the image of a surly dog snarling at everything it sees.

▶ *"A cynic is one who never sees a good quality in a man and never fails to see a bad one."*

— Henry Ward Beecher

What is a cynic and in what manner does his vision see things?

▶ Cynic: n. "a blackguard whose faulty vision sees things as they are, not as they ought to be."

— Ambrose Bierce

"Idealism is what precedes experience.

▶ Cynicism is what follows."

A cynic and his absence of knowledge about value.

▶ "A cynic is a man who knows the price of everything, and the value of nothing."

— Oscar Wilde

"A cynic is a man who, when he smells flowers,...

▶ looks around for a coffin."

— H. L. Mencken

D

• THE DANCER •

He's a great dancer.

▶ *"He has eloquent feet."*

— B. Chad

How we used to
dance in the good old
pre-disco days.

▶ *"We really danced when we were
kids. The guys got close
'cause they knew that was all they
were going to get."*

• DANGER! •

When you court danger,
approach with caution!

▶ *"Only a fool tests the depth of water
with both feet."*

That's a hopeless manoeuver.

▶ *"That's like trying to tattoo a soap
bubble."*

— John Mason Brown

Sign on hydro pole —

▶ *"To touch these wires means instant
death. Anyone disregarding this notice
will be placed under arrest."*

• DATING! •

Going out on a Blind Date is...

▶ *when you expect to meet a Vision and
she turns out to be a Sight!*

• DEAFNESS •

Which two things don't listen to reason?

▶ *"Neither great poverty nor great riches will hear reason."*

— Henry Fielding

"There are none so deaf as...

▶ *those who will not hear."*

• DEATH •

What are your views on death?

▶ *"I don't believe in it!"*

— George Burns (at age 90)

What will many people fear most about dying?

▶ *"People are not afraid of death per se, but of the incompleteness of their lives."*

— Lisl Marburg Goodman

Where everybody ends up!

▶ *"Earth to earth, ashes to ashes, dust to dust, in sure and certain hope of the resurrection."*

— Book of Common Prayer

Death's echo!

▶ *"Death plucks at my ear and says — Live. I am coming!"*

— Oliver Wendell Holmes

Since everybody eventually dies, maybe death isn't as bad as it sounds.

▶ *"That which is so universal as death must be a benefit."*

— Friedrich von Schiller

Who to ask what it's like to be dead.

▶ *"The night approaches... Bringing dread Of that irrevocable journey to Eternal Sleep. Is it so awesome? Ask the Dead."*

— Lloyd Hartley

"I'm not anxious to die because...

▶ *that's been done so many times before!"*

— Woody Allen

"It is one of God's blessings that we cannot foreknow the hour of our death.

▶ *For a time fixed, even beyond the possibility of living, would trouble us more than doth this uncertainty."*

— James VI

What happens when you live too long?

▶ *"The long habit of living Indisposeth us to dying."*

— Sir Thomas Browne

Are we justified in regarding death as such an evil?

▶ *"It is by no means a fact that death is the worst of all evils; when it comes it is an alleviation to mortals who are worn out with sufferings."*

— Metastasio

"It is very singular how the fact of a man's death often seems to give people a truer idea of his character, whether for good or evil than...

▶ *they have ever possessed while he was living and acting among them."*

— Nathaniel Hawthorne

A reminder on where we're all going.

▶ *"For dust thou art, and unto dust shalt thou return."*

— Book of Genesis

What will a man pay to avoid death?

▶ *"All that a man has will he give for his life."*

— The Bible

When we come to die, what will we conclude life is?

▶ *"Life's a succession of tremendous trifles."*

If you don't want to be totally forgotten when you die, do some kindnesses to those dear to you.

▶ *"To live in hearts we leave behind is not to die."*

— Thomas Campbell

Death —

▶ *"Nature's way of suggesting we slow down."*

How much will the world be affected by your death?

▶ *"The three words I have learned about life is that it goes on!"*

— Robert Frost

"If I could drop dead right now,...

▶ *"I'd be the happiest man alive!"*

— Samuel Goldwyn

"That which is often so terrible when we come to die is...

▶ NOT *that life should end is so terrible in itself — but that it should end with so many disappointments."*

— Saul Bellow

"The reports of my death are...

▶ *greatly exaggerated!"*

— Mark Twain

If you want a decent turnout at your funeral, you better start being nicer to a lot of people!

▶ *"I hate funerals, and would not attend my own if it could be avoided, but it is well for every man to stop once in a while to think of what sort of a collection of mourners he is training in his final event."*

— Robert T. Morris

Woody Allen's views on death.

▶ *"I'm not afraid to die. I just don't want to be there when it happens."*

— Woody Allen

"You can't tell how good it is to be alive, till you are facing death, because...

▶ *you don't live till then."*

— John Galsworthy

The nice thing about not knowing when we're going to die.

▶ *"No man is so old as to believe he cannot live one more year."*

— Sean O'Casey

• DECADENCE •

"The difference between our Decadence and the Russians' is...

▶ *that while theirs is brutal, ours is apathetic."*

— James Thurber

• DECISIONS •

Guide on when say Yes or No when making decisions!

▶ *When, against one's will, one is high pressured into making a hurried decision, the best answer is always "No," because "No" is more easily changed to "Yes", than "Yes" is changed to "No".*

— Charles E. Nielson

He's always undecided.

▶ *"He's a man of instant indecision!"*

Should you cross that bridge
or burn it?

▶ *"The hardest thing to learn in life is
which bridge to cross and which to
burn."*

— David Russell

Should you meekly resign
yourself to troubles — or battle
and get rid of them?

▶ *"To be or not to be — that
is the question;
Whether 'tis nobler in the
mind to suffer
The slings and arrows of
outrageous fortune,
Or to take arms against a
sea of troubles,
And by opposing end them?"*

— William Shakespeare

To the fellow who's forced to
make the final decision.

▶ *"The buck stops here!"*

— Harry S. Truman

Shakespeare's soliloquy in
Hamlet — "To be or not to be."

▶ *"It is the most famous speech in
modern literature, with an appeal that
neither repetition nor parody can
destroy.
It dramatizes for each one of us the
baffled individual in the agony of
indecision."*

— H. Peterson

Don't rush into
decisions!

▶ *"Second thoughts are ever
wiser."*

— Euripides

"The man who insists upon
seeing with perfect clearness
before he decides,...

▶ *never decides."*

— Henri Frederic Amiel

The ease and difficulty of
making a decision.

▶ *"It's easy to make decisions on matters
for which you have no responsibility!"*

Give your decisions, never
your reasons. Why?

▶ *"Your decisions may be right, your
reasons are sure to be wrong."*

— Earl of Mansfield

Reply to the person who says "I never change my mind."

▶ *"Only fools and dead men don't change their minds."*

Consolation when you're frustrated in wanting to decide something one way or the other!

▶ *"Not to decide is to decide."*
— Harvey Cox

Don't torment unduly on a decision.

▶ *"Don't stand shivering upon the bank; plunge in at once and have it over."*
— T.C. Haliburton

• DEFEAT •

How to take defeat.

▶ *"Defeat isn't bitter if you don't swallow it."*

• DELEGATING! •

The question the smart executive asks.

▶ *"Does this require my personal attention, or can it be done just as well by somebody else?"*

What a real delegater is.

▶ *"He doesn't put his hand on any work he delegates but his fingerprint is on every job."*

• THE DEMAGOGUE •

When can Demagoguery become useful?

▶ *"When ideas fail, words come in very handy."*
— Johan Wolfgang von Goethe

"A demagogue is a person who preaches doctrines he knows to be untrue to...

▶ *men he knows to be idiots."*
— H.L. Mencken

• DEMOCRACY •

That which a democracy can do to its government.

▶ *"The people's right to change what does not work is one of the greatest principles of our system of government."*

— Richard M. Nixon

Weakness of our political system.

▶ *"Under democracy, one party always devotes its chief energies to trying to prove the other party is unfit to rule — and both commonly succeed, and are right."*

— H. L. Mencken

The great advantage of democracy over dictatorship.

▶ *"No man is good enough to govern another man without that other man's consent."*

— Abraham Lincoln

The profound reason why democracy is possible and necessary!

▶ *"Man's capacity for justice makes democracy possible, but man's inclination to injustice makes democracy necessary."*

— Reinhold Niebuhr

Is the rule of a 51% vote in a democracy, a true reflection of the people?

▶ *"The rule of 51% is a convenience... We have lost all of its true meaning when we imagine the opinion of 51% is in some high fashion the true opinion of the whole 100%, or indulge in the sophistry that the rule of a majority is based upon the ultimate equality of man."*

— Walter Lippmann

Is it true that in a democracy the majority make the decisions?

▶ *"People often say that, in a democracy, decisions are made by a majority of the people. Of course, that is not true. Decisions are made by a majority of those who make themselves heard and who vote — a very different thing."*

— Walter H. Judd

Asked during the Watergate investigation —
"Whose fault is it in a democracy if we get a bad government?"

▶ "If men and women of capacity refuse to take part in politics and government, they condemn themselves, as well as the people, to bad government."

— Sam Ervin

"We must either fight for democracy throughout the world or...

▶ learn to eat rice and do the goose-step."

— Sumner Welles

• DENTAL •

"You don't have to floss your teeth every day...

▶ just those you want to keep!"

Toothache —

▶ "A pain that drives you to extraction!"

Sign in dentist's office in Tokyo —

▶ "Teeth Extracted by Latest Methodists."

• DEPRAVITY •

Definition of Debauchee —

▶ "One who has so earnestly pursued pleasure that he has had the misfortune to overtake it."

— Ambrose Bierce

• DEPRESSED! •

"When you're down in the mouth...

▶ remember Jonah. He came out alright."

• DESIRES •

Never expect too much!

▶ "Blessed is he that expecteth nothing, for he shall not be disappointed!"

The difference between Desires and Wants.

▶ "Discontents arise from our desires oftener than from our wants."

Are man's wants and desires ever satiated?

▶ *"Man is a wanting animal — as soon as one of his needs is satisfied, another appears in its place. This process is unending. It continues from birth to death."*

— Douglas McGregor

"The stoical scheme of supplying our wants by lopping off our desires is like...

▶ *cutting off our feet when we want shoes."*

— Jonathan Swift

Man is a fool always wanting what he can't get.

▶ *"As a rule man is a fool.
When it's hot, he wants it cool.
When it's cool he wants it hot.
Always wanting what is not!"*

• DESPAIR •

How to handle despair.

▶ *"Beware of desperate steps; the darkest day,
Lived till tomorrow, will have passed away."*

— William Cowper

• DETERMINATION •

"If there's a will, there's a way." ▶ *"If there is an IS there ought not to be a NOT!"*

A person of determination will transform his potential into maximum performance.

▶ *"Before the gates of excellence the high gods have placed sweat."*

— Greek proverb

That vital spark we call "Spirit" is half the battle.

▶ *"My left is broken; my right shattered; therefore I will advance with the centre."*

— Marshal Foch

If there is no wind...

▶ *"Row."*

— Latin proverb

What a man of guts
will do after a
major failure.

▶ *"I am hurt but I am
not slain! I will lie
me down and bleed awhile
— then I'll rise and
fight again."*

— St. Barton's Ode

• THE DEVIL •

Who attracts more followers?
God or the Devil?

▶ *"Wherever God erects a house of
    prayer
The Devil always builds a chapel there
And 't will be found upon examination
The latter has the largest
    congregation!"*

"Speak of the Devil...

▶ *and he will hear about it!"*

— Ambrose Bierce

Warning!
"If you don't come face to face
with the devil...

▶ *you may be travelling the same way he
is."*

Caution to society when
there's too much
unemployment!

▶ *"The Devil finds jobs for idle hands."*

Is the Devil a creation of God?

▶ *"The Devil would be the best way out
as an excuse for God... But even so,
one can hold God responsible for the
existence of the Devil."*

— Sigmund Freud

"The devil makes work for...

▶ *idle glands!"*

Why the devil is so prevalent!

▶ *"The devil is a gentleman who never
goes where he is not welcome."*

— John A. Lincoln

• THE DIAMOND •

The Diamond —

▶ *"A diamond is a hunk of coal that
made good under pressure."*

"Better a diamond with a flaw ▶ *a pebble without!"*
than...

• YOUR DIET •

What happens when you gain ▶ *"It's a caloric calamity!"*
weight?

A diet guaranteed to work! ▶ *"Another good reducing exercise*
consists in placing both hands against
the table edge and pushing back."
— Robert Quillen

God's way of telling you what ▶ *"Indigestion is charged by God with*
to avoid eating. *enforcing morality on the stomach."*
— Victor Hugo

"Diet Failure is... ▶ *when your wife tells you to pull in your*
stomach — and you already have."

The toughest part of dieting ▶ *"It's watching what your friends eat!"*
isn't watching what you eat.

Does mental effort consume a ▶ *"The extra calories needed for one*
lot of calories? *hour of intense mental effort would be*
completely met by eating one oyster
cracker or one half of a salted peanut."
— Francis G. Benedict

There's a new radical diet ▶ *"Eat Less!"*
out —

What happens when the weak ▶ *"The weak shall inherit the girth."*
give up on their diet?

"The trouble with a diet is that ▶ *not being fed."*
you get fed up with... — Erskine Johnson

How food can make the day ▶ *"Go on a diet!"*
longer.

"I've been on a diet now for twenty-one days. ▶ *"All I lost was three weeks."*

The doctor just put me on a No Starch diet. ▶ *"Now I can have all the detergent I want."*

Me lose weight? ▶ *"I'd rather starve first!"*

"My wife has put on so much weight that... ▶ *I'm not even legally married to thirty pounds of her."*

Calories don't count! ▶ *"They multiply!"*

Can gluttony be kept a secret? ▶ *"Gluttony is not a secret vice."*
— Orson Welles

Diet and your Figure. ▶ *"Watching my figure is rough on me. The more I watch it the more I see."*

"Nothing Stretches Slacks... ▶ *like Snacks!"*

Everything I like is a disaster! ▶ *"Everything I like is either illegal, immoral, or fattening!"*

Eating versus Fasting. ▶ *"The pleasures of eating are fleeting. The pleasures of fasting are lasting."*

• THE DILEMMA! •

What a dilemma is — ▶ *"In front a precipice, Behind a wolf."*
— Latin proverb

When you're on the Horns of a Dilemma you've got to look at the alternatives, think clearly and make a decision. ▶ *"A certain jackass, which had an exceptional intelligence quotient, was placed midway between two equally attractive bundles of hay, and he died of starvation because he could not find reason to choose between them."*
— Jean Buridan

The dilemma that always damns you. ▶ *"You can and you can't, You will and you won't; You'll be damn'd if you do, You'll be damn'd if you don't."*
— Lorenzo Dow

• DIPLOMACY •

"A diplomat is someone who can tell you to go to hell in such a way that...

▶ *you look forward to the trip."*

The quintessential Diplomat —

▶ *"When a diplomat says yes he means perhaps; when he says perhaps he means no; when he says no he is no diplomat."*

Secret strategies in the world of diplomacy.

▶ *"A one-time U. S. Ambassador in Europe, astonishing in view of his age, is said to have approached all problems with a closed mind and an open fly."*
— John Kenneth Galbraith

What art is there to diplomacy?

▶ *"Diplomacy is the art of concealing one's thoughts."*

"Sincere diplomacy is no more possible than...

▶ *dry water."*
— Joseph Stalin

How to practice diplomacy.

▶ *"Diplomacy is to do and say The nastiest thing in the nicest way."*
— Isaac Goldberg

How a diplomat tells you you're stupid.

▶ *"A diplomat is a man who says you have an open mind instead of telling you that you have a hole in your head."*

• DIRECTION •

You've got to know where you're going!

▶ *"No wind is a good wind if you don't know where the harbor is."*

• THE DIRECTIONS •

How people react to reading the directions.

▶ *"Many of us would rather risk catastrophe than read the directions."*

Make sure you know where you're going if you want to get there!

▶ *"The direction we are facing has a lot to do with our destination."*

• DISAPPOINTMENT •

Advice to a person who keeps griping about his disappointments.

▶ *"Disappointments should be cremated, not embalmed!"*

• DISCRETION •

If you're going to battle with somebody, what role should Discretion play?

▶ *"Discretion is the better part of valour."*

• DISCRIMINATION •

"End discrimination.

▶ *Hate everybody!"*

• DISSIDENTS •

How to silence dogs and other dissidents.

▶ *"A biting dog never barks — while its mouth is full."*

• DISSIPATING! •

The penalty of dissipation with a candle.

▶ *"People who burn the candle at both ends get caught in the middle!"*

Maybe burning your candle at both ends is the right philosophy.

▶ *"My candle burns at both ends*
It will not last the night.
But ah my foes — and oh my friends
It gives a lovely light."

— Edna St. Vincent Millay

• DIVORCE •

"Common sense could prevent most divorces...

▶ *and almost most marriages!"*

"After a divorce I feel like...

▶ *a new man!"*

— Mae West

The smart strategy to practice after divorce.

▶ *"I was married once. Now I just lease."*

The couple who were divorced after 76 years of marriage.

▶ Q. *"Why did you wait so long?"*
A. *"We wanted to wait till all our children were dead."*

• HOW TO "DO" IT •

Sign on Church bulletin board —

▶ *"Do unto others as if you were others!"*

"I hear and I forget. I see and I remember.

▶ *I do and I understand."*
— Chinese proverb

How to do unto the other fellow.

▶ *"Do unto the other feller the way he'd like to do unto you an' do it fust!"*
— Edward N. Westcott

How to do an insuperable job.

▶ *"Nothing is particularly hard if you divide it into small pieces."*
— Henry Ford

Motto of the 4-H Club.

▶ *"Learn to Do by Doing."*

Adam Smith wasn't the only guy who knew about Division of Labour.

▶ *"Light is the task when many another shares the toil."*
— Homer

How to do unto others —

▶ *"Do unto others. Then run!"*

"Well done is...

▶ *better than well said!"*
— Benjamin Franklin

"If you don't have anything to do...

▶ *do it with style!"*
— James H. Boren

What to do if you don't want things to get better.

▶ *"Left alone — things go from bad to worse."*

"Don't just stand there...

▶ *undo something!"*
— Murray Weidenbaum

"Do not do unto others as you would that they should do unto you because...

▶ *their tastes may not be the same."*
— George Bernard Shaw

"If you have to suck a lemon...

▶ *suck it quickly!"*

What to do when you know you're beat.

▶ *"When defeat is inevitable it is wisest to yield."*

— Marcus Fabius Quintilianus

What to do when you don't know what to do first.

▶ *"I have so much to do that I am going going to bed."*

— Savoyard proverb

"There is no pleasure in having nothing to do. The fun is in...

▶ *having lots to do and NOT doing it."*

"If you want a thing to be well done...

▶ *order it rare!"*

"Ask not what your country can do for you.

▶ *Ask what you can do for your country."*

— John F. Kennedy

Do one thing at a time and each will get its turn.

▶ *"You can't get sugar and furniture out of a maple tree at the same time."*

"The early bird catches the worm.

▶ *So the smart worm learns to sleep in."*

I can do something about it!

▶ *"I am only one, but still I am one; I cannot do everything, but still I can do something; and because I cannot do everything I will not refuse to do the something that I can do."*

— Edward E. Hale

• WHEN TO "DO" IT! •

"Do it now but...

▶ <u>DON'T DO IT</u>"!

"Why you should do a disagreeable job today instead of tomorrow.

▶ *"It will save you 24 hours of dread — and give you 24 hours of relief that the job is done."*

"Never agains means...

▶ *not until the next time!"*

"When a man has not a good reason for doing a thing...

▶ *he has one good reason for letting it alone."*

— Walter Scott

"The day I'll do that is...

▶ *when hell freezes over!"*

Do all your dirty jobs first!

▶ *" 'Tis the dessert that graces all the feast, for an ill end disparages the rest."*

— William Shakespeare

• DOCTORS •

What an M.D. specialist is —

▶ *"A doctor who has his patients trained to become ill only during his office hours."*

Remember! Only doctors, and not patients, can appraise the qualifications of other doctors.

▶ *"Those that employ doctors know not their excellence — and those that reject them know not their deficience."*

— Samuel Johnson

Which is more important for the doctor to know? The patient or the patient's disease?

▶ *"It is much more important to know what sort of a patient has a disease than what sort of a disease a patient has."*

— William Osler

"The kind of doctor I want is...

▶ *one who, when he is not examining me, is home studying medicine."*

Regardless of the patient's outcome, doctors too are entitled to make a living.

▶ *"They answered, as they took their fees, 'There is no cure for this disease.'"*

— Hillaire Belloc

Do too many of us regard our Doctor as a God?

▶ *"We have confidence in our plumbers But we have faith in our doctors."*

Notice in an English doctor's waiting-room —

▶ *"To avoid delay, please have all your symptoms ready."*

Advertisement by a doctor in Athens —

▶ *"Specialist in Women and Other Diseases."*

Sign on doctor's office door —

▶ *"All Appointments Must be Made by Appointment."*

"I could have been a doctor but...

▶ *I had no patience!"*

A barometer by which you might appraise a doctor.

▶ *"Never go to a doctor whose office plants have died."*

— Erma Bombeck

In memory of
John Michael Forbes
1925-1985

▶ *"Beloved husband and father, and patient of Dr. Gary Nicolls of Memphis Tennessee!"*

Should you bequeath
a gift in gratitude
to your doctor?

▶ *"He's a fool that makes his doctor his heir."*

How doctors practice their profession.

▶ *"Some doctors practice medicine with their brains — others with their tongues."*

— William Osler

• DOGMATISM •

The tragic consequences of dogmatism throughout history.

▶ *"Most of the greatest evils that man has inflicted upon man have come through people feeling quite certain about something which, in fact, was false."*

— Bertrand Russell

• DOWNGRADING! •

Downgrade a person enough, particularly a child, and he'll develop an inferiority complex.

▶ *"We are very much what other people think of us."*

— William Hazlitt

• DOGS •

"My dog is so smart, that...

▶ *while he was being paper-trained he learned to read."*

"The reason a dog has so many friends is...

▶ *that his tail wags instead of his tongue."*

What sense of pride and recognition does a dog give his owner that no other human is likely to give him?

▶ *"To his dog, every man is Napoleon; hence the constant popularity of dogs."*

— Aldous Huxley

"In Siberia, they've got the fastest dogs in the world because...

▶ *the trees are so far apart."*

When is a dog most friendly?

▶ *"Nothing in the world is friendlier than a wet dog!"*

Of all dogs, why is the hot dog the noblest of them all?

▶ *"It never bites the hand that feeds it, but always feeds the hand that bites it."*

How owning a dog rejuvenates your personality.

▶ *"The great pleasure of a dog is that you may make a fool of yourself with him and not only will he not scold you, but he will make a fool of himself too."*

— Samuel Butler

How much does your dog love you?

▶ *"A dog is the only thing on earth that loves you more than you love yourself."*

— Josh Billings

• DOUBTS •

Are our doubts our own worst enemies, making us afraid even to try?

▶ *"Our doubts are traitors And make us lose the good we oft might win, By fearing to attempt."*

— William Shakespeare

"When in doubt,...

▶ *tell the truth!"*

— Mark Twain

• DREAMS •

"To make a dream come true...

▶ *don't oversleep!"*

The dream that was
a nightmare!

▶ *"As I was going up the stair
I met a man who wasn't there.
He wasn't there again today.
I wish, I wish, he'd stay away."*

— Hughes Mearns

By all means dream!

▶ *"Build a dream and the dream will
build you."*

What happens when dreams
are realized?

▶ *"Waiting and hoping are the whole of
life, and as soon as a dream is realized
it is destroyed."*

— Gian-Carlo Menotti

• DUTIES! •

"When you have a number of
disagreeable duties to
perform...

▶ *always do the most disagreeable first!"*

— Josiah Quincy

E

• EASY GOING! •

President Warren G. Harding, noted for a regime of corruption, was warned by his father not to be so easy-going.

▶ *"If you were a girl, Warren, you'd be in the family way all the time. You can't say 'No'."*

• THE EASY WAY! •

He likes everything to come the "Easy Way".

▶ *"He'd like his green peas to grow ready buttered."*

• ECONOMICS •

Most economists never agree, thereby proving economics is not a science.

▶ *"If all economists were laid end to end, they would not reach a conclusion."*
— George Bernard Shaw

Caution about the "Trickle Down" theory.

▶ *"When the horse dies, the oats no longer pass through to the sparrows."*
— John Kenneth Galbraith

• ECONOMISTS •

"If economists were good at business...

▶ *they would be rich, instead of advisers to the rich."*

• ECSTASY •

"Another form of ecstasy is...   ▸ *happiness with its clothes off.*"

"What a thrill!"   ▸ *"I felt the wings of my spirit give a little flutter of delight!"*

• EDUCATION •

"If you think education is   ▸ *try ignorance!"*
expensive...
                                                           — Derek Bok

It pays to teach people to be   ▸ *"If you give a man a fish you feed him*
self sufficient.   *for a day, but if you teach a man to fish*
                                       he'll be fed for the rest of his life."

Boy, is he ever   ▸ *"He's got more degrees*
educated!   *than a thermometer!"*

What should be two   ▸ *"Education today, more than ever*
objectives of education?   *before, must see clearly the dual*
                                       objectives: education for living and
                                       education for making a living."
                                                           — James M. Wood

What's the best part of   ▸ *"To know where you can find a thing is*
education?   *in reality the best part of learning."*

Real education begins in the   ▸ *"I have never let my schooling interfere*
street — not in school.   *with my education."*
                                                           — Mark Twain

Do you need to go to   ▸ *"The best and most important part of*
university to become   *every man's education is that which*
educated?   *he gives himself.*
                                                           — Edward Gibbon

Education will never replace   ▸ *"The world is full of educated*
guts and determination.   *derelicts."*
                                                           — Calvin Coolidge

"Without our universities, there would be few serious readers. Without readers, there would be few books.

▶ *Without books, the fabric of our culture would disappear and our aspirations for the future would be destroyed."*

— Jack McClelland

"Today we need to combine learning with work, political struggle, community service and even play.

▶ *All our conventional assumptions about education need to be re-examined."*

— Alvin Toffler, futurist

"Education has for its object...

▶ *the formation of character."*

— Herbert Spencer

"Education begins ten seconds after you are born and lasts until you die.

▶ *School is a secondary part of your lifelong education. I think your real education comes through people you know and the books you choose to read."*

— Robert Fulford

"The future of work will consist in...

▶ *learning a living."*

— Marshall McLuhan

The tragedy of so many of today's over educated people.

▶ *"Many a man with a B.A., M.A., and Ph. D. has no J.O.B."*

What's wrong with our method of education?

▶ *"I know the economic theories of Malthus and Adam Smith, but I cannot live within my income. I can conjugate Latin verbs, but I cannot write legibly. I can explain the principle of hydraulics, but I cannot fix a leak in the kitchen faucet."*

— Bernadine Freeman

"It is a tragic fact that most of us know how to be taught but...

▶ *we haven't learned how to learn."*

— Malcolm S. Knowles

Plea by the American Negro Colleges Association —

▶ *"A mind is a terrible thing to waste."*

To what degree, if any, are educated men superior to uneducated?

▶ *When asked how much educated men were superior to those uneducated, Aristotle answered, "As much as the living are to the dead."*

• EFFICIENCY •

That which efficiency really is —

▶ *"The art of last motion."*

• EGOISM •

The four "Egos" that are odious!

▶ *"1. The Egocentric — who's all wrapped up in himself.*
2. The Egoist — who loves himself.
3. The Egotist — who boasts about himself.
4. The Egomaniac — who morbidly loves himself to an almost insane extreme."

What is an Egotist and how do you rate his taste?

▶ *"An egotist is a person of low taste, more interested in himself than in me."*
— Ambrose Bierce

"I'm not conceited...

▶ *though God knows I have every reason to be."*

I'm never wrong!

▶ *"I may have faults but being wrong is not one of them."*

The quintessential egotist who likes talking to himself for two reasons.

▶ *1. "I like talking to an intelligent man.*
2. I like listening to intelligent talk."
— N. Lamont Tilden

How an egotist reacts when you malign him or praise him.

▶ *"When you malign me I know how to defend myself — but when you praise me I'm defenseless."*
— Sigmund Freud

The dean of Egocentrics upon receiving a report from his advisers.

▶ *"There is somewhat of wisdom, but not much, in thy suggestions: had there been more, the notions would first have occurred to me."*
— Xerxes

How Disraeli described a
verbose egotist —

▶ *"He's a sophistical rhetorician
inebriated with the exuberance of his
own verbosity."*
— Benjamin Disraeli

"Of all my father's family...

▶ *I like myself the best!"*

The self-made egotist and his
opinion of himself.

▶ *"He is a self made man and worships
his creator."*
— Benjamin Disraeli

What is the nothingness of an
obnoxious egotist?

▶ *"He's a case of mistaken nonentity."*

He who is full of himself is...

▶ *"Empty."*

How many letters of the
alphabet are in the word
Egotism?

▶ *"Egotism is an alphabet of One
Letter."*

"An egotist's inflated opinion
of his importance is like...

▶ *the rooster who thought the sun had
risen to hear him crow."*
— George Eliot

The nicest thing about
egotists!

▶ *They never go around talking about
other people."*

"Talk to a man about himself
and...

▶ *he will listen for hours."*
— Benjamin Disraeli

You should be
an acrobat...

▶ *the way you pat
yourself on the back."*

The garrulous egotist.

▶ *"I'm tired of talking about myself. Let's
change the subject! Now, you talk
about me!"*

The egotist who doesn't know
for sure if he's a genius.

▶ *"I can't tell you if genius is hereditary,
because heaven has granted me no
offspring."*
— James McNeill Whistler

An egotist's view of his birth.

▶ *"An egotist is a man who thinks that if
he hadn't been born, people would
have wondered why."*
— Dan Post

Do egotists return affection?   ▶ *"We may not return the affection of those who like us, but we always respect their good judgment."*
— Libbie Fudim

To the self-interested egotist.   ▶ *"A man wrapped up in himself makes a very small package."*

How NOT to have any rivals in love.   ▶ *"He that falls in love with himself will have no rivals."*

An egotist's unjustified opinion of himself.   ▶ *"He's a legend in his own mind."*

About the conceited egotist —   ▶ *"I'd like to buy him at my price and sell him at his."*

"Those of you who think you know everything...   ▶ *are very annoying to those of us who do."*

Why I like to talk to myself.   ▶ *"I talk to myself because I like dealing with a better class of people."*
— Jackie Mason

The complaint of the egotist who likes to hear himself.   ▶ *"If other people are going to talk, conversation becomes impossible."*
— James McNeill Whistler

The man who's carried away with his self-deluded importance is like —   ▶ *the fly riding on a wagon-wheel who looked backward to remark, "My, my, look at the dust I'm kicking up."*

The world's greatest lover!   ▶ *"With the whole world of people to fall in love with — he chose himself."*

The Egocentric on being right.   ▶ *"I may not always be right — but I'm Never Wrong!"*

• ELECTRICITY •

Edison's prediction of the low cost of electricity.   ▶ *"I shall make electricity so cheap that only the rich can afford to burn candles."*
— Thomas Edison

• ELEVATORS •

Sign on an airport elevator
door in Sweden —

▶ *"The lifts is being fixed for the next
days. During that time we regret that
you will be unbearable."*

• ELOQUENCE •

The art of becoming
eloquent —

▶ *"Saying the proper thing and
stopping."*
— Stanley Link

Which has the greater
impact?
What you say or How you say
it?

▶ *"The manner of your speaking is as
important as the matter. More people
have ears to be tickled than
understandings to judge!"*
— Lord Chesterfield

Definition of Eloquence and
how eloquence can make you
colour blind.

▶ *"Eloquence is the art of orally
persuading fools that white is the color
that it appears to be. It includes the gift
of making any color appear white."*
— Ambrose Bierce

What takes top billing in
ruling the world?

▶ *"A mighty thing is eloquence...
nothing so much rules the world."*
— Pope Pius II

What kind of eloquence is
the eloquence that counts?

▶ *"The finest eloquence is that which
gets things done."*
— David Lloyd George

• EMBARRASSMENT •

Embarrassing birth —

▶ *"To my embarrassment I was born in
bed with a lady."*
— Wilson Mizner

• EMOTIONS •

Even if you win the lottery,
peak excitement is very short
lived!

▶ *"Time cools, time clarifies; no mood
can be maintained quite unaltered
through the course of hours."*
— Thomas Mann

"The mind will never
understand the heart.

▶ *The heart has its reason
which reason knows not."*

— French proverb

• EMPATHY •

Can anyone truly feel
empathy for another?

▶ *"No one really understands the grief or
joy of another."*

— Franz Schubert

There again but by
the grace of God
go I.

▶ *Quit saying
"You're clumsy,"
"You're stupid!"
Say — "Can I help you?"*

"This world is a comedy to
those who think...

▶ *a tragedy to those who feel."*

— Horace Walpole

Everybody needs at least one
empathetic friend.

▶ *"What an empty life it would be if you
had a grateful heart and nobody to
share it with!"*

Can the wealthy truly ever
have understanding of those in
need?

▶ *"Nothing is so hard for those who
abound in riches as to conceive how
others can be in want."*

— Jonathan Swift

Show empathy!

▶ *"When you are among the blind shut
your eyes."*

— Turkish proverb

"Anybody can sympathize
with the sufferings of a friend
but...

▶ *it requires a very fine nature to
sympathize with a friend's success."*

— Oscar Wilde

An oft-used ruthless
Watergate trial quote —

▶ *"Let him turn and twist slowly in the
wind."*

— John Ehrlichman

Why I can be empathetic to
your problem!

▶ *"I've walked that walk.
That's why I can talk that talk!"*

Is man capable of true empathy ▶ *"The least pain in our finger gives us*
for his fellow man? *more concern than the destruction of*
millions of our fellow beings."

— William Hazlitt

• EMPLOYERS AND EMPLOYEES •

Why you should treat your ▶ *"It is not the employer who pays*
customers right. *wages — he only handles the money. It*
is the customer who pays wages."

— Henry Ford

"Around here, I have ▶ *Every time something*
an important position *goes wrong,*
of responsibility. *I'm responsible!"*

When management applauds ▶ *"The deepest principle of human*
employees for good work, do *nature is the craving to be*
they tend to work better? *appreciated."*

— William James

"The only time some people ▶ *when the boss rides them."*
work like a horse is...

— Gabriel Heatter

"If thou has a loitering ▶ *send him on thy errand just before his*
servant... *dinner!"*

— Thomas Fuller

Don't be misled into ▶ *A boy will wake up one day and*
believing that somehow *find himself working for another*
the world owes you *boy who did not have that belief*
a living. *and, therefore, earned the right to*
have others work for him."

— David Sarnoff

The Chairman of the Board at ▶ *All those opposed —*
the Board of Directors' meeting *Say "I Quit".*
taking a vote —

Has the Master and Slave ▶ *"The man who gives me employment,*
syndrome really ever passed *which I must have or suffer, that man*
into history? *is my master, let me call him what I*
will."

— Henry George

"The employer generally gets... ▸ *the employees he deserves."*
— Sir Walter Bilbey

The Chairman of the Board firing a top executive. ▸ *"You're fired; go turn in your ulcer."*

"It isn't the number of people employed in a business that makes it successful. ▸ *It's the number working."*

Notice to employees — ▸ *"We have an excellent incentive plan. If you don't work your guts out, you're fired!"*

Can any company function successfully without contented employees? ▸ *"Take away my people but leave my factories and soon grass will grow on the factory floors. Take away my factories but leave my people and soon we will have a new and better factory."*
— Andrew Carnegie

Notice To All Employees "Due to increased competition and a keen desire to remain in business, we find it necessary to institute a new policy... ▸ *Effective Immediately We are asking that somewhere between starting and quitting time and without infringing too much on the time usually devoted to lunch period, coffee breaks, rest period, story telling, vacation planning, and the rehashing of yesterday's T.V. programs, that each employee endeavor to find some time that can be set aside and known as the 'Work Break'."*

• ENCOURAGE! •

"When someone does something good, applaud. ▸ *You will make two people happy!"*
— Samuel Goldwyn

• THE ENCYCLOPEDIA •

The mental drudgery that an encyclopedia saves you. ▸ *"To me the charm of an encyclopedia is that it knows — and I needn't."*
— Francis Yeats-Brown

• ENEMIES •

He's a wise man who avoids
making an enemy.

▶ *"He who has 1000 friends*
Has not a friend to spare
And he who has one enemy
Shall meet him everywhere."
— Omar Khayyam

How the Eskimo knows his
friend from his enemy.

▶ *"You do not know who is your friend*
or who is your enemy until the ice
breaks."

How the 19th century
Russian revolutionary
Sergei Nechayev viewed
the treatment of
an enemy.

▶ *"It is not enough to kill an adversary.*
He must first be dishonored."

Never underestimate the
potential of an enemy.

▶ *"If thy enemy is an ant, regard him as*
an elephant."
— Turkish proverb

How to handle your enemy so
that he can't retaliate.

▶ *"Never wound the Prince. If you're*
going to turn against him, kill him!"
— Niccolò Machiavelli

A person searching for
success should avoid making
enemies.

▶ *"It is far less difficult to march up a*
steep ascent without fighting than
along a level road with enemies on
each side."
— Xenophon

Before you make even one
enemy remember this!

▶ *"Every enemy a man makes has 10*
friends!"

Technique for getting even
with your enemy..

▶ *"Float like a butterfly.*
Sting like a bee!"
— Mohammed Ali

How enemies make
friendships.

▶ *"There is no stronger bond of*
friendship than to have a mutual
enemy."

"The enemy of my enemy is... ▶ *my friend."*
— Arabic proverb

Who is a country's greatest enemy?

▶ *"The deadliest enemies of nations are not their foreign foes; they always dwell within their own borders."*

— William James

One method by which a victor might treat his foe.

▶ *"Whoever has his foe at his mercy, and does not kill him, is his own enemy."*

— Sa'di

• ENERGY •

How long will the world's energy last?

▶ *"The twin 100-story towers of New York's World Trade Center, consume as much energy in a day as the entire city of Pittsburgh."*

— Barbara Ward

• ENTHUSIASM •

Nothing great was ever achieved without enthusiasm.

▶ *"Remember. Enthusiasm — or lack of it — is contagious."*

— Ralph Waldo Emerson

• ENVY •

How Love and Envy view things.

▶ *"Love looks through a telescope; envy through a microscope."*

— Josh Billings

Envy can eat your gut away.

▶ *"As a moth gnaws a garment so doth envy consume a man."*

— St. Chrysostom

A neighbour's possessions look bigger than they are.

▶ *"The neighbor's chicken looks to the neighbor like a goose."*

— Turkish proverb

Despite outward appearances, most other people are no happier than you are.

▶ *"O, how bitter a thing it is to look into happiness through another man's eyes!"*

— William Shakespeare

• EPIGRAMS •

"Epigram" — a short poem expressing a single thought with terseness and wit.

▶ *"Three things must epigrams, like bees, have all,*
A sting, and honey, and a body small."

— Latin Distich

What is an epigram?

▶ *"A dwarfish whole*
Its body brevity and wit its soul."

— Coleridge

"Epigram" — a cleverly worded statement making a pointed observation.

▶ *"He misses what is meant*
by epigram
Who thinks it only
frivolous flim-flam."

• EPITAPHS •

Definition of an Epitaph —

▶ *"An inscription on a tomb showing that virtues acquired by death have a retroactive effect."*

— Ambrose Bierce

Reaction if people could read their own epitaphs.

▶ *"If men could see the epitaphs their friends write they would believe they had got into the wrong grave."*

— American proverb

Epitaph for the Driver who didn't watch the road.

▶ *"Beneath this slab*
John Brown is stowed.
He watched the ads
And not the road."

— Ogden Nash

The difference between an Epitaph and an Epithet.

▶ *"An epitaph is a description of the dead; an epithet is a description of the living."*

Epitaph of a hypochondriac who really wasn't.

▶ *"I told you I was sick!"*

Apt epitaph for some Wives.

▶ *"Here lies my wife; here let her lie!*
Now she's at rest, and so am I."

— John Dryden

Epitaph on tombstone of a Pet Dog.

▶ *"If love could have saved you, you would never have died."*

Epitaph to Mother Earth.

▶ *"Lay heavy upon me O Earth For I have laid many a heavy load upon thee!"*

Epitaph on the Philosophy of Life.

▶ *"Life is a jest and all things show it. I thought so once and now I know it."*
— John Gay

"Here lies John Smith.

▶ *Age 102. The good die young."*

Self-composed Epitaph —

▶ *"Pardon me for not rising."*
— Clive Brook

Epitaphs on tombstones are generally flattering tributes to the deceased.

▶ *"If we truly believed the epitaphs we ought to dig up the dead and bury the living."*

Epitaph on an Infant.

▶ *"Ere sin could blight or sorrow fade, Death came with friendly care; The opening bud to Heaven conveyed, And bade it blossom there."*
— Samuel Taylor Coleridge

Epitaph for Better or for Worse.

▶ *"Here lies John Smith. He lived for better or for worse — but he died for good!"*

• EQUALITY •

Are all men created equal?

▶ *"All men are created equally corrupt."*
— Jules Feiffer

Aristotle said all men are equal under law — but not equal in their individual abilities.

▶ *"The worst form of inequality is to try to make unequal things equal."*
— Aristotle

• EQUAL RIGHTS •

Equal Rights!
Do women merit them?

▶ *"If God had wanted women to be equally clever as men — he would have made them all men."*
— Male Chauvinist Pig

One of the seeds that gave birth to Women's Lib.

▶ *"Sensible and responsible women do not want to vote. The relative positions to be assumed by man and woman in the working out of our civilization were assigned long ago by a higher intelligence than ours."*
— Grover Cleveland

The effect of Women's Lib on biblical names.

▶ *"They have renamed Adam and Eve to Adam and Even."*

After his press secretary reported complaints by women seeing Jackie Kennedy photographed always walking several steps behind the president, J.F.K.'s reply was...

▶ *"Tell Jackie to walk faster!"*

Why I'm in favour of Equal Rights for women.

▶ *"I'm all for ERA. I want to see women equal to men — not so damn superior like they've been."*
— Nipsey Russell

The case against Equal Rights for women.

▶ *"Women once made equal to man becomes his superior."*
— Plato

• TO ERR •

"To err is human.

▶ *To forgive is against departmental policy."*
— California Police

• ESTIMATES •

That which estimates should include —

▶ *"An estimate of how much more it will cost than the estimate."*

Guideline if you're going to build a house.

▶ *"Never build after you are five and forty; have five years income in hand before you lay a brick; and always calculate the expense at double the estimate."*
— Henry Kett

• ETERNITY •

A magnificent portrayal of the enormity of time and eternity.

▶ *"Forever and a Day. High up in the North in the land called Svithjod, there stands a rock. It is one hundred miles high and one hundred miles wide. Once every thousand years a little bird comes to this rock to sharpen its beak. When the rock has thus been worn away, then a single day of eternity will have gone by."*
— Hendrik Willem van Loon

• ETYMOLOGY •

What is an Etymologist?

▶ *"An etymologist is somebody who knows the difference between an etymologist (words) and an entomologist (insects)."*
— Earl Wilson

• EUTHANASIA •

A case for Euthanasia.

▶ *"The prime goal is to alleviate suffering, and not to prolong life. And if your treatment does not alleviate suffering, but only prolongs life, that treatment should be stopped."*
— Christian Barnard

• EVIL •

Does society continually fail to grapple with the basic roots of evil?

▶ *"There are a thousand hacking at the branches of evil to one who is striking at its root."*
— Henry David Thoreau

Does having vices mean you also have virtues?

▶ *"It has been my experience that folks who have no vices have very few virtues."*
— Abraham Lincoln

Why is there so little Good and so much Evil?

▶ *"There are times when it would seem as if God fished with a line, and the devil with a net."*

— Madame Swetchine

In what manner do people remember the deeds you do?

▶ *"An evil deed is written in marble; a good deed in dust."*

"In order for evil to succeed...

▶ good men need do nothing."

"See no evil.
Hear no evil.
Speak no evil!"
How should this be changed today?

▶ *"What we need these days are the three monkeys who see no upheaval, hear no upheaval and speak no upheaval."*

— R.J. Cvikota

• EXAGGERATION •

"He's such an obnoxious exaggerater that...

▶ he gives new meaning to the word hyperbole."

Are you free from exaggeration?

▶ *"There is no one who does not exaggerate!"*

— Ralph Waldo Emerson

• EXCESS •

Is too much of anything generally no good?

▶ *"Too much of a good thing is wonderful."*

— Mae West

• THE EXECUTIVE •

A good executive will ask questions, being on guard that the answers aren't from "Yes men"!

▶ *"You are not here, to agree with me, but to express your own views."*

— Napoleon to his counsellors

The executive who is behind in his "desk work!"

▶ *"In reply to your letter of March 18, 1949..."*

How the true executive does his thinking and preparation prior to negotiation.

▶ *"When I'm getting ready to reason with a man, I spend one-third of my time thinking about myself and what I am going to say — and two-thirds thinking about him and what he is going to say."*

— Abraham Lincoln

"Executive ability is deciding quickly...

▶ *and getting somebody else to do the work."*

— J.G. Pollard

Should the Chief Executive Officer always appreciate those beneath him?

▶ *"One reason why the big apples are at the top of the basket is because a lot of little apples are keeping them up there."*

• EXERCISE •

I don't have to jog or do exercise.

▶ *"I get enough exercise as a pallbearer for people who exercised too much."*

Jackie Gleason on exercise —

▶ *"I get plenty of exercise. Immediately after waking I always say sternly to myself, 'Ready now, Up...down...up... down...' And after three minutes I tell myself, 'Okay, boy, now we'll try the other eyelid.'"*

Exercise is bunk.

▶ *"If you are healthy, you don't need it; if you are sick, you shouldn't take it."*

— Henry Ford

How you should exercise —

▶ *"If there's no pain There's no gain."*

A comforting guide to exercise —

▶ *"Whenever I feel like exercise I lie down until the feeling passes."*

— Robert M. Hutchins

"The only drawback about exercise is...

▶ *that it makes you tired."*

• EXPENDITURES •

What happens as your income rises?

▶ *"Expenditure rises to meet income!"*
— C. Northcote Parkinson

• EXPERIENCE •

"When a person with experience meets a person with money...

▶ *the person with experience will get the money — and the person with money will get the experience!"*

That which experience teaches you to recognize.

▶ *"Experience is what lets you recognize the same mistake you made — when you make it again."*
— Franklin P. Jones

After doing lots of things, what does experience teach you?

▶ *"Experience is knowing a lot of things you shouldn't do."*
— William S. Knudsen

Has a man of 85 generally had 85 years of experiences?

▶ *"Most men have had one year of experience repeated 85 times."*

"Experience is what you have left after...

▶ *everything else is gone."*

Can everybody afford the school of experience?

▶ *"Experience is a good school but the fees are high."*
— Heinrich Heine

"If one hundred men each tell me something they have learned as the result of 10 years of experience...

▶ *I am in a position to profit by their combined wisdom; that is by 1,000 years of experience!"*
— E.T. Meredith

That which experience is to today's Teenager.

▶ *"Experience is what you've got left after you've forgotten her name."*

"There's only one thing more painful than learning from experience and that is...

▶ *not learning from experience."*
— Laurence J. Peter

"Experience of others is too often ignored. You've really got to live a problem yourself and find out the hard way.

▶ *"Nothing ever happens unless it happens to you."*
— Edward R. Murrow

Experience —

▶ *"The name everyone gives to his mistakes."*

— Oscar Wilde

"One thorn of experience is worth...

▶ *a whole wilderness of warning."*

• THE EXPERT! •

"An expert is a guy who tells you today what is going to happen tomorrow and then tell you what?

▶ *and explains the next day why it didn't."*

— Bob Hawk

What an expert knows —

▶ *"An expert is one who knows more and more about less and less."*

— Nicholas Murray Butler

"That which an expert is —

▶ *"Someone who brings confusion to simplicity."*

— Gregory Nunn

• EXTREMISM •

When can extremism be a virtue and when can moderation be a vice?

▶ *"I would remind you that extremism in the defence of liberty is no vice. And let me remind you also that moderation in the pursuit of justice is no virtue."*

— Barry Goldwater

How the eye and the ear differ.

▶ *"The ear tends to be lazy, craves the familiar and is shocked by the unexpected; the eye, on the other hand, tends to be impatient, craves the novel and is bored by repetition."*

— W.H. Auden

F

• FACING UP! •

Should you always take the
bull by the horns?

▸ *"There comes a time in the affairs of
man when he must take the bull NOT
by the horns, but by the tail and face
the situation!"*

How to face up
to the inevitable.

▸ *For every ailment under the sun.
There is a remedy or there is none.
If there be one, try to find it.
If there be none, never mind it."*

You looked as
nervous as...

▸ *a long tailed cat in a roomful of
rocking chairs."*

• FACTS •

"Get the facts first.

▸ *You can distort them later!"*
— Mark Twain

To the person who imagines
his alleged facts.

▸ *"To treat your facts with
imagination is one thing, but to
imagine your facts is another."*
— John Burroughs

When he doesn't know what
he's talking about.

▸ *"One thing I can say. He can't be
accused of being accurate on his
facts."*

"If the facts do not conform
to the theory...

▶ *they must be disposed of!"*

The flaw in saying —
"As a matter of fact."

▶ " 'As a matter of fact' is an expression
that precedes many an expression
that isn't."

— Laurence J. Peter

• FAILURE •

Beware of starting at the top!

▶ *"A lot of guys start at the top and work
their way down."*

"There are two kinds of
failures.

▶ *The man who will do nothing he is told,
and the man who will do nothing else."*

— Perle Thompson

I did it for better
or worse.

▶ *"I could have done it better but I
couldn't have done it worse."*

"Another born loser is...

▶ *the kleptomaniac who finds himself in
a piano store."*

The redeeming feature of
reaching the bottom.

▶ *"He that is down can fall no lower."*

— Samuel Butler

The key to Failure in dealing
with people.

▶ *"I don't know the key to success; but
the key to failure is trying to please
everybody."*

— Bill Cosby

If at first you fail, don't
despair!

▶ *"If at first you don't succeed, you're
running about average."*

— M.H. Alderson

When is it better to fail than to ▶ *"Better to fail at something great than
succeed?* *succeed at doing nothing."*

"The only time the world will ▶ *right after you decide to take a nap."*
beat a path to your door is...

How to turn failure into
success.

▶ *"When I was a yound man I observed
that nine out of ten things I did were
failures. I didn't want to be a failure, so
I did ten times more work."*

— George Bernard Shaw

Everybody loves a winner.

▶ *"Victory has 1000 fathers. Defeat is an orphan."*

"We rise to fortune by successive steps.

▶ *We descend by only one."*

Caution about Success and Failure!

▶ *"Success isn't final. Failure isn't fatal."*

"If life is a bowl of cherries...

▶ *what am I doing in the pits?"*

Sometimes all the early bird gets is...

▶ *"Up."*

What failing really is —

▶ *"Failing is a learning experience."*

Success requires no explanations. What about failure?

▶ *"Failure permits no alibis!"*

Success is within his grasp — yet he manages to fail.

▶ *"He has the faculty of snatching defeat out of the jaws of victory."*

The stultifying philosophy of the millions who could have improved their lives.

▶ *"I know my limitations and am content to live within the known boundaries of my life as I have found it up to now."*

How to use timing to assure failure.

▶ *"It's just as sure a recipe for failure to have the right idea fifty years too soon as five years too late."*

— J.R. Platt

"Failures are divided into two classes.

▶ *Those who thought and never did, and those who did and never thought."*

— John Charles Salak

"After everything fails...

▶ *try reading the instructions!"*

"Perfection is doing everything right." What is failure?

▶ *"Failure is doing one thing wrong."*

That which success is to the failure.

▶ *"Success is only a matter of luck. Ask any man who fails!"*

• FAITH •

The True Believer —

▶ *"I believe in LOVE even when I do not feel it.*
I believe in the SUN even when it is not shining.
I believe in GOD even when He is silent."

In what commodity do people of all faiths have the same faith?

▶ *"When it is a question of money, everybody is of the same religion."*
— Voltaire

Can a devout believer have doubt?

▶ *"Doubt isn't the opposite of faith. It is an element of faith."*
— Paul Tillich

Did God inspire the Bible? Did God direct the writing of the Bible?

▶ *"Disagreement about these two questions has torn apart more than one Protestant denomination. It has caused disagreement even among Catholic teachers."*
— Paul Kroll

Why are Faith Healers limited to curing only their own limited selection of diseases and infirmities?

▶ *"Evidently God can cure cancer and tuberculosis, but cannot grow a leg... this is blasphemy, but not mine — the priest and faith healers are guilty of limiting God's powers."*
— Abraham Myerson

Why Spinoza was regarded as abandoning his faith.

▶ *"I believe in a God, who reveals himself in the orderly harmony of all that exists, not in the God who concerns himself with fates and actions of human beings."*
— Baruch Spinoza

• FAME •

The relationship of fame and sleep.

▶ *"The man who wakes up to find himself famous hasn't been asleep."*

Fame is transient.

▶ *"The president of today is only a 50¢ stamp of tomorrow."*

• FAMILIARITY •

"Familiarity breeds contempt."

▶ "Where you're not wanted, don't go! Where you're liked don't go too often!"

Since familiarity breeds contempt, how should you behave?

▶ "Be civil to all; sociable to many; familiar with few."
— Benjamin Franklin

"Though familiarity may not breed contempt...

▶ it takes the edge off admiration."
— William Hazlitt

What else does familiarity do?

▶ "Familiarity breeds!"
— Mark Twain

"Be not too familiar with thy servants.

▶ At first it may beget love, but in the end 't will breed contempt."

What else does familiarity breed?

▶ "Familiarity breeds attempt."
— Goodman Ace

• THE FAMILY •

Take the word "family". Strike out the "m" for mother and the "y" for youth...

▶ and all you have left is "fail".
— Omar Burleson

"I've just spent a few days with my family...

▶ and it's a pleasure to be here among you strangers."

Wherein does a grandfather differ from many fathers towards the children?

▶ "There are fathers who do not love their children; there is no grandfather who does not adore his grandson."
— Victor Hugo

One thing about a daughter. She generally stays in the family.

▶ "My son is my son till he have got him a wife,
But my daughter's my daughter all the days of her life."
— Thomas Fuller

• FAMILY PLANNING •

Has woman the right to control her own body?

▶ *"No woman can call herself free who does not own and control her body. No woman can call herself free until she can choose consciously whether she will or will not be a mother."*

— Margaret Sanger

"Use Contraceptives.

▶ *The Unborn Will Bless You!"*

Is sex for pleasure between husband and wife a sin?

▶ *"Any use whatsoever of matrimony exercised in such a way that the act is deliberately frustrated in its natural power to generate life is an offense against the law of God and of nature, and those who indulge in such are branded with the guilt of a grave sin."*

— Pope Pius XI

• FANTASIZING •

If you fantasize about building castles in the air.

▶ *"If you have built castles in the air your work need not be lost; that is where they should be built; now put foundations under them!"*

— Henry David Thoreau

Fantasy of the Macho Man.

▶ *"He's the man who liked his women weak and his liquor strong."*

"To dream of the person you would like to be is...

▶ *to waste the person you are!"*

The role and fantasy that some women would take delight in.

▶ *"I'm a little tired. Send one of them home!"*

— Mae West

"Fantasy is nothing but the human dimension of reality...

▶ *that makes life tolerable and sometimes even fun."*

— Luis Bunuel

When neither partner can fantasize during love making.

▶ *"What's the matter, you can't think of anybody either!"*

— Rodney Dangerfield

• FARMING •

Farmer to son —

▶ *"I want you to go to school and learn how to be a middleman!"*

"Farming today is so expensive to get into that...

▶ *you're either born with it — or marry it!"*

• FASHION •

That which fashion is —

▶ *"Fashion is a form of ugliness so intolerable that we have to change it every six months.*
— Oscar Wilde

If you're in fashion you're well dressed. But! If you've got style you've got class.

▶ *"Fashions fade. Style is eternal!"*
— Yves Saint Laurent

How to handle fashion —

▶ *"Be neither too early in the fashion nor too long out of it; nor at any time in the extremes of it."*

What's the difference between Fashion and Style?

▶ *"Fashion can be bought. Style one must possess."*
— Edna Woolman Chase

• FATE •

How come fate smiles on some people and frowns on others?

▶ *"God plays dice with the world."*

"When fate summons...

▶ *even Monarchs must obey!"*
— John Dryden

It was the filthy finger of fate that did him in!

▶ *"He was diddled by the dirty digit of destiny!"*

Some peoples' lives are just plain lucky. Others are unending pain and torment.

▶ *"Some are born to sweet delight, Some are born to endless night."*
— William Blake

"The belief that fate will prevail no matter what is by no means confined to the superstitious.

▶ *"I have been versed in the reasonings of men, and fate is stronger than anything I have known."*
— Euripides

• FAULTS •

"Every man has a bag hanging before him, in which he puts his neighbor's faults...

▶ *another behind him in which he stows his own."*
— William Shakespeare

"Justifying a fault...

▶ *doubles it!"*
— French proverb

• THE FAVOUR •

When somebody's asking a favour!

▶ *"I'd like to help you out! Which way did you come in?"*

• FAVOURITISM •

When should you take sides?

▶ *"When in doubt who will win, be neutral."*
— Swiss Proverb

• FEAR •

"So let me assert my firm belief that the only thing we have to fear is...

▶ *fear itself!"*
— Franklin D. Roosevelt

"I was so nervous...

▶ *you could march an army to the beat of my heart."*

Fear gives intelligence to whom?

▶ *"Even to fools!"*
— French proverb

• FICKLE! •

"Don't rely on him. He's as changeable as...

▶ *a one-dollar bill!"*

• FILING CABINETS •

A filing cabinet is a place to lose things —

▶ *"Alphabetically."*

• FISHING •

Fisherman's prayer —

▶ *"Lord give me grace to catch a fish so big that even I, when telling of it afterwards, may never need to lie."*

Derision of the fishing rod and the fisherman!

▶ *"A fishing-rod is a stick with a hook at one end and a fool at the other."*
— Samuel Johnson

The ultimate accolade on the sport of "FISHING."

▶ *"God never did make a more calm, quiet, innocent recreation than angling."*
— Izaak Walton

"The fish that escaped is...

▶ *always big!"*
— Turkish proverb

• FLATTERY •

A practical guide on how to practice flattery.

▶ *"The most skilful flattery is to let a person talk on, and be a listener."*
— Joseph Addison

"Flattery is telling the other person...

▶ *what he already thinks of himself."*
— Hal Wilshire

"Commend a fool for his wit, or a knave for his honesty...

▶ *and they will recieve you into their bosom."*
— Henry Fielding

When can a flatterer be a hypocrite?

▶ *"A flatterer is one who says things to your face he wouldn't say behind your back."*
— G. Millington

Breathes there any man on earth who doesn't like flattery at one time or another?

▶ *" 'Tis an old maxim in the schools, That flattery's the food of fools; Yet now and then your men of wit Will condescend to take a bit."*
— Jonathan Swift

"Flattery will get you nowhere but..." ▸ *bribery will get you everywhere.*"

"Flattery will get you somewhere." ▸ *Start talking!*"

• FLEXIBILITY •

Always Be Flexible. ▸ *"Better bend than break!"*

— Scottish proverb

• THE FLORIST •

World famous slogan for the Society of American Florists which influenced people's method of sending congratulations! ▸ *"Say it with flowers."*

— Patrick O'Keefe

• FLYING •

Aeroplane turbulence — ▸ *"Makes you think doesn't it? This plane was built by the lowest bidder."*

Did God mean man to fly? ▸ *"If God had wanted us to fly, he'd have given us tickets."*

Will man ever be able to fly? ▸ *"Heavier than air flying machines are impossible."*

— Lord Kelvin

• FOOD •

The relationship of appetizers to appetite. ▸ *"Appetizers are those little bits you eat until you lose your appetite."*

Is food in England really that bad? ▸ *"In England there are sixty different religions, and only one sauce."*

— Marquis Caraccioli

What is Edible and to what cycle of life does it liken itself?

▶ *"Edible is good to eat, and wholesome to digest, as a worm to a toad, a toad to a snake, a snake to a pig, a pig to a man and a man to a worm."*
— Ambrose Bierce

"The trouble with eating Italian food is...

▶ *that five or six days later you're hungry again."*

Who said food in England isn't great?

▶ *"Food is great in England if you have three breakfasts a day!"*

The hangups that most people have about certain foods.

▶ *"A gourmet challenged me to eat A tiny bit of rattlesnake meat, Remarking, "Don't look horror-stricken, You'll find it tastes a lot like a chicken." It did. Now chicken I cannot eat Because it tastes like rattlesnake meat."*

"On cold days food tastes better when you are hungry.

▶ *This is also true on warm days."*

How to get a nice figure.

▶ *"Everything you see I owe to spaghetti."*
— Sophia Loren

• THE FOOL •

Every man is a damn fool for at least five minutes every day. What should a man of wisdom do about it?

▶ *"Wisdom consists of not exceeding the limit."*
— Elbert Hubbard

"There's no fool like an old fool, except...

▶ *an older fool."*

"A fool and his money...

▶ *are soon popular."*

Where does an educated fool rate as against an uneducated one?

▶ *"A learned fool is more of a fool than an ignorant fool."*

"God must have loved fools.

▶ *He made so many of them."*

What bearing do fools have on our success?

▶ *"Let us be thankful for the fools. But for them the rest of us could not succeed."*
— Mark Twain

Are you always the fool when you remain silent?

▶ *"Better to remain silent and be thought a fool than to speak and remove all doubt!"*

Where do fools set foot?

▶ *"Fools rush in where angels fear to tread."*
— Alexander Pope

"You can fool some of the people some of the time but...

▶ *most of the time, they fool themselves."*

Is a fool's own utterances that which does him in?

▶ *"What kills a skunk is the publicity it gives itself."*
— Abraham Lincoln

"It's impossible to make anything foolproof...

▶ *because fools are so ingenious!"*

"You may lead an ass to water but you cannot make him drink!"

▶ *"You may lead an ass to knowledge, but you cannot make him think!"*

What should you do if more than one person calls you an ass?

▶ *"If one man calleth thee a donkey, pay, him no mind. If two men calleth thee a donkey, get thee a saddle."*
— Yiddish proverb

Even a clock that has stopped going is right twice a day. How about fools?

▶ *"A fool must now and then be right by chance."*
— William Cowper

"The educated man without common sense is...

▶ *the most learned of all fools!"*

"The wisdom of a fool is...

▶ *always conspicuous by its absence."*

"You can't fool all the people all of the time but...

▶ *never forget that you are one of all of the people who can be fooled some of the time!"*

• FORECASTING •

How to be a successful
forecaster on prices.

▶ *"Some think prices will go up;
some think they will go down. I
do, too."*

• FOREIGN AFFAIRS •

What degree of military
strength should nations have in
negotiating treaties?

▶ *"The lesson of all history warns
us that we should negotiate only
when our military superiority is so
convincing that we can achieve our
objective at the conference table, and
deny the aggressor theirs."*
— Richard M. Nixon

In international affairs, how
many and what kind of
countries are required to form
an Alliance?

▶ *"In international politics, an
alliance is the union of two thieves
who have their hands so deeply
inserted in each other's pocket that
they cannot separately plunder
a third."*
— Ambrose Bierce

Where our foreign aid money
ends up in Third World
countries.

▶ *"Foreign aid is taxing poor people
in rich countries for the benefit
of rich people in poor countries."*
— Bernard Rosenberg

How to conduct foreign
policy —

▶ *"Walk softly and carry a big
stick!"*
— Theodore Roosevelt

• FORGIVE! •

When you bury the hatchet, is
everything really forgotten?

▶ *"Nobody ever forgets where he
buried the hatchet."*
— Kin Hubbard

A poet might call Forgiveness
a fragrance and would liken it
to the violet.

▶ *"Forgiveness is the fragrance the
violet sheds on the heel that has
crushed it."*
— Mark Twain

"Doing an injury puts you
below your enemy. What about
Revenging and Forgiving?

▶ *"Revenging one makes you even
with him. Forgiving one sets you
above him."*
— Benjamin Franklin

How we react to a transgression of a friend or an enemy.

▶ *"It is easier to forgive an enemy than a friend."*

• FORESIGHT •

"Having foresight is...

▶ *to dig a well before you are thirsty."*

• FORGETTING! •

What to say when you forget your wife's birthday.

▶ *"How can you expect me to remember your birthday, when you don't look a day older?"*

What's the best way NOT to forget?

▶ *"To endeavor to forget any one is the certain way to think of nothing else."*

— Jean de la Bruyère

• FORTUNE •

How we measure our fortune.

▶ *"We don't measure our good fortune by counting what we have, but by comparing it with what we haven't."*

• THE FOREWARNING! •

I told you so!

▶ *Of all the horrid, hideous notes of woe, Sadder than low-songs on the midnight blast, Is that portentous phrase, "I told you so."*

— Lord Byron

• FREEDOM •

A reminder to those who take freedom for granted.

▶ *"Posterity! You will never know how much it cost the present generation to preserve your freedom. I hope you will make good use of it."*

— John Quincy Adams

Money and freedom.

▶ *"There is no freedom in this world —
unless you have money."*

What a free land means
according to our constitution.

▶ *"A free land is where you aren't
insulted, abused or intimidated except
on the witness stand."*

The unavoidable price society
must pay in order to
preserve human freedom in
a democracy.

▶ *"The trouble about fighting
for human freedom is that
you have to spend much
of your life defending SOBs;
for oppressive laws are always
aimed at them, and oppression
must be stopped in the
beginning if at all."*

— H.L. Menken

• FRIENDS •

Caution! Your friend and
your enemy can unpredictably
change roles!

▶ *"Treat your friend as though
one day he will be your enemy.
Treat your enemy as though one
day he will be your friend"*

If you get rich and want to
keep your friends, should you
flaunt your wealth?

▶ *"Prosperity makes few friends."*

— Marquis de Vauvenargues

"A friend in need is...

▶ *a friend you don't need!"*

How to make friends.

▶ *"You can make more friends in
two months by becoming interested
in other people than you can in
two years by trying to get people
interested in you."*

— Dale Carnegie

There are limits to what you
can do to your friend.

▶ *"You can pick your friends. You
can pick your nose. But you can't
pick your friend's nose!"*

We never know the true
value of friends.

▶ *"While they live we are
too sensitive of their faults:
when we have lost them we
only see their virtues."*

How a walk is affected when taken with a friend.

▶ *"A mile walked with a friend has only one hundred steps!"*

Definition of a friend in our materialistic society.

▶ *"A friend is someone who is doing slightly worse than you are."*

"The ideal of friendship is...

▶ *to feel as one while remaining two."*

The test of "friendship" is to be interested in the trifle happenings of your friend!

▶ *"Tell me about your adventures on the voyage from Troy. I gain nothing by knowing it, but because you are dear to me I want to share in all you have experienced."*
— As Helen said to Menelaus:

How many real friends does one have in a lifetime?

▶ *"One friend in a lifetime is much; two are many; three are hardly possible."*
— Henry Adams

Some people can forgive anything in a friend except —

▶ *"Success."*

The vast difference in the interests that link men as against what link nations.

▶ *"Men may be linked in friendship. Nations are linked only by interests."*
— Rolf Hochhuth

Which of the two is higher — Love or Friendship?

▶ *"Love is all very well in its way, but friendship is much higher. Indeed, nothing in the world is either nobler or rarer than a devoted friendship."*
— Oscar Wilde

"There are two types of friends.

▶ *Those who are around when you need them, and those who are around when they need you."*

"That friendship will not continue...

▶ *to the end that is begun for an end."*
— Francis Quarles

How to have a friend —

▶ *"The only way to have a friend is to be one!"*
— Ralph Waldo Emerson

"We cherish our friends not for their ability to amuse us, but for...

▶ *our ability to amuse them."*
— Evelyn Waugh

Is friendship affected when your friend attains a position of power?

▶ *"A friend in power is a friend lost."*
— Henry Adams

"Talking with a friend is...

▶ *nothing else but thinking aloud."*
— Joseph Addison

What's a good test of friendship between two people?

▶ *"True friendship comes when silence between two people is comfortable."*

"A friend that you have to buy won't be worth what you pay for him...

▶ *no matter what that may be."*
— George D. Prentice

What kind of person do you call an Acquaintance?

▶ *"An acquaintance is a person whom we know well enough to borrow from but not well enough to lend to. A degree of friendship called slight when its object is poor or obscure, and intimate when he is rich or famous."*
— Ambrose Bierce

To find a friend how much should you overlook?

▶ *"To find a friend one must close one eye — to keep him, two."*
— Norman Douglas

"Is a friend in need really a friend in deed?"

▶ *"A friend in need is a pest!"*

The give and take of friendship.

▶ *"Friendship is the gift that goes on giving and is a gift to both the person given to and to the giver as well. But to really make it work it isn't enough to give to another person, you have also to let them give to you."*
— Merle Shain

Is it expedient or wise to examine our friends too closely?

▶ *"Few persons are raised in our esteem by a close examination."*
— Duc de la Rochefoucauld

How Prosperity and Adversity
affect friendship.

▶ *"In time of prosperity friends will
    be plenty;
    In time of adversity not one in
    twenty."*

— English proverb

"A married man's best friend
is...

▶ *his wife's husband!"*

"A friend in need is a friend in
deed."
Who else is?

▶ *"A friend that ain't in need is a
friend indeed!"*

— Kin Hubbard

"A true test of friendship is...

▶ *to sit or walk with a friend for an
hour in perfect silence without
wearying of one another's company."*

— N. Gebel

What is Platonic friendship
and how long does it last?

▶ *"Platonic friendship is the interval
between the introduction and the
first kiss."*

— Sophie Irene Loeb

Visit your friend often or you'll
soon be forgotten!

▶ *"Go often to the house of thy
friend; for weeds soon choke up the
unused path."*

— Scandinavian proverb

"A true friend is...

▶ *one who likes you despite your
achievements."*

What to say to retain friends.

▶ *"Lots of friends are retained by not
saying the smart things we might
have said."*

• FUN •

"Fun is like insurance.

▶ *The older you get the more it costs."*

"I haven't had so much fun
since...

▶ *I had root canal work!"*

• THE FUTURE •

"If we don't roll up
our sleeves and wrestle
with the problem of
slovenly education of
our children, our
future will inherit...

▶ *— Bad leaders*
— Bad scientists
— Bad generals
— Bad engineers
— Bad doctors
— Bad executives
— and not bad — but HORRIFIC
nightmares!"

Making your future.

▶ *"What you are to be,*
you are now becoming."

Should you plan for your
future?

▶ *"People who fail to plan, plan to*
fail!"

Why you should be
concerned about the Future.

▶ *"My interest is in the future*
because I am going to spend the rest of
my life there."
— Charles F. Kettering

Who and when can anybody
predict anything?

▶ *"You can only predict things after*
they've happened."
— Eugene Ionesco

Is it ironic to be concerned
about the future?

▶ *"This is the first age that's paid*
much attention to the future, which
is a little ironic since we may
not have one."
— Arthur C. Clarke

"The wise man guards against
the future as if...

▶ *it were the present."*

"Live only for today...

▶ *and you ruin tomorrow!"*
— Charles Simmons

G

• GAMBLING •

That which happens to so many who go to Las Vegas.

▶ *"He went to Vegas in a $40,000 Mercedes and went home in a $400,000 Greyhound bus."*

"There are two times in a man's life when he should not speculate.

▶ *When he can't afford it, and when he can."*
— Mark Twain

Bookmaker's warning to the sporting man!

▶ *"No horse can go as fast as the money you put on it!"*
— Earl Wilson

What's the best way to gamble at Craps?

▶ *"The best way to throw with the dice is to throw them away."*
— C. Simmons

How to gamble using your head.

▶ *"Gamble with your head. Not over it."*

Some people are not against gambling. They're against government run lotteries.

▶ *"Government is encouraging people to gamble instead of merely letting them gamble."*

"The world's greatest gambler was Lady Godiva.

▶ *She put everything she had on one horse."*

"Don't gamble; take all your savings and buy some good stock and hold it till it goes up, then sell it.

▶ *If it don't go up, don't buy it."*
— Will Rogers

The ingredient that motivates horse racing!

▶ *"A difference of opinion is what makes horse racing and missionaries."*

— Will Rogers

The only sure thing about gambling!

▶ *"It's the sure way of getting nothing for something!"*

— Wilson Mizner

"I had a great horse in the last race.

▶ *It took seven horses to beat him!"*

• GAMES •

How people react to your talent at playing bridge and poker.

▶ *"If you play bridge badly you make your partner suffer; but if you play poker badly you make everybody happy."*

— Joe Laurie, Jr.

Denigrating people who play games.

▶ *"Games are for people who can neither read nor think."*

— George Bernard Shaw

• GARDENING •

Sign on vehicle of landscape gardener —

▶ *"We Just Keep Rolling a Lawn."*

Where there is one Englishman there is a garden. When there are two Englishmen there will be a club. But...

▶ *this does not mean any falling off in the number of gardens. There will be three. The club will have one too."*

— A.W. Smith

"It is not enough for a gardener to love flowers.

▶ *He must also hate weeds!"*

• THE GENERATION GAP •

How will the next generation behave towards us?

▶ *"It's an immutable law of nature that each generation will dress, speak, make love — listen to music in the way best calculated to infuriate their elders."*

• GENEROSITY •

The true test of generosity.

▶ *"When you give, take to yourself no credit for generosity unless you deny yourself something in order that you may give."*

— H. Taylor

"Takers eat well.

▶ *Givers sleep well!"*

• THE GENIUS •

If you receive a shirt as a gift — how can that make you a genius?

▶ *"A genius is somebody who can rewrap a new shirt and not have any pins left over."*

— Dino Levi

You don't become a genius just by wishing.

▶ *"Before I was a genius I was a drudge."*

— Ignace Jan Paderewski

"Genius is...

▶ *eternal patience!"*

— Michaelangelo

What is the driving force of Genius — and what are the limitations of Talent?

▶ *"Genius does what it must, talent does what it can."*

— Edward Bulwer-Lytton

It was not only Edison's mechanical talent — but his business acumen that was his genius.

▶ *"I am more of a sponge than an inventor. I absorb ideas from every source. I take half-matured schemes for mechanical development and make them practical. My principal business is giving commercial value to the brilliant but misdirected ideas of others."*

— Thomas A. Edison

"Genius is one per cent inspiration and...

▶ *ninety-nice per cent perspiration."*

— Thomas A. Edison

Genius is an infinite capacity to do what?

▶ *"To pick brains!"*

Genius always beats a new path.

▸ *"Towering genius disdains a beaten path. It seeks regions hitherto unexplored."*
— Abraham Lincoln

What distinguishes a genius in the handling of a complex problem?

▸ *"Genius is the ability to reduce the complicated to the simple."*
— C.W. Ceram

• GENOCIDE •

Why history half shuts its eye to genocide.

▸ *"A single death is a tragedy, a million deaths is a statistic."*
— Joseph Stalin

• GENTLEMAN •

"To be born a gentleman is an accident.

▸ *To die one is an achievement!"*
— Bob Goddard

"The gentleman is solid veneer."

▸ *The fashionable man is only mahogany."*
— J.G. Holland

Definition of Gentleman —

▸ *"One who never hurts another's feelings unintentionally."*

• GEOMETRY •

"Geometry is...

▸ *as easy as π "*

• GIFTS •

About the acceptance of gifts.

▸ *"It is not good to refuse a gift."*
— Homer

Be gracious in accepting gifts.

▸ *"Friends must understand Exchange of gifts is an art, Give with an open hand, Receive with an open heart."*
— M.J. Huston

What is the most noble gift you can give?

▶ *"The only gift is a portion of thyself."*

— Ralph Waldo Emerson

A hedonist is his own best friend when it comes to indulgence.

▶ *"A friend is a present you give yourself."*

— Robert Louis Stevenson

• GLAMOUR •

That which much of glamour is today under the guise of designer labels.

▶ *"When the value of the package exceeds that of its contents!"*

That which glamour is on Rodeo Drive, Hollywood, California.

▶ *"Glamour is a web of enchantment 'cast' by retailers."*

• HOW TO GO! •

Three Ways To Go!

▶ *The first is "Go", the second is "Keep Going", and the third is "Help someone else to go."*

— Theo Adams

• YOUR GOAL! •

On reaching your goal.

▶ *"The worst thing that can happen to you is to have your dreams realized."*

• GOD •

How God would view life in today's world.

▶ *"Nay: I have no remembrance of such a place: Such world I fashioned not!"*

If man pictures God in his own image, what image would inanimate things visualize?

▶ *"If triangles had a god, he would have three sides."*

— Montesquieu

Why Galileo preferred the use of reason and intellect over blind faith in dogma or the supernatural.

▶ *"I do not feel obliged to believe that that same God who has endowed us with sense, reason, and intellect has intended us to forego their use."*

— Galileo Galilei

"If only God would give me some clear sign!

▶ *like making a large deposit in my name at a Swiss bank."*

— Woody Allen

Alas! Religion will always evolve.

▶ *"If there were no God, it would be necessary to invent him."*

— Voltaire

Why God gave man two ends.

▶ *"God gave man two ends, one to think with and one to sit on. A man's success depends upon which he uses most; a case of heads you win, tails you lose."*

How does one reconcile the omnipotence of God with so much world suffering?

▶ *"The greatest of all perplexities in theology has been to reconcile the infinite goodness of God with his omnipotence. Nothing puts a greater strain upon the faith of the common man than the existence of utterly irrational suffering in the universe."*

— Walter Lippmann

"God is not dead.

▶ *He simply refuses to get involved."*

• GOLD •

What could all the gold in the world NOT buy?

▶ *"If all the gold in the world were melted down into a solid cube it would be about the size of an eight —room house. If a man got possession of all that gold — billions of dollars worth, — he could not buy a friend, character, peace of mind, clear conscience, or a sense of etenity."*

— Charles F. Banning

"Money makes money."

▶ *"Gold that's put to use — more gold begets!"*

"More gold has been mined from the thoughts of men than...

▶ *has ever been taken from the earth."*

"Gold — what can it not do... ▶ *and undo!"*

— William Shakespeare

Is any man so virtuous that the ▶ *"There is no place so high that an*
Right Price won't reach him? *ass laden with gold cannot reach*
it."

Which has ruined fewer men? ▶ *"The possession of gold has ruined*
The lack of gold or its *fewer men than the lack of it."*
possession?

— Thomas Bailey Aldrich

"A mask of gold... ▶ *hides all deformities!"*

"All is not gold that glitters." ▶ *"Gold all is not that doth golden*
seem."

— Edmund Spenser

"All that glitters is not gold." ▶ *"Everything that coruscates with*
effulgence is not ipso facto aurous."

An aged version of "All is not ▶ *"All is not golde that outward*
gold that glitters." *shewith bright."*

— John Lydgate

"All is not gold that glitters." ▶ *"Polished brass will pass upon more*
people than rough gold."

— Lord Chesterfield

• THE GOLDEN RULE •

"The Golden Rule" — ▶ *How remarkable that the core*
Do Unto Others. *teaching in all major religions is the*
same!

Christianity: *"All things whatsoever you would*
that men should do to you, do you
so to them; for this is the law
and the prophets."
(Matthew 7:12)

Judaism: *"What is hateful to you, do not to*
your fellowman. That is the entire
Law; all the rest is commentary."
(Talmud, Shabbat 3id)

Islam:

"No one of you is a believer until he desires for his brother that which he desires for himself." (Sunnah)

Buddhism:

"Hurt not others in ways that you yourself would find hurtful." (Udana-Varga 5,18)

Hinduism:

"This is the sum of duty: do naught unto others which would cause you pain if done to you." (Mahabharata 5,1517)

Confucianism:

"Is there one maxim which ought to be acted upon throughout one's life? Surely it is the maxim of loving-kindness: Do not unto others what you would not have them do unto you." (Analects 15,23)

Taoism:

"Regard your neighbor's gain as your own gain, and your neighbor's loss as your own loss." (Tai Shang Kan Ying P'ien)

Zoroastrianism:

"That nature alone is good which refrains from doing unto another whatsoever is not good for itself." (Dadisten-i-dinik, 94,5)

Does the Golden Rule of the Bible really work?

▸ "I live by the Golden Rule: he who has the gold makes the rules."

"We have committed the Golden Rule to memory.

▸ Let us now commit it to life!"
— Edwin Markham

A beautiful reminder of when to practice the Golden Rule.

▸ "I shall pass through this world but once; any good that I can do, or any kindness that I can show, let me not defer it or neglect it, for I shall not pass this way again."
— John Wesley

• GOLF •

Golf —	▶ *"An outdoor recreation played on a course of spacious dimensions with a diminutive spherical object and variously shaped instruments, the objective being to maneuver the sphere into a series of cylindrical apertures."*
"Golf is...	▶ *Flog spelled backwards."*
A practical tip to golfers.	▶ *"A golf ball should be hit every time — but not too often!"*
Golf rule in Africa.	▶ *"A ball lying less than 10 yards from a lion need not be played."*
A golfer's chief handicap is...	▶ *"Honesty!"*

— Maclean's

If you watch a game, it's fun. If you play it, it's recreation. If you work at it, what is it?	▶ *"It's golf."*

— Bob Hope

How Shakespeare would have cursed the golf putts he missed.	▶ *"Cursed be the hand that made these fatal holes."*

— William Shakespeare

"The trouble with my Golf is...	▶ *that I have a handicap!"*
Caution to the business man who golfs!	▶ *"If you break 100, watch your golf; if you break 80, watch your business."*
Golfer's prayer:	▶ *"May I live long enough to shoot my age!"*

• GOOD-BAD-WORSE! •

Is the Good or the Evil you do remembered?	▶ *"The evil that men do lives after them. The good is oft interred with their bones."*

— William Shakespeare

How to do Good.

▶ "*Do all the good you can,*
In all the ways you can,
In all the places you can,
At all the times you can,
To all the people you can,
As long as ever you can!"

— John Wesley

Definition of Bad —

▶ "*Bad is good when worse happens.*"

"There's only one thing worse than a flooded basement.

▶ *It's a flooded attic.*"

Good versus Bad.

▶ "*There can be no rainbow without a cloud and a storm.*"

— J.H. Vincent

"The smallest good deed is better than...

▶ *the grandest good intention.*"

Every good has its bad — but how come the bad lasts so long?

▶ "*The rose does not bloom without thorns — true; but would that the thorns did not outlive the rose!*"

— Jean Paul Richter

What is better than "Ours"?

▶ "*Mine is better than ours.*"

— Benjamin Franklin

"Forget about wanting to be the best.

▶ *All you want to be is the best you can be!*"

Do good deeds always pay?

▶ "*No good deed goes unpunished.*"

Is "Good" — good enough?

▶ "*The good is the enemy of the best.*"

Is any man on earth so good as never to have been guilty of base thoughts and immoral actions?

▶ "*There is no man so good, who, were he to submit all his thoughts and actions to the laws, would not deserve hanging ten times in his life.*"

— Michel de Montaigne

• GOODBYE! •

"Goodbye...

▶ *I'm glad you saw me!*"

The least painful way of saying goodbye. ▶ *"Departure should be sudden!"*
— Benjamin Disraeli

• GOODNESS •

Machiavelli advises a government leader to practice Goodness but not in excess.

▶ *"A man who wished to make a profession of goodness in everything, must necessarily come to grief amongst so many who are not good."*
— Niccolò Machiavelli

• GOODWILL •

The precious treasure of Goodwill!

▶ *"The most precious thing anyone, man or store, anybody or anything can have is the good will of others.*
It is something as fragile as an orchid, And as beautiful.
As precious as a gold nugget, And as hard to find.
As powerful as a great turbine, And as hard to build.
As wonderful as youth, And as hard to keep."
— Amos Parrish

What one thing can your competition NOT beat you on?

▶ *"Goodwill is the one and only asset that competition cannot undersell nor destroy."*
— Marshall Field

Today's profits are yesterday's good will —

▶ *"Ripened."*

How goodwill is lost.

▶ *"Goodwill, like a good name, is won by many acts and lost by one."*

• GOSSIP •

What should you beware of in a person who gossips?

▶ *"Whoever gossips to you will gossip of you."*
— Spanish proverb

"Gossip is what no one claims to like, but... ▶ *everybody enjoys."*

— Joseph Conrad

What's the best kind of gossip you can hear? ▶ *"The best gossip is when you hear something you like about someone you don't."*

— Earl Wilson

"If we all said to people's faces what we say behind one another's backs... ▶ *society would be impossible."*

— Honoré de Balzac

"There's only one thing worse than a person who will gossip... ▶ *and that's the person who doesn't know any."*

"There is only one thing in the world worse than being talked about... ▶ *and that is not being talked about."*

— Oscar Wilde

• GOVERNMENT •

"The Law of Inevitable Contradiction" on election promises and government execution of the promises. ▶ *"Any government elected on a specific policy will do the precise opposite on reaching office."*

— Bruce Hutchison

"When you think of the government debt which the next generation must pay... ▶ *it's no wonder a baby cries when it is born!"*

"The legitimate object of government is... ▶ *to do for a community of people whatever they need to have done, but cannot do at all in their separate and individual capacities."*

— Abraham Lincoln

What is the Capital of any country or government? ▶ *"The capital is the seat of misgovernment."*

— Ambrose Bierce

The weak policies of most democratic governments. ▶ *"Short term gain Long term pain"*

In government, what one thing should we be truly grateful for? ▶ *"Be thankful we're not getting all the government we're paying for."*

— Will Rogers

Government Budgeting.

▶ *"Expenditures and revenues rise to meet each other no matter which one will be in excess!"*

If society and the media don't speak up, will governments tend to ignore fairness and justice?

▶ *"A society of sheep must in time beget a government of wolves."*
— Bertrand de Jouvenel

Machiavelli's perceptive and modern view of how a government leader should select his cabinet.

▶ *"The first impression one gets of a ruler and of his brains is by seeing the men he has about him."*
— Niccolò Machiavelli

"There are no bad people in government.

▶ *There are only good people doing bad things."*
— Art Buchwald

The kind of Light we're tired of seeing in government planning.

▶ *"We saw the light at the end of the tunnel, and it was out."*
— John Clancy

"The Law of Cyclical Time Lag". Governments are so slow in planning ahead, that the event planned for happens before the plan has evolved.

▶ *"This law ensures that the view held among the current majority is out of date, the government's latest policies designed for a situation already ended, as generals plan their strategy for the last war."*
— Bruce Hutchison

Guide to your status if you're in government.

▶ *"Where you stand depends on where you sit."*
— Rufus Miles

In government, where do the middle of the roaders and the extremists rate?

▶ *"The middle of the road is all of the usable surface. The extremes, right and left, are in the gutters."*
— Dwight D. Eisenhower

How well do governments deal with important problems of the day?

▶ *"Politics offers yesterday's answers to today's problems."*
— Marshall McLuhan

Why governments can get away with passing laws that so often ignore fairness for the less privileged.

▶ *"You'll never go wrong underestimating the morality of the public!"*
— Louis B. Mayer

Machiavelli on how a leader should maintain his control of government.

▶ *"A leader must be like the lion and the fox. Strong enough, like the lion, to fight when it is necessary, yet smart enough, like the fox, to avoid traps."*

— Niccolò Machiavelli

• GRAMMAR •

Never end a sentence with a preposition. Never say: "This is the sort of English I will not put up with."

▶ *Instead say —*
"This is the sort of English up with which I will not put."

— Winston Churchill

• BE GRATEFUL! •

"There — but by the grace of God go I!"

▶ *"I had the blues because I had no shoes.*
Until upon the street
I met a man who had no feet."

Express your love Today. Tomorrow may be too late!

▶ *"If you like him or love him tell him now.*
Don't wait till he has white lilies over his brow."

The ingratitude of a child.

▶ *"No serpents tooth is so sharp as that of a thankless child."*

— William Shakepeare

Who to get even with.

▶ *"The only people to get even with are those who have helped you."*

If you want to appreciate your condition, visit a nursing home.

▶ *"Think of the ills from which you are exempt."*

Do mere words and solicitous inquiries ever equal an act of actual friendship?

▶ *"If a friend is in trouble, don't annoy him by asking if there is any-thing you can do. Think up something appropriate and do it."*

How to feel grateful.

▶ *"Go back and take another look at your childhood sweetheart!"*

— Harry Ruby

"Gratitude is... ▶ *the memory of the heart.*"

The moral obligation Albert
Einstein felt towards his fellow
man.

▶ *"I realize how much of my own
outer and inner life is built upon the
labors of my fellow-men, both living
and dead, and how earnestly I must
exert myself in order to give in
return as much as I have
received."*

— Albert Einstein

Every adversity leaves room
for some gratitude.

▶ *"He who limps is still walking."*

There should always be
gratitude for those things you
take for granted.

▶ *"You never miss the water until the
well runs dry."*

The most important lesson
G.K. Chesterton had learned
during his lifetime.

▶ *"The critical thing was whether one
took things for granted or took them
with gratitude."*

— James Reston

Don't wait till it's too late!

▶ *"Let all the nice words now be said
For he can't read his tombstone when
he's dead."*

• GRAVITY •

Law of Selective Gravity —

▶ *"An object will fall so as to do the
most damage."*
Corollary —
*"The chance of the bread falling with
the buttered side down is directly
proportional to the cost of the
carpet."*

• GREATNESS •

Greatness comes to man in
three ways.

▶ *"Some are born great,
some achieve greatness,
and some have greatness thrust
upon them."*

— William Shakespeare

Is the greatness of a man determined by his scholarliness?

▶ *"The world's great men have not commonly been great scholars, nor the great scholars great men."*

— Oliver Wendell Holmes,

• GRIEF •

"It is foolish to tear one's hair in grief...

▶ *as though sorrow would be made less by baldness."*

— Cicero

Visible tears are not a yardstick for measuring grief.

▶ *"Some people suffer in silence louder than others."*

"Grief knits two hearts in closer bonds than happiness ever can.

▶ *And common sufferings are far stronger links than common joys."*

— Alphonse de Lamartine

• THE GROUCH! •

That which a grouch should learn from the whale.

▶ *"The whale never gets into trouble until he comes up to spout."*

• THE GRUDGE! •

"A chip on the shoulder is...

▶ *about the heaviest load a body carries."*

Does carrying a grudge serve your best interests?

▶ *"The art of being wise is the art of knowing what to overlook."*

— William James

• GUESTS •

"An ideal guest is

▶ *one who stays at home!"*

• GUILTY •

"You're as guilty looking as...

▶ *the cat that ate the canary!"*

• GULLIBILITY •

Isn't it time you started
being more skeptical?

▶ *"Believe nothing you read or hear
and half of what you see."*

— Talmud

Why gullible people swallow
the printed word.

▶ *"It's in print. So it
must be true"!*

Should suckers get a break?

▶ *"Too many people think it's morally
wrong to allow suckers to keep their
money."*

Whispering and Gullibility.

▶ *"Most people will believe anything if
it is whispered to them."*

What kind of people generally
get taken in?

▶ *"There is none deceived but he that
trusts."*

— Benjamin Franklin

Are Americans any different
from African aborigines in
gullibility?

▶ *"Americans are people who laugh
at African witch doctors and
spend 100 million dollars on fake
reducing systems."*

— Leonard Louis Levinson

Don't always get taken in by
the person who cries a lot!

▶ *"Nothing dries sooner than a tear."*

Do many people in general
believe the unbelievable?

▶ *"I never cease being dumfounded
by the unbelievable things people
believe."*

— Leo Rosten

"Fool me once, shame on you.

▶ *Fool me twice, shame on me!"*

— Chinese proverb

For every skeptic, is there an
equal and opposite gullible
sucker?

▶ *"For every credibility gap there is a
gullibility fill."*

— Richard Clopton

Are suckers hard to find?

▶ *"There's a sucker born every
minute!"*

— P.T. Barnum

It's a naive gullible person who allows himself to listen to an unconscionable gyp artist.

▶ *"It is a blind goose that cometh to the fox's sermon."*

— John Lyly

The naiveté of those who believe everything they read.

▶ *"Those who think a thing is true because it is in print — is a fool!"*

— Moses Maimonides

Better not to be a sucker than suffer after.

▶ *"Better shun the bait than struggle in the snare."*

— John Dryden

• GUTS! •

He has no guts.

▶ *"He's got a backbone as soft as a banana — and as yellow!"*

The philosophy of the guy with guts.

▶ *"To dry one's eyes and laugh at a fall*
And baffled — get up and begin again."

— Robert Browning

After appointing a disappointing judge to the U.S. Supreme Court —

▶ *"I could have carved a better backbone out of a banana!"*

— Theodore Roosevelt

Before a person becomes a mature "Pro" in life he's got to be able to take a lot of bumps!

▶ *"Before the diamond shows its brilliancy, it has to stand a great deal of cutting."*

A University degree often means little as against an ordinary man with "fight".

▶ *"I'd rather have an inch of dog than miles of pedigree."*

— Dana Burnet

The difference between Big shots and Little shots.

▶ *"Big shots are only little shots who keep shooting."*

— Christopher Morley

"If you can't stand the heat...

▶ *get out of the kitchen!"*

— Harry S. Truman

H

• HABITS •

Don't let the wrong habits start!

▶ *"Habits are at first cobwebs — then cables."*
— Spanish proverb

"The hardest habit to quit is...

▶ *that of quitting!"*

• YOUR HAIR •

"Long Hair"
How does it look on men?

▶ *"Lycurgus said that long hair enhances a handsome man but makes an ugly one ten times worse."*
— Plutarch

The transience of hair.

▶ *"Hair today and gone tomorrow!"*

How should a man react if his hair turns grey?

▶ *"No man should fret in case his hair Turns silver in his prime He's fortunate that some was there To turn at turning time."*
— William W. Pratt

Word of caution to the fellow who is losing his hair.

▶ *"A hair in the head is worth two in the brush."*
— Oliver Herford

"The only real cure for dandruff is...

▶ *the guillotine!"*

Sign in barber shop —

▶ *"We need your head to run our business."*

To the grey haired politician who dyes his hair.

▶ *"He doesn't dye his hair. He's just prematurely orange."*

A "hairdresser" usually attains an authority and intimacy few other men ever attain.

▶ *"Women tell a hairdresser things they wouldn't dare confess to a priest or a doctor!"*

• HANDWRITING •

"My handwriting is so bad that...

▶ *I sometimes think I should have been a doctor!"*

• HANGOVERS •

When a Frenchman suffers from that thing called a hangover, he says something roughly translatable as —

▶ *"My eyes aren't opposite the holes."*

• THE HAPPENING •

What can you expect to always happen?

▶ *"The unexpected always happens."*
— Lawrence J. Peter

• HAPPINESS •

"Everybody aspires to a lifetime of happiness but...

▶ *no man alive could bear it: it would be hell on earth."*
— George Bernard Shaw

"There is no happiness.

▶ *There are only moments of happiness."*
— Spanish proverb

"Man is never as unhappy as he thinks he is, nor...

▶ *as happy as he expects to be."*

In what ratio do Ecstasy and Anguish keep company?

▶ *For each ecstatic instant We must an anguish pay In keen and quivering ratio To the ecstasy."*
— Emily Dickinson

Happiness and its relationship to the body and to the mind.

▶ *"Happiness is not being pained in body or troubled in mind."*
— Thomas Jefferson

"If ignorance is bliss...

▶ *there should be more happy people."*
— Laurence J. Peter

"Happiness is...

▶ *no laughing matter!"*
— Richard Whately

No matter who you are, "You" affect the happiness of others!

▶ *"Every human being either adds to or subtracts from the happiness of those with whom he or she comes in contact."*

"Don't mistake pleasure for happiness.

▶ *They are a different breed of dogs."*
— Josh Billings

"Success is getting what you want...

▶ *Happiness is appreciating what you have!"*

"Every minute you're angry, you lose...

▶ *60 seconds of happiness."*

"Do not speak of your happiness...

▶ *to one less fortunate than yourself."*
— Plutarch

When does misery become even more sorrowful?

▶ *"There is no greater sorrow than to recall, in misery, the time when we were happy."*
— Dante Alighieri

If you can find contentment in your own company, your happiness will be less dependent on others.

▶ *"The man who has begun to live more seriously within begins to live more simply without."*
— Ernest Hemingway

Which makes you happier? Doing what you like or liking what you do?

▶ *"The secret of happiness is not in doing what one likes, but in liking what one has to do."*
— James M. Barrie

"As unhappy as...

▶ *a tap dancer in driver's shoes."*

What are two helpful ingredients for happiness?

▶ *"Happiness? That's nothing more than health and a poor memory."*
— Albert Schweitzer

What kind of happiness is Ecstasy?

▶ *"Ecstasy is happiness with its clothes off."*

Motto on Happiness!

▶ *"My creed is this:*
Happiness is the only good.
The place to be happy is here.
The time to be happy is now.
The way to be happy is to make others so."

— Robert G. Ingersoll

What in life is the loftiest element for happiness?

▶ *"The supreme happiness of life is the conviction that we are loved."*

— Victor Hugo

"Happiness adds and multiplies as...

▶ *we divide it with others."*

Happiness and your mortgage!

▶ *"Happiness is paying the last installment."*

"Happiness is not a state to arrive at but...

▶ *a manner of travelling."*

— Margaret Lee Runbeck

If your concern for others is too great, will you be happy?

▶ *"To be happy, we must not be too concerned with others."*

— Albert Camus

Happy is the man who knows he consciously lived today.

▶ *"Happy the man and happy he alone*
He who can call today his own.
He who secure within can say
Tomorrow, do thy worst for I have lived today."

Does anything make up for short-lived happiness?

▶ *"Happiness makes up in height for what it lacks in length."*

— Robert Frost

"Happiness is the peculiar sensation you get when...

▶ *you're too busy to be miserable."*

What is harder to conceal — Joy of Grief?

▶ *"He who can conceal his joys is greater than he who can hide his grief."*

— J.K. Lavater

How to diminish unhappiness. ▶ *"Acquire an enthusiasm. You can't be unenthusiastic and unhappy at the same time."*

Love and passion is great — but what is Ecstasy? ▶ *"Real ecstasy is discovering that you haven't lost your car keys after all."*

• HARD HEARTED •

Which type of people are most likely to grow hard-hearted? ▶ *"Extremely happy and extremely unhappy men are alike prone to grow hard-hearted."*

— Montesquieu

• HATRED •

Avoid turning Love to Hatred. ▶ *"Heaven has no rage like love to hatred turned."*

— William Congreve

• YOUR HEALTH •

The way to stay healthy. ▶ *"Eat what you don't want. Drink what you don't like. And do what you'd rather not!"*

Sign in Norwegian hospital — ▶ *"Visitors. Two to a Bed and Half-an-Hour Only."*

Procrastination to too many is what fails to discover the unknown in time. ▶ *"A man too busy to take care of his health is like a mechanic too busy to take care of his tools."*

— Spanish proverb

Valuable guide on making your heart live longer. ▶ *"Never do anything standing that you can do sititng, or anything sitting that you can do lying down."*

— Chinese proverb

Ten Golden Rules for Good
Health —

▶ *1. Have a checkup every year.*
   2. Be a non-smoker.
   3. Drink in moderation.
   4. Count each calorie.
   5. Watch your cholesterol.
   6. Learn nutritional values.
   7. Find time for leisure and vacations.
   8. Adjust to life's daily pressures.
   9. Develop an exercise program.
   10. Understand your physical assets
   and limitations."

— The American Health Foundation

"He who is not healthy at
twenty, wealthy at forty, or wise
at sixty will never be...

▶ *healthy, wealthy, or wise."*

"There's lots of people
who spend so much time
watching their health that...

▶ *they haven't got time to enjoy it."*

— Josh Billings

"If you want to be the picture
of health...

▶ *make sure you have a happy frame of*
mind."

Canadian Slogan urging you
to exercise and shape up!

▶ *"If you want to make everything you*
do better, start by making yourself
better."

— ParticiPaction

To cure a cold...

▶ *takes about a week of treatment to*
cure — and about seven days without
treatment."

"If I had known I was going to
live this long...

▶ *I would have taken better care of*
myself."

— Cary Grant

• HEAVEN •

"Everybody wants to go to
heaven but...

▶ *nobody wants to die to get*
there."

• THE HEDONIST •

Philosophy of the man who says — "This is my life, not a dress rehearsal."

▶ *"Me, my, and I —*
Before we die —
Want everything —
And don't ask why!"

• HELL •

Here in Hell lies the reward for all who are villainous.

▶ *"All Hope Abandon,*
Ye who enter here!"

— Aligheri Dante

"Count that day lost when...

▶ *you don't catch Hell for something!"*

"Hell is less torment than...

▶ *the road to Hell."*

Is Hell ever located on earth?

▶ *"When I die, I'll go to Heaven. I've already been to Hell."*

— George S. Patton

Who should be consigned to the lowest place in Hell?

▶ *"The lowest place in Hell is reserved for those who were neutral in the face of moral crisis."*

— Aligheri Dante

• HELP! •

"If there's anything I can do for you...

▶ *don't let me know!"*

A fallacious argument on why more help for the poor isn't necessary.

▶ *"The poor will always be with you."*
— Bible

Where should you look for a helping hand?

▶ *"The best place to get a helping hand is at the end of your arm."*

Is it futile to seek help from heaven?

▶ *"And that inverted Bowl they call the Sky,*
Whereunder crawling coop'd we live and die,
Lift not your hand to it for help — for it
As impotently moves as you or I."

— Omar Khayyam

The helper who leaves the heavy loads for you.

▶ *"Some fellows always reach for the stool when there is a piano to be moved."*

Be careful when you give a helping hand!

▶ *"Some people will never let go of a helping hand."*

When somebody won't help you out.

▶ *"He's such a nice guy. There's NOTHING he wouldn't do for me, and that's exactly what he's done — NOTHING!"*

"I'd like to help you out.

▶ *Which way did you come in?"*

What is the second most beautiful verb in the world?

▶ *After the verb "To Love", "To Help" is the most beautiful verb in the world.*
— Baroness Von Suttner

"A man never stands straighter than...

▶ *when he stoops to help somebody smaller or less well off."*

• HELPFUL •

If everybody didn't do their little bit — no good cause would succeed.

▶ *"I am only one, but still I am one; I cannot do everything, but still I can do something; and because I cannot do everything I will not refuse to do the something that I can do."*
— Edward E. Hale

"It was as helpful as...

▶ *throwing a drowning man both ends of a rope."*
— Arthur "Bugs" Baer

• HEREDITY •

The Law of Heredity —

▶ *"All bad traits come from the other parent!"*

• HESITATING •

"He who hesitates is...

▶ *sometimes saved."*
— James Thurber

• THE HIGHBROW •

"A highbrow is a person educated beyond...

▶ *his intelligence.*"

• HINDSIGHT •

In the mistakes of life, how is hindsight related to foresight?

▶ *"Hindsight is how we explain the mistakes that foresight could have avoided."*

• HISTORY •

What's wrong with history?

▶ *"History repeats itself. That's one of the things that's wrong with history."*
— Clarence Darrow

Does history ever repeat itself?

▶ *"History is the science of what never happens twice."*
— Paul Valtry

"In 321, Constantine issues an edict forbidding work on 'the venerable day of the sun' (Sunday)...

▶ *the day that had come to be substituted for the seventh-day Sabbath."*

Do only the wise learn from the past?

▶ *"Those who cannot remember the past are condemned to repeat it."*
— Herbert Samuel

Is it infantile for man to ignore history?

▶ *"Not to know what has been transacted in former times is to continue always a child. If no use is made of the labors of past ages, the world must remain always in the infancy of knowledge."*
— Cicero

The nice part of being able to write your own history book.

▶ *"History will be kind to me for I intend to write it."*
— Winston Churchill

What is the relationship of news to history?

▶ *"News is the first rough draft of history."*

— Benjamin Bradlee

In International Relations, when do nations finally behave wisely?

▶ *"History teaches us that men and nations behave wisely once they have exhausted all other alternatives."*

— Abba Eban

What single basic act of man does the record of history portray?

▶ *"The history of the world is the record of a man in quest of his daily bread and butter."*

— Hendrik Willem van Loon

Is history generally written with the bias of the writer?

▶ *"History's lessons are no more enlightening than the wisdom of those who interpret them."*

— David Schoenbrun

Plutarch — 1800 years ago — set his formula for writing history.

▶ *"I record, not history, but human destiny. The evidences of vice or virtue are not confined to famous accomplishments; often some trivial event, a word, a joke, will serve better than great campaigns and battles as a revelation of character."*

— Plutarch

"After you've heard two different eyewitness accounts of the same automobile accident, you begin to wonder about the validity of history.

▶ *How do we know, for sure, what ever happened anywhere?"*

"History repeats itself" and "History never repeats itself" are about equally true. True or false?

▶ *"We never know enough about the infinitely complex circumstances of any past event to prophesy the future by analogy."*

— G.M. Trevelyan

"The only thing we learn from history is...

▶ *that we don't learn from history."*

— Napoleon

• HISTORIC DOCUMENTS •

World War II speech by
Churchill.

▶ *"We shall go on to the end, we shall
fight in France, we shall fight on the
seas and oceans, we shall fight with
growing confidence and growing
strength in the air, we shall defend our
Island whatever the cost may be, we
shall fight on the landing grounds, we
shall fight in the fields and in the
streets, we shall fight in the hills; we
shall never surrender, and even if,
which I do not for a moment believe,
this Island or a large part of it were
subjugated and starving, then our
Empire beyond the seas, armed and
guarded by the British Fleet, would
carry on the struggle, until, in God's
good time, the New World, with all its
power and might steps forth to the
rescue and the liberation of the old."*

— Winston Churchill

"All men are created equal."

▶ *"Fourscore and seven years ago, our
fathers brought forth on this continent
a new nation, conceived in libery, and
dedicated to the proposition that all
men are created equal."*

— Abraham Lincoln

Excerpt from the "Magna
Carta", treasured forerunner of
liberty for democracies of the
world.

▶ *"No freeman shall be taken or
imprisoned or proceeded against
except by the lawful judgment of his
peers or by the law of the land."*

Revered inscription on the
"Statue of Liberty", New York
City.

▶ *"Give me your tired, your poor,
Your huddled masses, yearning to
  breath free.
The wretched refuse of your teeming
  shore.
Send these, the homeless, tempest
  tossed, to me:
I lift my lamp beside the golden door."*

— Emma Lazarus

From "The Oath of Hippocrates", about 400 B.C. Greece.
"Life is short, and the Art long; the occasion fleeting; experience fallacious, and judgment difficult. The physician must not only be prepared to do what is right himself, but also to make the patient, the attendants, and externals cooperate."

▶ (excerpts)
1. "I swear by Apollo the physician to teach this Art (of medicine) without fee or stipulation."
2. "I will follow that system of regimen which, according to my ability and judgment, I consider for the benefit of my patients, and abstain from whatever is deleterious and mischievous."
3. "Into whatever houses I enter, I will go into them for the benefit of the sick."
4. "Whatever, in connection with my professional practice, or not in connection with it, I see or hear, I will not divulge."
5. "While I continue to keep this Oath unviolated, may it be granted to me to enjoy life. But should I trespass and violate this Oath, may the reverse be my lot."

Churchill's historic eleven words during World War II that gave courage to the free world.

▶ "I have nothing to offer but blood, toil, sweat and tears."

— Winston Churchill

Abridged version of the "Ten Commandments". (Exodus 20:3-17)

▶ "I. Thou shalt have no other gods before me.
II. Thou shalt not make unto thee any graven image.
III. Thou shalt not take the name of the Lord thy God in vain.
IV. Remember the sabbath day, to keep it holy.
V. Honor thy father and thy mother.
VI. Thou shalt not kill.
VII. Thou shalt not commit adultery.
VIII. Thou shalt not steal.
IX. Thou shalt not bear false witness against thy neighbor.
X. Thou shalt not covet thy neighbor's house, nor thy neighbor's wife...nor anything that is thy neighbor's."

Government of, by, and for the People.

▶ "We here highly resolve that these dead shall not have died in vain; that this nation, under God, shall have a new birth of freedom, and that government of the people, by the people, and for the people, shall not perish from the earth."

— Abraham Lincoln (Gettysburg Address)

Life, Liberty and the pursuit of Happiness. (USA)

▶ "We hold these truths to be self-evident, — that all men are created equal; that they are endowed by their Creator with certain unalienable rights; that among these are Life, Liberty, and the pursuit of happiness."

— Declaration of Independence

Trial by Jury.

▶ "The trial of all crimes, except in cases of impeachment shall be by jury."

— American Constitution

Freedom of Speech.

▶ "Congress shall make no law abridging the freedom of speech or of the press."

— American Constitution

A statement made prior to the USA Declaration of Independence.

▶ "Is life so dear, or peace so sweet, as to be purchased at the price of chains and slavery? Forbid it, Almighty God! I know now what course others may take; but, as for me, give me liberty, or give me death!"

— Patrick Henry

Prayer for World Peace.

▶ "They shall beat their swords into ploughshares, and their spears into pruninghooks: nation shall not lift up sword against nation neither shall they learn war any more."

— Isaiah II.4

Famous words of Churchill during World War II, regarding the handful of British flyers who staved off the much larger German Luftwaffe.

▶ "Never in the field of human conflict was so much owed by so many to so few."

— Winston Churchill

The Communist Manifesto by Karl Marx and Friedrich Engels that changed the world.

▶ *"Let the ruling classes tremble at a Communist revolution. The proletarians have nothing to lose but their chains. They have a world to win. Working men of all countries, unite!"*

Preamble to the Charter of the "United Nations".

▶ *"WE THE PEOPLES OF THE UNITED NATIONS*
Determined
"To save succeeding generations from the scourge of war, which twice in our lifetime has brought untold sorrow to mankind, and
To reaffirm faith in fundamental human rights, in the dignity and worth of the human person, in the equal right of men and women and of nations large and small..."

• HOME •

What the new home buyer should be aware of when he sacrifices himself on the altar of Home Ownership.

▶ *"A man builds a fine house; and now he has a master, and a task for life."*
— Ralph Waldo Emerson

How clean should your house be for a harmonious marriage?

▶ *"A house must be clean enough to be healthy and dirty enough to be happy!"*

Does the opulence of a home determine how much happiness it can hold?

▶ *"A cottage will hold as much happiness as would stock a palace."*
— James Hamilton

What a house is NOT.

▶ *"A House is not a Home."*
— Polly Adler

Is there any place like home?

▶ *"Mid pleasures and palaces though we may roam.*
Be it ever so humble there's no place like home."
— J. Howard Payne

The three most important points to remember when buying a home.

▶ *"Location, location and location!"*
— Real estate agents' motto

• HOMOSEXUALITY •

In defense of homosexuality.

"If the concept of God has any validity or use, it can only be to make us larger, freer, and more loving. If God cannot do this, then it is time we got rid of Him."

— James Baldwin

In support of homosexuals, who also have rights under our constitution.

▶ *"The world isn't worth a damn If I can't stand up and say I am what I am!"*

—"La Cage aux Folles"

• HONESTY •

If you're going to be a crook, plan the event efficiently.

▶ *"Many men fail in wickedness for want of going deep enough in."*

— Henry Fielding

A person who has once perceived what makes greatness of spirit, cannot be happy if he allows himself to fall short of the best that he has it in him to be.

▶ *"To thine own self be true, And it must follow, as the night the day, Thou canst not then be false to any man."*

— William Shakespeare

"There are no such things as honest people.

▶ *There are only people less crooked."*

— Gerald F. Lieberman

Go straight!

▶ *"No man ever got lost on a straight road."*

What is the unexpected attribute in finding honesty in public men?

▶ *"Honesty in public men is generally attributed to Dumbness and is seldom rewarded."*

— Will Rogers

• THE HONEYMOON •

50,000 honeymooners in Niagara Falls every year! The lesson?

▶ *"Niagara Falls is the second greatest disappointment for the American bride."*

— Oscar Wilde

• HOPE •

The troubles of today generally look worse than they do tomorrow.

▶ *"It is always darkest just before the day dawneth."*

— Thomas Fuller

Consoling words spoken to Richard M. Nixon after his his demoralizing resignation.

▶ *"Whether you have been knocked down or are on the ropes, always remember that life is 99 rounds."*

— Walter Annenberg

How to hope.

▶ *"Hope ever urges on and tells us tomorrow will be better."*

Remember! There's hope when you hit bottom.

▶ *"The lowest ebb is the turn of the tide."*

What is most often the ultimate destination of hope?

▶ *"Hope is merely disappointment deferred."*

— W. Burton Baldry

"The man who lives only by hope...

▶ *will die with despair."*

— Italian proverb

Does hope make life more tolerable?

▶ *"It is necessary to hope; for hope itself is happiness, and its frustrations, however frequent, are less dreadful than its extinction."*

— Samuel Johnson

So long as there is some hope, the incentive is there to continue battling for tomorrow's goal!

▶ *"There is no medicine like hope, no incentive so great, and no tonics so powerful as expectation of something better tomorrow."*

— Orison Swett Marden

"He who lives on hope...

▶ *will die fasting!"*

• HOPELESS! •

Don't pursue a lost cause.

▶ *"Don't flog a dead horse!"*

• HOSPITALITY •

Definition of Hospitality via lodging.

▶ *"The virtue which induces us to feed and lodge certain persons who are not in need of food and lodging."*

— Ambrose Bierce

The ultimate in hospitality. Welcome!

▶ *"Through this wide opening gate None come too early, none return too late.*

• THE HOST •

The art of a tactful host.

▶ *"Making guests feel at home even though you wish they were."*

• THE HOTEL •

Sign in a Zurich hotel —

▶ *"Because of the impropriety of entertaining guests of the opposite sex in the bedroom, it is suggested that the lobby be used for this purpose."*

Letter in tortured English from an Italian hotel.

▶ *"I can offer you a commodious chamber with balcony imminent to the romantic gorge and I hope you want to drop in."*

• HUMANITARIANS •

Are there any really sincere humanitarians?

▶ *"A humanitarian is always a hypocrite."*

— George Orwell

• THE HUMBLE •

"Never be haughty to the humble.

▶ *Never be humble to the haughty."*

— Jefferson Davis

• HUMILIATION •

Don't be a weakling and smile when somebody is insulting you.

▶ *"If you let your smile be your umbrella, you get a mouthful of rain."*

• HUMILITY •

How to keep humble.

▶ *"Carry a mirror with you!"*

Why it is difficult to be humble.

▶ *"Even if you aim at humility, there is no guarantee that when you have attained the state you will not be proud of the feat."*
— Bonamy Dobrée

If you were testing a man for greatness, what prime quality would you look for?

▶ *"I believe the first test of a truly great man is humility."*
— John Ruskin

What quality does humility elicit?

▶ *"The quality of feeling ashamed while telling how good you are."*

It's OK to be proud but never lose humility.

▶ *"Walk tall but remember how to stoop!"*

• HUMOUR •

The weakness of dragging a joke out too long.

▶ *"Brevity is the soul of wit."*
— William Shakespeare

What is the difference between Tragedy and Comedy?

▶ *"Tragedy is if I cut my finger. Comedy is if you walk into an open sewer and almost drown."*

— Mel Brooks

Where does a Pun rate in humour?

▶ *"A pun is the lowest form of wit — unless you say it first."*

Cultivate a sense of humour in adversity.

▶ *"One of the best things to have up your sleeve is a funny bone."*

A valuable tip to comedians and joke tellers!

▶ *"To provoke laughter without joining in it greatly heightens the effect."*
— Honoré de Balzac

The rare quality of the true comedian.

▶ *"The test of a real comedian is whether you laugh at him before he opens his mouth."*

— George Jean Nathan

The test of humour.

▶ *"A jest's prosperity lies in the ear of him that hears it — and never in the tongue of him that makes it!"*

— William Shakespeare

What flavour do Variety and Humour give to life?

▶ *"Variety is the spice of life. Good humour is the salt."*

What purpose in life does comedy serve?

▶ *"Mankind without comedy is unthinkable. If all laughter were suddenly to disappear from the face of the earth, man would revert from a human being to being non-human."*

Do men of wisdom avoid nonsense?

▶ *"A little nonsense now and then Is relished by the wisest men."*

"Surprise is so essential an ingredient of wit that no wit will bear repetition.

▶ *The original electrical feeling produced by any piece of wit can never be renewed."*

— Sydney Smith

The role of humour in everyday life.

▶ *"Jokes and humour are the cayenne of conversation and the salt of life."*

How people react if they're told they have no sense of humour.

▶ *"Any man will admit if need be that his sight is not good, or that he cannot swim or shoots badly with a rifle, but to touch upon his sense of humour is to give him mortal affront."*

— Stephen Leacock

"A jest loses its point when...

▶ *he who makes it is the first to laugh."*

What's the worst kind of failure in humour?

▶ *"Of all failures to fail in, a witticism is the worst, and the mishap is the more calamitous in a drawn out and detailed one."*

— Samuel Johnson

Definition of Comedian —

▶ *"A person with a good memory who prays no one else has."*

— Red Skelton

• HUNGER •

How is Hunger related to the Morse Code?

▶ *"Hunger is an SOS from the stomach."*

• HUSBANDS AND WIVES •

"Any man who thinks he's more intelligent than his wife...

▶ *is married to a very intelligent woman."*

"Marriage is a legal and religious alliance entered into by a man who can't sleep with the window shut...

▶ *and a woman who can't sleep with the window open."*
        — Ogden Nash

How come after 40 years, you both get along so well!

▶ *"We attribute our harmony to a growing loss of hearing."*

When should husband and wife yell at each other?

▶ *"Never speak loud to one another unless the house is on fire!"*
        — B. Evelyn

A tribute to my wife.

▶ *"My pleasure and torment —*
The empress of my heart."

Beware of calling your wife stupid.

▶ *"When you question your wife's judgment remember she married you."*

The cavewoman wife.

▶ *"I came — I saw — I conked him."*

"The man who holds the car door open for his wife...

▶ *has either a new wife or a new car."*

As the Cavewoman said to the caveman —

▶ *"You never drag me anyplace anymore!"*

There are two kinds of party-goers —

▶ *"One wants to leave early — the other wants to stay late. Usually, they're married to each other."*

WIFE: "If this canoe capsizes, who would you save first, the children or me?"

▶ *HUSBAND: "Me."*

"For every woman on earth there's a man.

▶ *So how come I got you!"*

What you'd like to say when your wife is driving you up the wall!

▶ "Breathes there the man, with
soul so dead,
Who never to his wife
hath said,
Shut up!"

Indebtedness to my wife.

▶ "I hereby publicly acknowledge that all I owe in this world is DUE to my wife."

"A wife is a gift bestowed upon a man...

▶ to reconcile him to the loss of paradise."

—J.W. von Goethe

"Never go to bed mad.

▶ Stay up and fight!"

— Phyllis Diller

"Behind every successful husband, there's...

▶ another woman!"

• THE HYPOCHONDRIAC •

Warning about talking to a hypochondriac!

▶ "A hypochondriac is a person, who when you ask him how he is — He tells you."

The hypochrondriac that everybody knows.

▶ "I complain about my ailments,
To everyone I know;
And the more I talk about
them,
The more my ailments grow."

As the hypochondriac said —

▶ "My last doctor was obsessed with the idea that all my illnesses were imaginary."

"The trouble with being a hypochondriac these days is...

▶ that antibiotics have cured all the good diseases."

Hypochondriac —

▶ "Someone who won't leave well enough alone."

"The way medical costs are rising...

▶ I can't afford to be a hypochondriac any more."

Advice to a hypochondriac.

▶ *"The best cure for hypochondria is to forget about your own body and get interested in somebody else's."*

— Goodman Ace

"How to say good-bye to a hypochondriac.

▶ *"So long! Keep on breathing."*

What the retired hypochondriac does.

▶ *"I get up early, read the obituary column, and if my name isn't there, I go back to bed."*

Has a hypochondriac more than five senses?

▶ *A hypochondriac is a person with a "sick" sense.*

He's such a hypochondriac!

▶ *"He wouldn't visit the Dead Sea without finding out what it died of."*

• HYPOCRISY •

How a hypocrite treats your face and your back.

▶ *"A hypocrite is somebody who pats you on your back to your face — and kicks you in the face to your back."*

— Dennis O'Keefe

Which hyprocrisy does society accept?

▶ *Politeness is the most acceptable hyprocrisy."*

"When I have to choose between honest arrogance and hypocritical humility...

▶ *I choose honest arrogance."*

— Frank Lloyd Wright

"A hypocrite is like a pin.

▶ *It points one way and heads the other."*

What hypocrisy is —

▶ *"Hypocrisy is the homage that vice pays to virtue."*

I

• THE IDEAL •

The Ideal that mankind dreams of achieving.

▶ *"Behold how good and how pleasant it is for brethren to dwell together in unity!"*

— Psalms

• IDEALISM •

How an ideal world could abolish poverty.

▶ *"If youth but knew and age were able, then poverty would be a fable."*

How idealistic can you be when the problem adversely affects you?

▶ *"Idealism increases in direct proportion to one's distance from the problem."*

— John Galsworthy

• IDEAS •

The power of a timely idea!

▶ *"There is one thing stronger than all the armies in the world, and that is an Idea whose time has come."*

— Victor Hugo

The feeling you experience when you get a great idea — and its anticlimax.

▶ *"Exhilaration is that feeling you get just after a great idea hits you and just before you realize what's wrong with it."*

Should you blame ideas for the crazy things people believe in?

▶ *"An idea isn't responsible for the people who believe in it."*

— Don Marquis

What an idea is and how it's affected by a metaphor.

▶ *"An idea is a feat of association and the height of it is a good metaphor."*

— Robert Frost

Don't be the guinea pig on new ideas — and don't be a bulldog clinging to old ones!

▶ *"Be not the first by when the new is tried.*
Nor yet the last to lay the old aside."

— Alexander Pope

First come the facts. Then follow ideas.

▶ *"The telephone book is full of facts but it doesn't contain a single idea."*

— Mortimer J. Adler

With the threat of nuclear world destruction, the battle for peace must now be fought with words.

▶ *"Ideas are weapons!"*

— V. I. Lenin

How to make an idea work.

▶ *"An idea is something that won't work unless you do."*

"Every time a man puts a new idea across he finds ten men who thought of it before he did but...

▶ *they only thought of it."*

How two people multiply ideas.

▶ *"If you have an idea and I have an idea, and we both keep them to ourselves, we each have only one idea. But if you tell me your idea and I tell you mine we each have two ideas."*

• IDLENESS •

What else is bad about having absolutely nothing to do?

▶ *"The bad thing about having nothing to do is you never know when you're finished."*

• IGNORANCE •

What is Gross Ignorance?

▶ *"Gross ignorance is 144 times worse than ordinary ignorance."*

— Bennett Cerf

• IMAGINATION •

As we grow older, do our powers of imagination increase or lessen?

▶ *"Imagination grows by exercise, and contrary to common belief, is more powerful in the mature than in the young."*

— W. Somerset Maugham

• THE IMMIGRANTS •

The reality of what so many immigrants found out upon arrival in America.

▶ *"I learned —*
First that the roads in America weren't paved with gold.
Second that the roads weren't paved.
And third that I had to pave them!"

• IMMORTALITY •

Can anybody produce any proof whatever in the belief that man has personal immortality?

▶ *"In spite of all the yearnings of men, no one can produce a single fact or reason to support the belief in God and in personal immortality."*

— Clarence Darrow

• YOUR IMPORTANCE •

"To judge of the real importance of an individual...

▶ *we should think of the effect his death would produce."*

Is any man indispensable?

▶ *"The cemeteries are full of irreplaceable people!"*

• THE IMPOVERISHED •

How the impoverished and the hungry yearn for aid from any source!

▶ *"And with no language but a cry!"*

— Alfred Lord Tennyson

• IMPRESSING •

Our false values in trying to impress others.

▶ *"Why is it we spend, money we can't afford — on things we don't need — to impress people we can't stand the sight of."*

Are first impressions important?	▸ *"Your first appearance,"* he said to me, *"is the gauge by which you will be measured."* — Jean Jacques Rousseau

• THE IMPRESSION •

I'll always cherish my First Impressions about you.	▸ *"I will always cherish the initial misconceptions I had about you."*
Do people really reveal their true character?	▸ *"God has given us one face. We make ourselves another."*
Should we trust our First Reactions — and why?	▸ *"Let us distrust our first reactions; they are invariably too favorable."* — Friedrich Nietzsche
First Impressions do impress.	▸ *"Remember! You don't get a second chance to make a first impression!"*

• IMPROBABLE •

"As unlikely as...	▸ *— a mousetrap chasing a mouse!"*
"As much chance as... "As much chance as... "As much chance as...	*— a fish has of perspiring!"* *— a meatball has of bouncing!"* *— a hot dog has of biting!"*
"As much chance as...	▸ *smuggling daylight past a rooster!"*
"You've got about as much chance as...	▸ *getting sap from a totem pole."* — Nikita Krusehev
When's that going to happen?	▸ *"You'll have to wait until a shrimp learns to whistle."* — Nikita Krusehev

• THE INCOMPETENTS •

The Law of Clowns when you hire a bunch of incompetents —	▸ *"If you have a bunch of clowns, you're going to have a circus."* — R.J. Boettcher

• INDEPENDENCE •

What is the one necessary
ingredient for independence?

▶ *"To be poor and independent is very
nearly an impossibility."*
— William Cobbett

What financial independence
really means.

▶ *"Lord of myself. Accountable to
none!"*
— Benjamin Franklin

• INDIFFERENCE •

"Affection can withstand very
severe storms of rigor but...

▶ *NOT a long polar frost of downright
indifference."*
— Walter Scott

What is worse for a
politician than to be
insulted?

▶ *"Insults would be more
tolerable than indifference."*
— Charles De Gaulle

• INDIGESTION •

What's the worst kind of
indigestion?

▶ *"There is no indigestion worse than
that which comes from having to eat
your own words."*

• INDIVIDUALITY •

Doing your own thing and not
following the pack.

▶ *"Two roads diverged in a wood and I
took the one less travelled by —
And that has made all the difference."*
— Robert Frost

"Don't be a carbon copy of
someone else...

▶ *make your own impression"*

"Be yourself.

▶ *There's nobody else like you!"*

"I am the architect of myself.

▶ *I am not compelled to be simply a
creature of others, molded by their
experiences, shaped by their
demands."*
— Carl Rogers

Don't always go with the trend!

▶ "Kites rise against, NOT with the wind."

— John Neal

Why you should be yourself.

▶ "Whatever you are by nature, keep to it; never desert your own line of talent. Be what nature intended you for, and you will succeed; be anything else and you will be ten thousand times worse than nothing."

— Sydney Smith

Be true to yourself!

▶ "This above all: to thine own self be true,
And it must follow, as the night the day,
Thou canst not then be false to any man."

— William Shakespeare

Be yourself. Mimic nobody. It It won't work!

▶ "The cow that mimics a cormorant gets drowned."

— Japanese proverb

Of the billions on planet earth, take pride that you and "You Alone" are unlike any other and are uniquely you!

▶ "A million million spermatozoa,
All of them alive:
Out of their cataclysm but one poor Noah
Dare to hope to survive.
And among that billion minus one
Might have chanced to be
Shakespeare, another Newton, a new Donne —
But the One was Me."

— Aldous Huxley

If you think you're the only person who thinks or does the things you do — you're not alone.

▶ "Whatever you may be sure of, be sure of this — that you are dreadfully like other people."

— James Russell Lowell

"When in Rome be individualistic.

▶ Do as the Romanians do!"

Is there any rational basis for deploring those who dress and wear their hair differently?

▶ "Individuals create their own style."

"Adam was the only man who, when he said a good thing...

▶ *knew that nobody had said it before him."*

— Mark Twain

He's a one of a kind!

▶ *"There never was such beauty in another man.*
Nature made him, and then broke the mould."

— Ludovico Ariosto

Include me...

▶ *"Out."*

— Sam Goldwyn

Theme of the Hippie Generation of the 1960's.

▶ *"I do my thing and you do yours.*
I am not in this world to live up to your expectations —
And you are not in this world to live up to mine.
You are you — and I am I
And if by chance we find each other It's beautiful!"

— Fritz S. Perls

• INDOLENCE •

Who, if anybody, can achieve results just by indolence?

▶ *"The hen is the only creature that can produce dividends just by sitting around."*

• DON'T INDULGE •

"Give a man an inch...

▶ *and he'll want to become a ruler."*

• INEFFECTIVENESS •

Don't try to do two tasks at the same time.

▶ *"Don't try to spear two fish with one lance!"*

— Chinese proverb

• INEPTNESS •

"He's so inept...

▶ *that when he tries to put his feet in his mouth — he misses."*

He always makes a mess of things.

▶ *"He suffers from FOOT IN THE MOUTH disease."*

"He's so inept that...

▶ *if he had to cross a field with four cowpies in it — he'd manage to step in all of them before he'd reach the other side."*

Why you shouldn't give him the job to do.

▶ *"He's the kind of guy who always hits the nail right on the thumb."*

• INFANTS •

Must any man who loves dogs and babies necessarily be good?

▶ *"Any man who hates dogs and babies can't be all bad."*

— Leo Rosten

That which a Baby is.

▶ *"Something that gets you down in the daytime and up at night."*

— Kate M. Owney

"I wonder if infants enjoy their infancy...

▶ *as much as adults enjoy their adultery."*

• INFERIORITY •

What you have felt at one time or another in the presence of somebody superior to yourself.

▶ *"So far is it from being true that men are naturally equal, that no two people can be half an hour together, but one shall acquire an evident superiority over the other."*

— Samuel Johnson

• THE INFERIORITY COMPLEX •

"The trouble with an inferiority complex is...

▶ *that the people who should have it — don't!"*

• INFIDELITY •

If you want to go broke, start cheating on your wife.

▶ *"Many a man goes broke trying to bluff with two queens."*

How infidelity started.

▶ *As Adam said to Eve —*
"How come the kids don't look like
me!"

• INFLATION •

The effect of inflation!
"Last week my dentist put in a
gold crown.

▶ *I think it belonged to Queen*
Elizabeth."

How the prices in
supermarkets bring out the
religious in us.

▶ *"It was like being in church. People*
were wandering up and down the
aisles saying, 'Oh my God, oh my
God.'"

Despite all the salary raises
I got — how come I'm not eating
as well as I dreamed I would be?

▶ *"When I first started working, I used*
to dream of the day when I might be
earning the salary I'm starving on
now."

"The most annoying inflation
is...

▶ *an inflated head."*

So what else is new?

▶ *"Who has not seen with his own eyes*
the present spirit...which forces up the
price of commodities to such a degree
that human language cannot find
words to express the transaction?"
— Diocletian, A.D. 284-305

"Inflation is...

▶ *a drop in the buck."*

How inflation is killing us!

▶ *"A chocolate bar wrapper now weighs*
more than the chocolate bar."

"If a quarter knew what it is
worth today...

▶ *it would feel like two cents."*

"The only good thing for me
about inflation is...

▶ *that my gold teeth have gone up in*
value."

"When it comes to telling a
quarter and a nickel apart
these days...

▶ *only a vending machine knows for*
sure."

Two used to be able to live as
cheap as one.

▶ *"Inflation has changed things. Now*
one can live as cheap as two used to."

Is inflation making life almost impossible to live?

▶ *"In spite of the cost of living, it's still popular."*

— Kathleen Norris

"I hope they don't raise the standard of living any higher.

▶ *I can't afford it now."*

• INNOVATIONS •

How the radical innovations of one generation are viewed by the following generation.

▶ *"That which seems the height of absurdity in one generation often becomes the height of wisdom in another."*

— Adlai Stevenson

• INSECTS •

"We hope that, when the insects take over the world, they will remember...

▶ *with gratitude how we took them along on all our picnics."*

• INSOMNIA •

"Insomnia is suffering from not sleeping a wink all night...

▶ *for at least an hour."*

"An insomniac is a man who is unable to sleep...

▶ *or who, when he does sleep, dreams that he is awake."*

"If you can't sleep, then get up and do something instead of lying there and worrying...

▶ *It's the worry that gets you, not the loss of sleep."*

— Dale Carnegie

"For most people insomnia is not serious.

▶ *So don't lose any sleep over it!"*

• INSTINCT •

Motto of the man who operates NOT on logic or analysis, but on instinct.

▶ *"Always be sure if you're right or wrong. Then go either way!"*

— Roy Rowan

If you don't have a compelling reason to act — should you act on a hunch?

▶ *"Let him make use of instinct who cannot make use of reason."*

• INSULTS •

"About his personality...

▶ *he had a charisma bypass."*

"I never said he was scum.

▶ *I said he should be treated like scum!"*

"He's one of those guys who has nothing to say...

▶ *and generally says it."*

He's got a dirty crooked past.

▶ *"There's so much dirt under his rug, you have to walk up hill to get near him."*

"I'll say this for you!

▶ *You can't be accused of being accurate on facts!"*

Malicious Insult.

▶ *"If I ever run into him again, I hope I'm driving a truck!"*

"I'll tell you this. Before they made him...

▶ *they broke the mould!"*

"It matters not what epithet you hurl...

▶ *the average person thinks he isn't."*

"He thinks he's a diamond but...

▶ *all he is — is a rhinestone in the rough!"*

"I can't believe that out of 100,000 sperm...

▶ *you were the quickest."*

He's the caveman type!

▶ *He's got rocks in his head!"*

What is one of the greatest personal insults?

▶ *"It is a way of calling a man a fool when no attention is given to what he says."*

"He's a going concern but...

▶ *he doesn't know which way he's going."*

"They said you weren't fit to sleep with pigs but...

▶ *I said you were!"*

"They may call you a HIT but...

▶ *I spell it with an "S"."*

"He's so brainless that...

▶ *if his brains were rubber, he wouldn't have enough to stretch over a mosquito!"*

He's what I call a real "Dope".

▶ *"If he were cloned we'd have two dopes."*

Get Lost!

▶ *"Pawn yourself into a pawn shop and then lose the ticket!"*

A non flattering comment by O.J. Simpson about Howard Cosell.

▶ *"He has a tremendous grasp for the obvious."*

Sarcastic insult!

▶ *"Those of you who think you know everything are annoying to those of us who do."*

Said about Ramsay MacDonald —

▶ *"You're a sheep in sheep's clothing!"*

— Ernest Bevin

"I've seen a lot of dim light bulbs in my lifetime but...

▶ *you're a power failure!"*

— Stern Jerome

He's a real Headache.

▶ *"I take everything he says with a Migraine of Salt."*

"He who allows himself to be insulted deserves to be so...

▶ *and insolence, if unpunished, goes on increasing."*

— Pierre Corneille

How to insult a person who is feigning Wisdom.

▶ *"Wisdom often comes with age. With you, age came alone."*

About some people whose presence you can't stand.

▶ *"Some people are electrifying. They light up a room when they leave."*

Never forget the impact of an insult — as against that of receiving an injury.

▶ *"An injury is much sooner forgotten than an insult."*

— Lord Chesterfield

You misquoted me.

▶ *"I didn't say you were incompetent. I said you were eminently incompetent!"*

"They should call him THEORY because...

▶ *everything he suggests rarely works!"*

"He's a NONENTITY.

▶ *He's an absolute ZERO!"*

You're a low down scoundrel!

▶ *"If dirt were trumps what hands you would hold"!*

— Charles Lamb

A belittling insult.

▶ *"I was at the top when you were practicing to be a Never Was!"*

Insult to somebody acting stupid.

▶ *"You're behaving like stupidity is a virtue!"*

He's the utmost for inducing heart attacks.

▶ *"For bringing on heart attacks, he replaces tobacco and cholesterol."*

— J. Edward Breslin

Insult to somebody you dislike.

▶ *"He has no enemies. His friends don't like him either!"*

— Oscar Wilde

How to insult somebody you despise.

▶ *"I don't despise you — but if I ever gave you any thought I probably would."*

• INTELLECT •

That which superior intellect really is.

▶ *"Superior intellect is a large development of the faculty of association by similarity."*

— Alexander Bain

"Two heads are not better than one if...

▶ *both are empty heads."*

"Some people confuse 'knowledge' with 'intelligence.'

▶ *Very often the ones with the greatest 'book learning' have a remarkably poor understanding of life in general."*

• INTELLIGENCE •

The derivation and the meaning of the word "intelligence."

▶ *"Intelligence is derived from two words — inter and legere — inter meaning 'between', and legere meaning 'to choose.' An intelligent person, therefore, is one who has learned 'to choose between.' He knows that good is better than evil, that confidence should supersede fear, that love is superior to hate, that gentleness is better than cruelty, forbearance than intolerance, compassion than arrogance, and that truth has more virtue than ignorance."*

— J. Martin Klotsche

Intelligence is like sex appeal.

▶ *"It's 50% of what you've got — and 50% of what people think you've got."*

"I may not be right but...

▶ *I'm never wrong!"*

— Stern Blake

Do humans have the right to think they're so intelligent?

▶ *"When I play with my cat, who knows whether I do not make her more sport than she makes me."*

— Michel de Montaigne

"Intelligence is...

▶ *the capacity to wonder."*

"You can't talk intelligently about something you don't know about anymore than...

▶ *you can come back from some place you haven't been."*

Military Intelligence is...

▶ *a contradiction in terms!"*

Do IQ tests truly portray inherent intelligence?

▶ *"If the aborigine drafted an IQ test, all of Western civilization would presumably flunk it."*

— Stanley Garn

• INTENTIONS •

When you have no intention of doing anything.

▶ *"I'll do that when I get back!"* *"When is that?"* *"I don't know. I'm not going!"*

• THE INTERNATIONALIST •

Ancestral lineage of an
Internationalist.

▶ *"He had a Russian father and an
Egyptian Mummy."*

• INTERRUPTING •

"You interrupted me so much
that you made me lose my train
of thought.

▶ *Don't worry! No one was aboard
anyhow."*

"Nobody complains of being
interrupted...

▶ *if it's by applause."*

• INTUITION •

What is intuition?

▶ *"The strange instinct that tells me
I'm right whether I am or not."*

Our science, our philosophy,
and our business are built
upon truths obtained through
intuition.

▶ *Science calls such truths "axioms",
philosophy calls them "innate ideas",
and business people call them
"horse-sense".*

— John Heron

• INVENTIONS •

Asked of the Director of the
U.S. Patent office — "Has not
man run out of inventions?"

▶ *"Everything that can be invented has
been invented."*

— Charles H. Duell (1899)

"I am more of a sponge
than an inventor.

▶ *My principal business is giving commercial
value to the brilliant but misdirected
ideas of others."*

— Thomas A. Edison

• INVESTING •

Wall Street maxim on
investing in stocks —

▶ *"When interest is low Stocks will grow.
When interest is high Stocks will die."*

The immortal words of J.P. Morgan when asked his views on the stock market.

▶ *"Stocks will fluctuate."*

— J.P. Morgan

The aloofness of the stock market.

▶ *"The stock market giveth and the stock market taketh away without remorse."*

How to avoid financial losses.

▶ *"Take care to sell your horse before he dies. The art of life is passing losses on!"*

When to sell stocks.

▶ *"It's better to have a short profit than a long face."*

How to buy and sell stocks.

▶ *"Buy on the rumor; sell on the news!"*

— Wall Street proverb

What shouldn't you invest your money in?

▶ *"Never invest your money in anything that eats or needs repairing."*

— Billy Rose

Which month is the most dangerous for buying stocks?

▶ *"October. This is one of the peculiarly dangerous months to speculate in stock. The others are July, January, September, April, November, May, March, June, December, August and February."*

— Mark Twain

Wall Street maxim on how to invest.

▶ *"Always be cautious when you're investing, especially if it's your own money!"*

Caution when investing!

▶ *"There's a world of difference between a good sound investment and an investment that sounds good."*

J

• JITTERY •

"He's so jittery...

▸ *he can thread a sewing machine needle with the motor on."*

"He's such a nervous guy that as a nail-biter he needs...

▸ *an additional hired hand."*

• YOUR JOB •

Sometimes the toughest part of a job is getting started.

▸ *"He has half the deed done who has made a beginning."*

— Horace

How you can often get the job done fastest.

▸ *"He travels the fastest who travels alone."*

— Rudyard Kipling

Maybe there's a way you can make your job less boring.

▸ *"You may know for a certainty that if your work is becoming uninteresting, so are you; for work is an inanimate thing and can be made lively and interesting only by injecting yourself into it. Your job is only as big as you are."*

— George C. Hubbs

To those lucky people who love their job.

▸ *"You're lucky if people pay you money to do what you would pay to do if you had the money."*

How not to lose you job.

▶ *"Learn to get along with those you can't get ahead of!"*

Is the job you're now doing necessarily a dead end?

▶ *"Somewhere within the job you do now is the beginning of a bigger and better job."*

"The less one has to do...

▶ *the less time one finds to do it in."*
— Lord Chesterfield

Never be irreplaceable at your job.

▶ *"If you can't be replaced, you can't be promoted!"*

• JOGGING •

The way many people feel about jogging.

▶ *"My doctor told me it could add years to my life. He's right! I feel ten years older already."*

• JUDGMENT •

What damaging trait will ignore good judgement?

▶ *"Enthusiasm is that temper of the mind in which the imagination has got the better of the judgment."*
— William Warburton

Does a person with a prodigious memory necessarily possess good judgment?

▶ *"It is commonly seen by experience that excellent memories do often accompany weak judgements."*
— Michel de Montaigne

Judgment is the final act of making up your mind.

▶ *"Good judgment begins with difficulties which force us to think which test our assumption and tell us the consequences of our decision."*
— John Heron

"Judge a man by his questions" rather than by what?

▶ *"Rather than by his answers."*
— Voltaire

Good and bad luck is a synonym in the great majority of instances...

▶ *for good and bad judgment."*
— John Chatfield

How to be a judge.

▶ *"Four things belong to a judge; to hear courteously, to answer wisely, to consider soberly, and to decide impartially."*

— Socrates

Before you judge, put yourself in the other fellow's shoes.

▶ *"Before I judge my neighbor, let me walk a mile in his moccasins."*

— Sioux proverb

The right road taken at the right moment can lead to fortune; the wrong road to misery.

▶ *"There is a tide in the affairs of men, Which, taken at the flood, leads on to fortune; Omitted, all the voyage of their life Is bound in shallows, and in miseries."*

— William Shakespeare

• JUSTICE •

Is justice dispensed by our best legal minds?

▶ *"The dispensing of injustice is always in the most capable hands."*

K

• KINDNESS •

It's grossly inadequate to merely say to a Kind Act — "Thank you — I appreciate it."

▶ *"Words pay no debts!"*
— William Shakespeare

Kindness pays.

▶ *"Kindness is something tough to give away. It is generally paid back."*

A creed on kindness worthy of remembering.

▶ *"Let me be a little kinder,*
Let me be a little blinder
To the faults of those around me."
— Edgar A. Guest

How the deaf and dumb view kindness.

▶ *"Kindness is a language the dumb can speak and the deaf can hear and understand."*

"Count that day lost whose low-descending sun...

▶ *Views from they hand no worthy action done."*

What's the greatest pleasure you can have in doing an act of kindness?

▶ *"The greatest pleasure I know is to do a good action by stealth, and to have it found out by accident."*
— Charles Lamb

Repay a kindness with a
kindness!

▸ *"Have you had a kindness shown?*
Pass it on;
'Twas not given for thee alone,
Pass it on;
Let it travel down the years,
Let it wipe another's years,
Let it wipe another's tears,
Till in Heaven the deed appears —
Pass it on."

— Henry Burton

• THE KISS •

"A kiss is something like a
straight whiskey.

▸ *It always needs a chaser."*

How to enjoy kisses.

▸ *"Stolen kisses are always sweetest."*

— Leigh Hunt

• KNOWING HOW •

"The most difficult thing in
the world is to know how to do
a thing...

▸ *and to watch somebody else doing it*
wrong, without comment."

— T.H. White

• KNOWLEDGE •

The discipline required to
achieve knowledge.

▸ *"Men should train their minds as*
Olympic athletes train their bodies."

— Socrates

The envy and awe of a
prodigious memory.

▸ *"And still they stared*
And still the wonder grew
That one small head
Could carry all he knew."

— Oliver Goldsmith

"The next best thing to
knowing something is...

▸ *knowing where to find it."*

— Samuel Johnson

In looking up information or knowledge, does serendipity play a role?

▶ *"I find that a great part of the information I have was acquired by looking up something and finding something else on the way."*

— Franklin P. Adams

Why the game of Trivial Pursuit won world wide popularity.

▶ *"There is much pleasure to be gained from useless knowledge."*

— Bertrand Russell

"It isn't what you know that counts.

▶ *It's what you think of in time!"*

Definition of an Ignoramus, relating to knowledge.

▶ *"An ignoramus is a person unacquainted with certain kinds of knowledge familiar to yourself, and having certain other kinds that you know nothing about."*

— Ambrose Bierce

How to identify one who knows.

▶ *"To know what you know — and know what you don't know — is the characteristic of one who knows."*

— Confucius

About "He who Knows".

▶ *"Men are four:*
He who knows not and knows not he knows not, he is a fool — shun him;
He who knows not and knows he knows not, he is simple — teach him;
He who knows and knows not he knows, he is asleep — wake him;
He who knows and knows he knows, he is wise — follow him!"

— Arabic apothegm

Only the shallow think they know a subject.

▶ *"There is no subject, however complex, which — if studied with patience and intelligence — will not become more complex."*

It is said — "Knowledge is power".

▶ *"Knowledge is power only if a man knows what facts not to bother about."*

— Robert Lynd

To what degree does man possess knowledge about anything?

▶ *"We do not know one millionth of one percent about anything."*

— Thomas A. Edison

L

• LABELLING •

What a shrink resistant label on a pair of socks means.

▶ *"It means the socks do shrink — but they don't want to!"*

• LAISSEZ FAIRE •

"The policy of nonintervention by the government in the economic affairs of the individual has come to be known as economic liberalism or laissez faire.

▶ *In order to use labor most effectively, the great mass of rules and regulations should be removed so that the rising merchants and business leaders could operate in freedom for the benefit of all."*

— Adam Smith

• LAMENTING •

What everybody laments at one time or another.

▶ *For of all sad words of tongue or pen, The saddest are these: "It might have been!"*

— John G. Whittier

• LANGUAGE •

Of all man's inventions, which has been the most powerful?

▶ *"Words are the most powerful drug used by mankind."*

The advantage to Churchill for being a dunce in English class.

▶ *"By being so long in the lowest form (at Harrow school) I gained an immense advantage over the cleverest boys ... I got into my bones the essential structure of the normal British sentence — which is a noble thing."*
— Winston Churchill

Can language reveal personality and character?

▶ *"Language most shows a man; speak that I may see thee."*
— Ben Jonson

Salty language by a President!

▶ *"I don't give a shit what happens. I want you all to stonewall it. Let them plead the Fifth Amendment, cover up, or anything else if it'll save the plan."*
— Richard M. Nixon

Will fancy language enhance an insignificant thought?

▶ *"Whitewashing the pump will not purify the water!"*

The greatest wonder of all human invention — "Language".

▶ *"The triumph of human ingenuity — surpassing even the intricacies of modern technology."*
— Alfred North Whitehead

If language does not have clarity — ambiguity will result and confusion!

▶ *"If language is not correct, then what is said is not what is meant; if what is said is not what is meant, then what ought to be done remains undone."*
— Confucius

How long is the life cycle of slang?

▶ *"No age ever borrows the slang of its predecessor."*
— Oscar Wilde

• LAUGHTER •

What is unique to laughter all over the world?

▶ *"Laughter is the only thing that doesn't have a foreign accent."*

"He who laughs last...

▶ *didn't get the joke at first!"*

"He who can laugh at himself...

▶ *is not laughed at."*

"A good laugh is...

▶ *sunshine in a house."*
— William Makepeace Thackeray

Why man is the only animal that laughs and weeps.

▶ *"Man is the only animal that is struck by the difference between what things are and what they might have been."*
— William Hazlitt

"He who laughs last not only laughs best but...

▶ *he who laughs, lasts."*

The relationship of a laugh to a smile.

▶ *"A laugh is a smile that burst."*
— John E. Donovan

"The most wasted of all days is...

▶ *the day when we have not laughed."*
— French proverb

Is laughter an ingredient in sex?

▶ *"Sex is one of the only things you can have fun doing without laughing!"*

• LAW •

In court, what should you expect? Law or Justice?

▶ *"This is a court of law, young man, not a court of justice."*
— Oliver Wendell Holmes

In any Contract make sure you write it all down.

▶ *"A verbal contract isn't worth the paper it's written on!"*
— Sam Goldwyn

Why our adversarial judicial system defends criminals, allowing heinous crimes to go unpunished.

▶ *"It is less evil that some criminals should escape than that the government should play an ignoble role."*
— Oliver Wendell Holmes

What the word Jury often unfortunately means.

▶ *"Twelve men chosen to decide which has the better lawyer."*

Will people who are desperate obey laws?

▶ *"Self preservation is the first law of nature."*

The difference between "Unlawful" and "Illegal".

▶ *"Unlawful" is against the law. "Illegal" is a sick bird.*

Why you should read the small print in a contract.

▶ *"The large print giveth and the small print taketh away."*

If you go on trial, make sure your lawyer selects a right Jury for you.

▶ *"A fox should not be on the jury at a goose's trial."*

— Thomas Fuller

Is it futile to pass laws that too many others oppose?

▶ *"It is useless for the sheep to pass resolutions in favor of vegetarianism while the wolf remains of a different opinion."*

— William R. Inge

How two disputants can avoid going to court.

▶ *"Four out of five potential litigants will settle their disputes the first day they come together, if you will put the idea of arbitration into their heads."*

— Moses H. Grossman

Is Contempt of Court sometimes justifiable under our judicial system?

▶ *"Sir! Are you showing contempt for this court?" "No your Honour! I'm trying to conceal it!"*

"A lawyer specializing in medical malpractice...

▶ *better beware when he has to undergo major surgery"!*

Why the courts won't let you plead ignorance of the law.

▶ *"Ignorance of the law excuses no man; not that all men know the law, but because 'tis an excuse every man will plead, and no man can tell how to confute him."*

— William Scott

The sad thing about our congested courts.

▶ *"Justice delayed is justice denied."*

— William E. Gladstone

In what way is law applied equally to both Rich and Poor?

▶ *"The law, in its majestic equality, forbids the rich as well as the poor, to sleep under bridges, to beg in the streets and to steal bread."*

— Anatole France

• LAWS •

Law of Jars —

▶ *"Any jar that can't be opened by force will open instantly if picked up by the lid."*

The law of the barbecue.

▶ *"Wherever you sit, the wind will always blow the smoke in your face."*

Why did Newton make trouble and invent gravity!

▶ *Why did Isaac Newton make a law where everything has to fall down!*

• LAWYERS •

Prosecuting attorney to Eskimo on witness stand in northern Alaska.

▶ *"Where were you on the night of October 21 to April 7?"*

Even lawyers have nightmares trying to read and understand laws.

▶ *"If laws could speak for themselves, they would first complain of the lawyers who wrote them."*
— Lord Halifax

"The kind of lawyer I want to defend me is...

▶ *one who can make the jury think a rainbow looks black and white."*

Are there lawyers practicing law who shouldn't be?

▶ *"Ignorance of the law excuses no man from practicing it."*
— Addison Mizner

Why lawyers should be grateful for crooks!

▶ *"If there were no bad people, there would be no good lawyers."*
— Charles Dickens

Caution about giving "Power of Attorney"!

▶ *"Before giving your lawyer the power of attorney, remember that power corrupts."*

A lawyer is like a carpenter.

▶ *"He can file a bill.*
Split a hair.
Chop logic.
Get up a case.
Put in a box.
Bore a court.
And chisel a client!"

• LAZY! •

"He's so lazy that...
▶ *when he gets the urge to work he lies down until the urge passes!"*

I'm not lazy.
▶ *I work so fast I'm always finished!"*

You'll never get anywhere just loafing.
▶ *"The hen is the only creature that can produce dividends by just sitting around."*

• LEADERS •

How Managers and Leaders do things.
▶ *"Managers do the right thing, leaders do things right."*

Sign on the desk of Ted Turner, of Turner Broadcasting, indicating his version of "leadership."
▶ *"Lead, Follow, or Get OUT!"*
— Ted Turner

"The great leader is one who never permits his followers to discover...
▶ *that he is as dumb as they are."*

Executive Technique.
▶ *"1. Analyse*
   2. Organize
   3. Deputize
   4. Supervise!"

How to separate the men from the boys.
▶ *"Put Potatoes in a cart over a Rough Road, — and the Big Ones come to the Top."*

A smart executive will find time for his staff.
▶ *"Free time is made, not found, in the manager's job; it is forced into the schedule."*
— Henry Mintzberg

Does an executive stick to the rules?
▶ *"The executive exists to make sensible exceptions to general rules."*
— E. Morison

What is the greatest ability of a leader?
▶ *"It is a fine thing to have ability, but the ability to discover ability in others is the true test."*
— Elbert Hubbard

"A man who wants to lead the orchestra... ▶ *must turn his back on the crowd."*

— James Crook

Does a leader lead or follow? ▶ *"I've got to follow them — I am their leader."*

— Alexandre Ledru-Rollin

Many great men of history were not egoists but psychopaths. ▶ *"The megalomaniac differs from the narcissist by the fact that he wishes to be powerful rather than charming, and seeks to be feared rather than loved. To this type belong many lunatics and most of the great men of history."*

— Bertrand Russell

A bustling manner and a commanding voice are not evidences of "good leadership". The leader does not say "Get going!" ▶ *He says "Let's go!". He leads all the way, always a step in front. He carries a banner, not a whip.*

— Wilfred A. Peterson

The difference that a strong leader can make. ▶ *"An army of sheep led by a lion would defeat an army of lions led by a sheep."*

— Arab proverb

How to become Chairman of the Board. ▶ *"There is something that is much more scarce, something rarer than ability. It is the ability to recognize ability."*

— Robert Half

The organized Executive's blueprint on how to plan life. ▶ *"I'm trying to arrange my life so that I don't even have to be present."*

What is the test of a good manager in the training of people? ▶ *"Good management consists in showing average people how to do the work of superior people."*

— John D. Rockefeller

Don't go around in circles! ▶ *"He who goes around in circles will never become a big wheel."*

How a smart leader of a company operates. ▶ *"The best leaders are those most interested in surrounding themselves with assistants and associates smarter than they are — being frank in admitting this — and willing to pay for such talents."*

— Amos Parrish

Respect for Leadership and automatic deference is no longer attained by a title on the door.

▶ *"Authority is entitled only to the respect it earns, and not a whit more."*

— Arthur Schlesinger Jr.

What the leader who knows his stuff must do.

▶ *"The leader must know, must know that he knows, and must be able to make it abundantly clear to those about him that he knows."*

— Clarence B. Randall

• LEARNING •

The limitations of learning.

▶ *"It is easy to learn something about everything, but difficult to learn everything about anything."*

For the first time in the history of our country, the educatonal skills of our generation will not equal...

▶ *will not even approach, those of our parents.*

— Ronald D. Kelly

• LEISURE •

"A perpetual holiday is a good working definition of hell...

▶ *If all the year was playing holidays, To sport would be as tedious as to work."*

— William Shakespeare

If only I didn't have to work! Is it a false fantasy?

▶ *"Absence of occupation is not rest."*

— William Cowper

• LETTERS •

A powerful lesson in letter writing.

▶ *"Never answer a letter when you're angry!"*

— Chinese proverb

A "good business letter" should be written conversationally! It should sound like...

▶ *"I wish I could be my letter and so go to talk with you!"*

—John Heron

A postcard you'd like to send.

▶ *"Am having a great time. Glad you're NOT here!"*

Should you reply to a letter when you're angry?

▶ *"When a man sends you an impudent letter, sit right down and give it back to him with interest ten times compounded — and then throw both letters in the wastebasket."*

— Elbert Hubbard

Don't forget those letters!

▶ *"In a letter to a friend the thought is often unimporant, and the feeling, if it be only a desire to entertain him, is everything."*

—Sir Walter Raleigh

A letter of resignation to the Friar's Club, Hollywood.

▶ *"Please accept my resignation. I don't want to belong to any club that will accept me as a member."*

— Groucho Marx

A nice way to end a letter.

▶ *"Yours more than you can imagine or I express!"*

When NOT to write a letter.

▶ *"If you are in doubt whether to write a letter or not, don't!"*

— Edward Bulwer-Lytton

• LIBERTY •

What price does the Western world pay to preserve liberty?

▶ *"Eternal vigilance is the price of liberty."*

— Wendell Phillips

Inscription on the Jefferson Memorial. Washington, D.C.

▶ *"I have sworn upon the altar of God eternal hostility against every form of tyranny over the mind of man."*

— Thomas Jefferson

What does liberty really mean to an inferior man?

▶ *"The only liberty an inferior man really cherishes is the liberty to quit work, stretch out in the sun, and scratch himself."*

— H.L. Mencken

Liberty from Leviticus as inscribed on the U.S. Liberty Bell.

▶ *"Proclaim liberty throughout the land and all the inhabitants thereof."*

"Liberty is always dangerous but...

▶ *it's the safest thing we have."*

— Harry Emerson Fosdick

• THE LIBRARY •

A library is the repository of man's thoughts.

▶ *"A library is thought in cold storage."*

— Herbert Samuel

• LIES AND LIARS •

Think twice before you practice to deceive.

▶ *"Oh, what a tangled web we weave, when first we practice to deceive."*

—Walter Scott

"This is the punishment of a liar.

▶ *He is not believed even when he speaks the truth."*

— Talmud

"The man who says he tells no lies...

▶ *is telling one!"*

"The beauty of truth is...

▶ *it never has to be memorized."*

"A half truth is...

▶ *a whole lie."*

— Yiddish proverb

What are sometimes the worst liars?

▶ *"Of all the liars in the world, sometimes the worst are you own fears."*

— Rudyard Kipling

What's worse than lying to others?

▶ *"We lie loudest when we lie to ourselves."*

— Eric Hoffer

What other thing in time saves nine?

▶ *"A lie in time saves nine."*

Ladies beware! Many males exaggerate the degree of their sexual achievements.

▶ *"Some men kiss and don't tell. They're called Gentlemen. Some men tell but don't kiss. They're called Liars."*

"A liar begins with making falsehood appear like truth." How does he end up?

▶ *"He ends with making truth itself appear like falsehood."*

— William Shenstone

A white lie often saves a lot of hurt and a lot of words.

▶ *"A little inaccuracy sometimes saves tons of explanation."*

— Saki

What's the worst kind of lie you can tell?

▶ *"A truth that's told with bad intent Beats all the lies you can invent."*

— William Blake

"The cruellest lies are often told...

▶ *in silence."*

— Robert Louis Stevenson

Could we get along in life successfully without lying?

▶ *Lying is an indispensable part of making life tolerable.*

— Bergen Evans

"You made your bed. Now what?

▶ *Now try to lie out of it!"*

He's such a liar!

▶ *"Even when he admits he's lying, you can't believe him."*

The greater the lie, the greater the gullibility!

▶ *"In the size of the lie is always contained a certain factor of credulity, since the great masses of the people... will more easily fall victims to a great lie than to a small one."*

— Adolf Hitler

"The effect of 'He who approves a white lie' is that...

▶ *he soon grows colour-blind."*

• LIFE •

What's life all about!

▶ *"Life is meaningless!"*

— Leo Tolstoy

Three stages in a person's life

> 1. *"My daddy can whip your daddy."*
> 2. *"Aw, Dad, you don't know anything."*
> 3. *"My father used to say..."*

The first half of our life is ruined by our parents and...

> *the second half by our children."*
> —Clarence Darrow

As Methuselah said ...

> *"The first hundred years are the hardest."*

Caution! Is this the journey your life is pursuing?

> *"If thou art rich, thou'rt poor; For, like an ass whose back with ingots bows, Thou bear'st thy heavy riches but a journey, And death unloads thee."*
> —William Shakespeare

• ADVICE ON "LIFE" •

Can one truly enjoy to the full the good things in life without first having tasted the bitter?

> *"To really enjoy the better things in life, one must first have experienced the things they are better than."*
> — Oscar Homolka

How seriously should we take life?

> *"Do not take life too seriously. You will never get out of it alive!"*
> — Elbert Hubbard

Hedonist's philosophy of life.

> *"You're on this earth for a very short time. Milk it for all it's worth!"*

How to live life.

> *"Live your life so that you'll have an after life!"*

For a good life how long should you live?

> *"Don't outlive yourself!"*
>
> — George Bernard Shaw

"It's better to add life to your years than...

> *to add years to your life."*

"Life is short.

> *The sooner that a man begins to enjoy his wealth the better!"*
> — Samuel Johnson

Guideline on whether or not you should cross that bridge when you come to it.

▶ *"The hardest thing to learn in life is which bridge to cross and which to burn."*

— David Russell

How do Hindsight and Foresight serve as guides to living life?

▶ *"Life can only be understood backwards; but it must be lived forwards."*

— Soren Kierkegaard

"Let us endeavor so to live" in what way?

▶ *"That when we come to die even the undertaker will be sorry."*

— Mark Twain

• THE CYCLE OF "LIFE" •

The cycle of life that awaits you.

▶ *"There was a young man from Perth, Who was born on the day of his birth. He was wed, so they say, On his wife's wedding day, And he died on his last day on earth."*

How much will you be missed when you're gone?

▶ *"The three words I have learned about life is that...'It goes on'."*

— Robert Frost

What's a depressing version of the goal of life?

▶ *"The goal of all life is death!"*

— Sigmund Freud

• THE GOOD "LIFE" •

A Good life is made up of three classes of goods dependent on the Public conditions of his life.

▶ *"1. Political goods as peace, laws and liberty.*
2. Economic goods as medical, leisure, income, education.
3. Social goods as equality of rights and opportunity."

— James Michener

A Good life is made up of four classes of goods belonging to the Private life of the individual.

▶ *"1. Goods of the body as health.*
2. Goods of the mind as knowledge.
3. Goods of character such as moral virtue.
4. Goods of personal association."

— James Michener

A comparison between the long life and the good life.

▶ *"A long life is not good enough. But a good life is long enough."*

— Talmud

• THE JOYS OF "LIFE" •

What the four joys of life used to be.

▶ *"Courtship, Love, Marriage, Children."*

• THE MEANING OF "LIFE" •

Guru to student trying to discover the meaning of religion and life.

▶ *"There are several meanings to life — a $50 meaning — a $100 and I have one for $500!"*

Does life have a meaning?

▶ *"What the meaning of human life may be I don't know; I incline to suspect that it has none."*

— H.L. Mencken

• PHILOSOPHY OF "LIFE" •

"Life is...

▶ *a zoo in a jungle."*

That which misery, gloom, and depression, so often is to many people.

▶ *"Depression is anger turned inward."*

A brief summary of what life is.

▶ *"Birth, copulation and death. That's all the facts when you come to brass tacks."*

— T.S. Eliot

What's life really all about?

▶ *"Life is what happens while we're making other plans."*

— John Lennon

"Life is...

▶ *what you make!"*

How you learn about life.

▶ *"The more I go this world about The more I find, by golly out!"*

— Pennsylvania Dutch maxim

The true function of time in living.

▶ *"Living is transforming time into experience."*

— J.J. Servan-Schreiber

The Electron Microscope reveals that each minute life form has even smaller life forms preying upon it.

▶ *"So, naturalists observe, a flea Hath smaller fleas that on him prey, And these have smaller fleas to bite 'em, And so proceed ad infinitum."*

— Jonathan Swift

"Life is a Sea of Troubled Waters...

▶ *where your soul is tossed upon waves of pain and pleasure."*

What kind of lives do the majority of mankind live?

▶ *"The mass of men lead lives of quiet desperation."*

— Henry David Thoreau

Life is a flower...

▶ *of which love is the honey."*

— B. Darren

Can anybody ever avoid or control the torturous episodes of one's life?

▶ *"My whole life is a movie. It's just that there are no cuts. I have to live every agonizing moment of it. My life needs editing."*

— Mort Sahl

After every disappointment or catastrophe in life where do we start our life all over again?

▶ *"Life begins on the other side of despair."*

— Jean-Paul Sartre

To how many people is life a bowl of cherries?

▶ *"Life is just a bowl of pits!"*

— Rodney Dangerfield

Is too much of life delayed for tomorrow?

▶ *"Life, as it is called, is for most of us one long postponement."*

— Henry Miller

The four "L's"

▶ *"May the fates inspire you to Live — Laugh — Learn and Love!"*

Of the billions of planets in the universe, why is there life, and where is it going on?

▶ *"Life is an experiment being conducted on one of the minor planets."*

Why is life something like a life sentence?

▶ *"Life is the sentence a man has to serve for the crime of being born."*

— Calderon

How to face up to living each day.

▶ *"I have a new philosophy. I'm only going to dread one day at a time."*

— Charles Schulz

Before it's too late, everybody should re-examine his life's priorities.

▶ *"The unexamined life isn't worth living!"*

— Socrates

• THE PURPOSEFUL "LIFE" •

For a purposeful life —

▶ *"Make yourself necessary to somebody."*

— Ralph Waldo Emerson

Guide to giving purpose to your life.

▶ *"If I can stop one heart from breaking,*
I shall not live in vain;
If I can ease one life the aching,
Or cool one pain,
Or help one fainting robin
Unto his nest again,
I shall not live in vain."

— Emily Dickinson

There must be a need for you in this world, otherwise there would have been no reason for you to be born.

▶ *"Every single man is a new thing in the world and is called upon to fulfill his particularity in this world."*

— Martin Buber

• THE QUALITY OF "LIFE" •

If I will it — I can make my world more enjoyable.

▶ *"The world's mine oyster,*
Which I with sword will open."

— William Shakespeare

"I don't want to be a Maharajah.

▶ *I just want to live like one!"*

What is better — the quality of life or the quantity of life?

▶ *"It's better to live one day as a lion than 1000 days as a sheep."*

—Italian proverb

What is NOT Standard of Living?	▸ *"Standard of living is not quality of living."*

• LITERATURE •

"The appreciation of literature is a question of temperament,...	▸ *not of teaching."* — Oscar Wilde

• LIVE NOW! •

If you've got it, spend it now while you can before it's too late.	▸ *"If you don't travel first class, your heirs will!"*
"If you're about 40 years old, have you lived 15000 days...	▸ *or have you lived one day 15000 times?"*
Eight guides on how to live.	▸ *"1. Do more than exist, live.* *2. Do more than touch, feel.* *3. Do more than look, observe.* *4. Do more than read, absorb.* *5. Do more than hear, listen.* *6. Do more than listen, understand.* *7. Do more than think, ponder.* *8. Do more than talk, say something."* — John H. Rhoades
"There is only one important moment in your life.	▸ *That is now!"*
"He who postpones the hour of living rightly...	▸ *is like the rustic who waits for the river to run out before he crosses."* — Horace
Live it up now!	▸ *"Remember — life is not a stage play. You're not coming back."*
"Try as much as possible to be wholly alive, with all your might, and when you laugh, laugh like hell...	▸ *and when you get angry, get good and angry. Try to be alive. You will be dead soon enough."* — William Saroyan

Warning on how to grow old! ▶ *"It is better to wear out than to rust out."*

— George Whitefield

It's up to you to spend your time enjoyably. ▶ *"Life itself can't give you joy,*
Unless you really will it;
Life just gives you time and space —
It's up to you to fill it."

How will most of us feel at death? ▶ *"Most of us dread finding out when we come to die that we have never really lived."*

— Henry David Thoreau

How you should live this very very day? ▶ *"Live this day as if it were the last!"*

Bumper sticker reminding you to be a little better to yourself. ▶ *"I'm spending my kid's inheritance now."*

Somehow I must force myself to make something beautiful or enjoyable today. ▶ *"Only that day dawns to which we are awake."*

— Henry David Thoreau

The tortured decision! Should I live today or tomorrow? ▶ *"Tomorrow will I live, the fool does say;*
Today itself's too late; the wise lived yesterday."

— Martial

A clock reminder to live a little bit more today. ▶ *"The clock of life is wound but once*
And no man has the power
To tell just when the hands will stop
At late or early hour.
Now is the only time you own
Live, love, toil with a will
Place no faith in "tomorrow" for
The clock may then be still."

• LOGIC •

A lesson in logic. ▶ *"Major Premise: No cat has two tails.*
Minor Premise: Every cat has one tail more than no cat.
Conclusion: Therefore, every cat has three tails."

• LONELINESS •

There is no loneliness to equal that of a stranger in a big city. ▶ *"No man can be as solitary as when he is surrounded by a multitude of friendly strangers."*

What unpleasantness is better than being lonesome? ▶ *"Better be quarrelling than lonesome!"*

— Irish proverb

• LOST AND FOUND •

The reason you can't find what you lose. ▶ *"People always look where it isn't — instead of where it is."*

"As hard to find as... ▶ *a grocery cart with the four wheels pointing in the same direction!"*

• GET LOST! •

"Any time you happen to pass by my city... ▶ *I'll appreciate it!"*

Make me happy and get lost! ▶ *"Never miss an opportunity to make others happy even if you have to leave them alone to do it."*

How John Ruskin dodged "nuisance visitors" when he wanted to work! ▶ *"Mr. J. Ruskin is about to begin a work of great importance and therefore begs that in reference to calls and correspondence, you will consider him dead for the next two months."*

— John Ruskin

• "LOVE" IN GENERAL •

How we treat those we love. ▶ *"Why do we speak harshly to those who love us — and kindly to those who neither know nor care about us?"*

What kind of word is Love? ▶ *"Love is the tenth word in a telegram."*

— Western Union

"A woman can fall in love with an ugly man, even an old man if he rouses her imagination but...

▶ *a man cannot fall in love with a woman unless she rouses his sexual instinct."*

No woman ever falls in love with a man unless what?

▶ *"Unless she has a better opinion of him than he deserves."*

— Ed Howe

That which true love is.

▶ *"It resembles a pair of shears, so joined that they cannot be separated; often moving in opposite directions, yet always punishing anyone who comes between them."*

— Sydney Smith

"Being in love is more than a dexterous manipulation of clothing."

▶ *You have to hold hands too!"*

"They sat...

▶ *holding eyes across the table."*

Does love endure when lovers merely love each other?

▶ *"Love endures when the lovers love many things together and not merely each other!"*

About somebody you have little love for —

▶ *"I've just learnt about his illness; let's hope it's nothing trivial."*

— Irvin S. Cobb

Child expressing love for her mother.

▶ *"I love you as many times as God can count."*

— B. Lauren

"Love is biology...

▶ *set to music."*

— M.J. Huston

Which is the greatest love? That of a mother, a dog, or a sweetheart?

▶ *"The greatest love is a mother's; then comes a dog's; then a sweetheart's."*

— Polish proverb

The relationship between Giving and Loving.

▶ *"You can give without loving, but you can't love without giving."*

"All the world loves...

▶ *a four-letter word!"*

What does love become
under monogamy?

▶ *"Love is the effort a man makes to be
satisfied with only one woman."*

"He who determines to love
only those who are faultless...

▶ *will soon find himself alone."*

"I never liked you...

▶ *and I always will!"*

If you retain love solely for
yourself, is it love?

▶ *"A bell isn't a bell if you don't ring it.
A song isn't a song if you don't sing it.
Love isn't love unless you give it
away."*

"Though gray be your hair
With little to part...

▶ *This does not denote
The age of your heart."*

— Michael Franklin Ellis

• "LOVE" AND HATE •

How do Love and Hatred
behave?

▶ *"Love and hatred exaggerate."*

I don't like you.

▶ *"I like your smile
I like your style
I like your walk
I like your talk
But I don't like you!"*

When love turns to Hatred
what degree of rage and fury
follow?

▶ *"Heaven has no rage like love to
hatred turned,
Nor hell a fury like a woman scorned."*

— William Congreve

The effect on life of Hate
versus Love.

▶ *"Love makes everything lovely; hate
concentrates itself on the one thing
hated."*

— George MacDonald

Do you need a reason to love
or hate?

▶ *"We love without reason, and without
reason we hate!"*

• ARDENT "LOVE" •

The ardent insatiable lover.

▶ *"Give me a kiss, and to that kiss a score;*
Then to that twenty, add a hundred more;
A thousand to that hundred; so kiss on,
To make that thousand up a million,
Treble that million, and when that is done,
Let's kiss afresh, as when we first begun."

— Robert Herrick

The anguish of a man in love having to say Good-night to his sweetheart.

▶ *"Good-night, good-night! parting is such sweet sorrow,*
That I shall say good-night till it be morrow."

— William Shakespeare

• EXPRESSIONS OF "LOVE" •

A man trying to express the heavenly bliss and infinite love he feels.

▶ *"Oh, pearl of all things, woman! Adored be the artist who created thee!"*

— J.C. von Schiller

An expression of love.

▶ *"I saw something today and was sorry you weren't there to share it."*

— C. Carere

An expression of love by a man transported by love.

▶ *"Her eyes, her lips, her cheeks, her shape, her features, seem to be drawn by love's own hand, by love himself in love."*

— John Dryden

How a man deeply in love describes his maiden.

▶ *"Her very frowns are fairer far Than smiles of other maidens are."*

— Samuel Taylor Coleridge

• FIRST "LOVE" •

Does a man's first love lead him to believe that this experience is unique to him alone and that it will remain timeless?

▶ *"The magic of first love is our ignorance that it can ever end."*
— Benjamin Disraeli

First love answers a lot of mysteries.

▶ *"First love is only a little foolishness and a lot of curiosity."*
— George Bernard Shaw

• THE FRAGILITY OF "LOVE" •

The fragility of love and how NOT to handle it.

▶ *"Love is a glass which shatters if you hold it too tightly or too loosely."*
— Russian proverb

Don't ever let Love's Fire go out!

▶ *"Love's fire, if once goes out, is hard to kindle."*
— Alfred Lord Tennyson

"The way to love anything is...

▶ *to realize that it might be lost."*
— G.K. Chesterton

• THE GAME OF "LOVE" •

Can only one win at the game of love?

▶ *"Love is the only game two can play — and both can win!"*

How to make good chemistry.

▶ *"Me Tarzan, you Jane. Me fire, you spark."*

Is a woman wise to yield herself too easily and too readily?

▶ *"The woman who has too easily and ardently yielded her devotion will find that its vitality, like a bright fire, soon consumes itself."*

• THE GOAL OF "LOVE" •

In the long run, what is the ultimate goal of love?

▶ *"At the end of what is called the 'sexual life' the only love which has lasted is the love which has everything, every disappointment, every failure and every betrayal, which has accepted even the sad fact that in the end there is no desire so deep as the simple desire for companionship.""*
— Graham Greene

• GUIDELINES TO "LOVE" •

Why would I want you to love me less?

▸ *"Love me a little less, but longer."*

Love is not what you get — it's what YOU GIVE! Love is thoughtfulness, concern, sensitivity to the needs of another.

▸ *"I love you more today than yesterday, but not as much as tomorrow"* — *needs working on. Love may begin small, but it can grow and has no end.*

What you should never fall in love with.

▸ *"Never love anything that can't love you back."*

• MAKING "LOVE" •

"Making Love...

▸ *is the most fun you can have without laughing."*

"A gentleman may love like a lunatic but not like...

▸ *a beast!"*

— French proverb

• NEIGHBOURLY "LOVE" •

Love thy neighbour.

▸ *"It is easier to love humanity as a whole than to love one's neighbor."*

— Eric Hoffer

"Love thy neighbor as thyself but...

▸ *choose your neighborhood."*

— Louise Beal

• PLATONIC "LOVE" •

That which platonic love is —

▸ *"Love from the neck up."*

— Thyra S. Winslow

• THE REALITY OF "LOVE" •

Which demands more — Love or Friendship?

▸ *"Love demands infinitely less than friendship."*

— George J. Nathan

• THE TEST OF "LOVE" •

A barometer for determining when a state of love exists.

▸ *"When the satisfaction or the security of another person becomes as significant to one as one's own satisfaction or security, then the state of love exists."*

— Henry Stack Sullivan

The joy of being loved for ourselves.

▸ *"The supreme happiness of life is the conviction that we are loved; loved for ourselves, or rather loved in spite of ourselves."*

— Victor Hugo

• BAD LUCK •

Is a black cat bad luck?

▸ *"Whether a black cat following you is bad luck depends on whether you're a man or a mouse."*

"Don't sit tight hoping that bad luck goes away because...

▸ *if you've got bad luck, you've missed something somewhere!"*

"The only sure thing about luck is...

▸ *that it will change."*

"He's so unlucky...

▸ *that he runs into accidents which are starting out to happen to someone else."*

Definition of Misfortune —

▸ *"Misfortune is the kind of fortune that never misses."*

— Ambrose Bierce

What is the worst misfortune that can happen to an ordinary man?

▸ *"It is to have an extraordinary father!"*
— Austin O'Malley

"Today has not been my day.

▸ *I should have stood in bed!"*
— Casey Stengel

Misfortune is bad enough when it gets here. Therefore what?

▸ *"Why suffer in advance by worrying over it?"*

— Talmud

Do Misfortunes leave a mark?   ▶ *"What deep wounds ever closed
without a scar?"*

— Lord Byron

When is Friday bad luck?   ▶ *"It is bad luck to fall out of a
thirteen-story window on Friday."*

When you get a lemon —   ▶ *"When Fortune empties her
smile and say — "We're going to   chamberpot on your head, smile and
have lemonade.   say "We are going to have a summer
shower."*

— John A. Macdonald

The difference between a   ▶ *"If Gladstone fell into the Thames that
Misfortune and a Calamity.   would be a misfortune. If anybody
pulled him out that would be a
calamity."*

— Benjamin Disraeli

How do we react to the   ▶ *"All of us have sufficient fortitude to
misfortunes of others?   bear the misfortunes of others."*

— Duc de La Rochefoucauld

When are Mishaps funny?   ▶ *"Everything is funny as long as it is
happening to somebody else."*

— Will Rogers

Is the fault of your bad luck   ▶ *"The fault, dear Brutus, is not in our
merely fate or what other likely   stars.
cause?   But in ourselves."*

— William Shakespeare

Is every wind that comes along   ▶ *"It's an ill wind that doesn't give
a bad one?   somebody a lift."*

To the poor fellow who's a   ▶ *"The poor schlemiel is man who falls
truly unlucky guy.   on his back and breaks his nose."*

— Hebrew proverb

This is not "my   ▶ *"This is a day — one of those —
day"!   when everything backwards goes"!*

• GOOD LUCK! •

The relationship between Luck and Intelligence.

▶ *"You don't need intelligence to have luck — but you do need luck to have intelligence!"*

— Talmud

How luck happens!

▶ *"Luck is what happens when preparation meets opportunity."*

Which is more important? Luck or Discipline?

▶ *"One half of life is luck; the other half is discipline — and that's the important half, for without discipline you wouldn't know what to do with your luck."*

"True luck consists not in holding the best of the cards at the table.

▶ Luckiest is he who knows just when to rise and go home."

— John Hay

The relationship of luck to work.

▶ *"I am a great believer in luck, and find the harder I work the more I have of it."*

— Stephen Leacock

In what quantities do blessings and misfortunes come?

▶ *"Blessings never come in pairs; misfortunes never come alone."*

— Chinese proverb

"Fortunate is being better off...

▶ *than you are!"*

Luck was with me. It was -

▶ *"The happy combination of fortuitous circumstances."*

— Charles Dickens

"Good and bad luck is a synonym in the great majority of instances...

▶ for good and bad judgment."

— John Chatfield

Don't exhaust your Quota of Luck!

▶ *"Never expose yourself unnecessarily to danger. If you're lucky and a miracle saves you, it will be deducted from your quota of luck."*

— Talmud

"Two kinds of people are always in tough luck. Those who did it but never thought...

▸ *and those who thought but never did it."*

— Franklin Field

What luck would be if you were a farmer?

▸ *"Luck is to own a farm and have your roosters lay eggs."*

• LUXURY •

"Living in the lap of luxury isn't bad except...

▸ *that you never know when luxury is going to stand up."*

— Orson Welles

M

• THE MAFIA •

The philosophy of La Cosa Nostra.

▶ *"Dead men tell no tales!"*

• THE MAGICIAN •

"I could have been a magician...

▶ *but the urge suddenly vanished."*

Sign on Magic Shop Door —

▶ *"Disappeared for Lunch."*

• MAN •

"Biological man is...

▶ *an omnivorous biped that wears pants — a forked straddling animal with bandy legs — descended from the hair-mantled, flint hurling Aboriginal Anthropophagus."*

Man is the only animal that eats when he is not hungry, and...

▶ *drinks when he is not thirsty."*

Such is the human race that it would have been bettter had Noah done what?

▶ *"Often is does seem such a pity that Noah...didn't miss the boat."*

— Mark Twain

What is the most valued right treasured by civilized man?

▶ *"The right to be let alone is the most comprehensive of rights and the right most valued in civilized man."*

— Justice Louis D. Brandeis

What are man's two basic passions of first importance?

▶ *"The natural man has only two primal passions: to get and to beget."*

— William Osler

Are great men good? Or are good men great?

▶ *"Great and good are seldom the same man."*

— Thomas Fuller

"A man whom nobody pleases is much more unhappy than...

▶ *a man who pleases nobody."*

— French proverb

"Man is an animal that makes bargains; no other animal does this.

▶ *One dog does not change a bone with another."*

— Adam Smith

What degree of pain is experienced when you find you're no longer needed by anybody?

▶ *"No man can live with the terrible knowledge that he is not needed."*

"Man hates what he is not good at but...

▶ *every man loves what he is good at."*

— Thomas Shadwell

"God must hate the common man." Why?

▶ *"He made him so common."*

— Philip Wylie

"God must love the common man." Why?

▶ *"He made so many of them!"*

— Abraham Lincoln

What is man and under what circumstances did God make him?

▶ *"Man is a creature made by God at the end of the week when he was tired!"*

What is one of man's greatest needs?

▶ *"The deepest need in human nature is the craving to be appreciated."*

— William James

Two inherent traits of man.

▶ 1. *"Man is Acquisitive."*
2. *"Man is Competitive."*
— Adam Smith

The capacity of a busy man.

▶ *"If you want a job done, give it to a very busy man."*

What is almost the greatest tragedy that can befall a man?

▶ *"Lack of something to feel important about is almost the greatest tragedy a man may have."*
— Arthur E. Morgan

"Man with all his noble qualities with his god-like intellect still bears in his bodily frame...

▶ *the indelible stamp of his lowly origin."*
— Charles Darwin

Name one physical facial quality unique to man!

▶ *"Man is the only animal that blushes, or needs to."*
— Mark Twain

• MANAGERS •

The effective Time manager.

▶ *"Effective time managers are the ones who leave the office just at quitting time with light briefcases."*

Caution if you're not indulging in the many joyful pursuits of life.

▶ *"If you consistently choose work over these alternatives, then you really do have a problem managing time."*

"Good management consists in...

▶ *showing average people how to do the work of superior people."*
— John D. Rockefeller

• MANNERS •

"In the early 1900s Henry James referred to aristocracy as...

▶ *bad manners organized."*

"The woman who goes to bed with a man should put off her modesty with her skirt and...

▶ *put it on again with her petticoat."*
— Michel de Montaigne

A father's advice to his son on cultivating good manners.

▶ *"A genteel manner prepossesses people in your favour, bends them towards you, and makes them wish to like you."*

— Lord Chesterfield

"The hardest job kids face today is learning good manners...

▶ *without seeing any."*

— Fred Astaire

Deep down, what is the true meaning of manners?

▶ *"Manners are the hypocrisy of a nation."*

— Honoré de Balzac

Today's seemingly normal behaviour.

▶ *Mom: "John, would you swear on the Bible you didn't do it?" John: "Sure, Mom, I'd even say the 'F' word!"*

"A gentleman is one who is always as nice as...

▶ *he sometimes is."*

Learning Manners.

▶ *"One learns manners from those who have none."*

— Persian proverb

That which too many women of this generation have forgotten.

▶ *"It is gentle manners which prove so irresistible in women."*

— Theophile Gautier

"Good breeding consists in concealing how much we think of ourselves...

▶ *and how little we think of the other person."*

— Mark Twain

• MARRIAGE •

"Matrimony...

▶ *the high sea for which no compass has yet been invented."*

"The aging process of married men goes through two stages.

▶ *When they want to be faithful and are not — and when they want to be unfaithful and cannot."*

— Joey Adams

Loneliness in marriage.

▶ *"No man — unless he is married — knows true loneliness."*

"I brought my girlfriend home to meet my parents.

▶ *They liked her but couldn't stand me!"*

"Marriage is like sitting in a bathtub.

▶ *Once you get used to it, it isn't so hot."*

Why Lincoln shunned marriage.

▶ *"I have come to the conclusion never again to think of marrying and for this reason: I can never be satisfied with anyone who would be blockhead enough to marry me."*
— Abraham Lincoln

"My wife and I just celebrated our Tin Anniversary...

▶ *12 years eating out of cans."*

Marriage —

▶ *"The alliance of two people, one of whom never remembers birthdays and the other never forgets them."*
— Ogden Nash

"Blessed is the couple who believe in multiplying...

▶ *rather than dividing."*

The ultimate lofty principle of marriage.

▶ *"The value of the marriage knot,*
Contrary to popular thought,
Is not,
To give you a body to sleep with,
But to give you a soul to weep with."
— M.J. Huston

Is there a mate for everybody?

▶ *"There never was so ugly a saucepan but it found a pot to match."*

"Marriage starts with Billing and Cooing but...

▶ *only the billing lasts!"*

What's the unique relationship between Marriage and War?

▶ *"Marriage is the only war where you sleep with the enemy."*

"If there is such a thing as a good marriage it is because...

▶ *it resembles friendship rather than love."*
— Michel de Montaigne

"Marriage is a mutual partnership if...

▶ *both parties know when to be mute."*

How to pronounce the word Marriage.

▶ *"Marriage is a word which should be pronounced Mirage!"*

What to do before and after marriage.

▶ *"Keep your eyes open before marriage, half shut afterwards."*
— Benjamin Franklin

• MARRIAGE AND ARGUING! •

A jocular remark you can make that can help appease an argument between husband and wife.

▶ *"When a husband and wife see eye to eye, they're generally the same height."*

What kind of marriage is it if there are no arguments?

▶ *"The conception of two people living together for 25 years without having a cross word suggests a lack of spirit only to be admired in sheep."*
— A.P. Herbert

"All married couples should learn the art of battle as they should learn the art of making love.

▶ *Good battle is healthy and constructive, and brings to a marriage the principle of equal partnership."*

— Ann Landers

• MARRIAGE AND BOSSINESS •

To the bossy wife "When a wife insists on wearing the pants...

▶ *it's usually some other woman who wears the fur coat."*

• MARRIAGE COMPATIBILITY •

"My wife and I are always unanimous...

▶ *except when we disagree."*

They're well mated!

▶ *"He's a Hypochondriac and she's a Pill!"*

• MARRIAGE COUNSEL •

For more harmony in marriage.

▸ *"Be to her virtues very kind.
Be to her faults a little blind."*
— Matthew Prior

A love formula for a successful marriage.

▸ *"A successful marriage requires falling in love many times with the same person."*
— Mignon McLaughlin

How NOT saying things can affect a marriage.

▸ *"Often the difference between a successful marriage and a mediocre one consists of leaving about three or four things a day unsaid."*
— Harlan Miller

Sign in marriage counselor's office —

▸ *"Back in an hour. Don't fight!"*

How many persons are needed to make marriage a success or a failure?

▸ *"It takes two to make a marriage a success and only one a failure."*
— Herbert Samuel

• MARRIAGE VERSUS ELOPEMENT •

The redeeming feature of a wedding.

▸ *"If it were not for the presents, an elopement would be preferable."*
— George Ade

• MARRIAGE THE INSTITUTION •

A lesson in logic about marriage.

▸ *"1. Love is blind
2. Marriage is an institution
3. Therefore marriage is an institution for the blind."*

The anomaly and uncertainty of wanting to be married.

▸ *"Is not marriage an open question, when it is alleged, from the beginning of the world, that such as are in the institution wish to get out, and such as are out wish to get in?*
— Ralph Waldo Emerson

• MARRIAGE AND LOVE •

Has marriage an innate
tendency to diminish itself?

▸ *"There lies within the very flame of love
a kind of wick or snuff that will abate
it."*

— William Shakespeare

• MARRIAGE PACT •

Marriage Pact —

▸ *"Let us make our regards to each
other mutual and unchangeable that
whilst the world around us is
enchanted with the false satisfactions
of vagrant desires our persons may be
shrines to each other and sacred to
conjugal faith, unreserved confidence
and heavenly society."*

Marriage Pact —

▸ *"We, Lloyd and Dorothy, after a close
companionship of several years, have
come to the conclusion that life
without the other is quite unthinkable.
Our interests being one, we have
decided to live as a unit."*

• MARRIAGE PARTNERSHIP •

The fallacy of marriage being
a 50/50 proposition.

▸ *"Anybody who thinks matrimony is a
50/50 proposition doesn't understand
women or fractions."*

— Danny Thomas

• MARRIAGE AND TROUBLE •

Why one out of two marriages
aren't working out.

▸ *"Needles and pins, needles and pins,
When a man marries his trouble
begins."*

— Nursery rhyme

Three out of four marriages
today live happily...

▸ *"Never After!"*

• MARRIAGE AND TRUTH •

Should a man lie to his wife?
▸ *"The man who won't lie to his wife —
has little regard for her feelings."*

Eleventh Commandment for a
good marriage.
▸ *"Thou shalt not tell thy wife
everything!"*

Is deception ever a requisite
for a charming marriage?
▸ *"The one charm of marriage is that it
makes a life of deception absolutely
necessary for both parties."*
Oscar Wilde

• MARRIAGE VOWS •

For those who have forgotten
how the Marriage Vows read.
▸ *"What therefore God hath joined
together, let no man put asunder."
(New Testament, Matthew XIX,6)
"To have and to hold from this day
forward, for better, for worse, for
richer, for poorer, in sickness, and in
health, to love and to cherish, till
death us do part."
(Book of Common Prayer)
"With this ring I thee wed, with my
body I thee worship, and with all my
wordly goods I thee endow."
(Book of Common Prayer)*

• MATHEMATICS •

The exquisite beauty of
mathematics.
▸ *"Mathematics possesses not only
truth, but supreme beauty — a beauty
cold and austere, like that of
sculpture."*
— Bertrand Russell

How to merit the august title
of Mathemetician.
▸ *"A mathemetician is a man who can
figure out his own income tax!"*

• MATURITY •

That which maturity is.
▸ *"Maturity is the ability to endure
uncertainty."*

• MAYBE! •

Synonym for Perhaps —   ▶ *"A definite maybe!"*

• MEANNESS •

He's so mean!   ▶ *"If he were rain, he would not fall on your field."*
— Turkish proverb

• MEDICAL •

"An apple a day keeps the doctor away but...   ▶ *an onion a day keeps everyone away."*

What could help you get cured?   ▶ *"It is part of the cure to wish to be cured."*
— Seneca

The convalescent hospital patient —   ▶ *"He took a turn for the nurse."*

"With the average hospitalized adult receiving 13 different drugs on multiple occasions...   ▶ *the opportunity both for the unexpected and for error is enormous!"*
—William O. Robertson

"All diseases of Christians...   ▶ *are to be ascribed to demons."*
— Saint Augustine

The good thing about illness.   ▶ *"I enjoy convalescence. It is the part that makes the illness worthwhile."*
— George Bernard Shaw

Is The Art of Medicine exaggerated in its ability to cure?   ▶ *"The art of medicine consists of amusing the patient while nature cures the disease."*
— Voltaire

The kind of pill a tranquilizer is!   ▶ *"A pill that helps you enjoy being tense."*

If only people knew that the human body cures most of its own ills without doctors!   ▶ *"God heals, and the doctor takes the fees."*
— Benjamin Franklin

M.D. to patient: "First the good news.

▶ *You're going to have a disease named after you."*

Evidence that more medical surgery takes place than is ever necessary.

▶ *"Those in the United States who, by and large, have the best medical care and advice readily available to them at the least expense are the families of the specialists in internal medicine. These families use less medicine and undergo less surgery on the whole than any other group, rich or poor."*

— Edward C. Lambert

• MEDIOCRE •

"Only a mediocre person is...

▶ *always at his best."*

— Somerset Maugham

Where does mediocrity rate throughout the world?

▶ *"The general tendency of things throughout the world is to render mediocrity the ascendant power among mankind."*

— John Stuart Mill

"He's so mediocre that...

▶ *he's giving mediocrity a bad name."*

• YOUR MEMORY •

"The only thing I can keep in my head...

▶ *for longer than an hour is a cold!"*

Always memo it!

▶ *"A short pencil is better than a long memory."*

What part of you is first to function and first to die?

▶ *"Of all the faculties of the mind, memory is the first that flourishes and the first that dies."*

"You never know what a good memory you have until...

▶ *you try to forget something."*

— Franklin P. Jones

As the elephant said —

▶ *"I don't care what people say — I can't remember."*

What is the relationship between a strong memory and good judgment?

▶ *"Experience teaches that a strong memory is generally joined to a weak judgment."*

— Michel de Montaigne

What is one of man's most treasured possessions?

▶ *"A man's real possession is his memory. In nothing else is he rich, in nothing else is he poor."*

— Alexander Smith

What's happening to my memory?

▶ *"I'm finding it harder all the time to remember my Ad Libs."*

Why God in his benificence gave us memory.

▶ *"So we could have roses in December."*

— James M. Barrie

"The advantage of a bad memory is...

▶ *that one enjoys several times the same good things for the first time."*

— Friedrich Nietzsche

"O memory, thou bitter sweet...

▶ *Both a joy and a scourge!"*

— Madame de Stael

"I never forget a face but...

▶ *in your case I'll make an exception!"*

"Seldom seen...

▶ *soon forgotten!"*

"A great memory does not make a mind...

▶ *any more than a dictionary is a piece of literature."*

— John Henry Newman

The majesty and awe of a photographic memory.

▶ *"And still they stared
And still the wonder grew,
That one small head
Could carry all he knew."*

— Oliver Goldsmith

How I wish I had your memory!

▶ *"My memory is what I forget with."*

— Alexander Chase

"A bad Memory is...

▶ *the skeleton in the liar's closet."*

How come a good memory forgets not to repeat the same story so often?

▶ *"How is that our memory is good enough to retain the least triviality that happens to us, and yet not good enough to recollect how often we have told it to the same person?"*
— Duc de La Rochefoucauld

"Every man complains of his memory, but" what does no man complain of?

▶ *"No man complains of his judgment."*
— French proverb

Do you remember me?

▶ *"Fortunately, I'm suffering from amnesia."*

As the elephant said —

▶ *"Aw, forget it!"*

"The secret of a good memory is...

▶ *always to write things down."*

Guide on how NOT to forget something.

▶ *"Nothing fixes a thing so intensely in the memory as the wish to forget it."*
— Michel de Montaigne

• HAVE MERCY! •

To the man pleading for unjustified mercy.

▶ *"He's like the man who murdered his parents — and when sentence was about to be announced — pleaded for mercy on the grounds that he was an orphan."*
— Abraham Lincoln

Why don't you put me out of my misery?

▶ *"They shoot horses, don't they!"*

Mercy is a Godly attribute when you season it with justice.

▶ *"The quality of mercy is not strain'd. It droppeth as the gentle rain from heaven
Upon the place beneath. It is twice blest
It blesseth him that gives and him that takes."*
— William Shakespeare

• THE METRIC SYSTEM •

Did God mean the world to go
Metric?

▶ *"If the Lord had meant us to go metric,*
He would have given us 10 apostles —
not 12."

• YOUR MIND •

The law of "Mental Discovery"
which most people don't
discover.

▶ *"There are many groups of cells of*
which many never develop throughout
life unless some upheaval in the mental
life of the individual himself initiates
their growth and springs them into life.
Fully one-third of the mental capacity
of all men lies dormant until death,
undisturbed by the easy demands of
an easy life."

— William James

Definition of Brain and how it
thinks.

▶ *"The brain is an apparatus with which*
we think that we think."

— Ambrose Bierce

If I will it — I can make my mind
see anything.

▶ *"Stone walls do not a prison make*
Nor iron bars a cage."

— Richard Lovelace

His mind doesn't impress me
at all.

▶ *"Intellectually he's a pygmy."*

He's very shallow.

▶ *"He's living proof that still waters*
run shallow."

The "materialist" claims
the mind is nothing more
than the work of the
brain. The "dualist"
says a "nonmaterial"
essence added to the
brain produces mind.

▶ *"It's a mistake to think that the*
brain does everything and that our
conscious experiences are simply a
reflection of brain activities."
— John Eccles
"My fundamental premise about the brain
is that its workings — what we call
'mind' — are a consequence of its
anatomy and physiology, and nothing more.

— Carl Sagan

Is the mind of man generally a
reasonable one?

▶ *"Man is a reasoning, rather than a*
reasonable mind."

— Robert B. Hamilton

Insult about his mind.

▶ *"What's on your mind? If you will forgive the overstatement."*

— Fred Allen

Can your mind alter
a state of discontentment?

▶ *"The mind is its own place and in itself can make a Heav'n of Hell, a Hell of Heav'n.*

— John Milton

Why are minds like
parachutes?

▶ *"Minds, like parachutes, won't function unless open."*

Who has not been in awe, at
one time or another, of an
encyclopedic mind!

▶ *"And still they stared
And still the wonder grew
That one small head
Could carry all he knew!"*

— Oliver Goldsmith

"He has nothing to say...

▶ *and generally says it!"*

When the severest physical
illness overtook Charles
Darwin he picked up his copy of
'Paradise Lost' and pondered
over Milton's lines.

▶ *"The mind is its own place and in itself Can make a Heav'n of Hell, a Hell of Heav'n."*

— John Milton

"The mind is a wonderful
thing.

▶ *It starts working the minute you're born and never stops until you get up to speak in public."*

"To call him a moron is...

▶ *a highly underrated tribute!"*

Many a Great Mind goes
through life not discovered and
not appreciated.

▶ *"Full many a flower is born to blush unseen
And waste its sweetness on the desert air."*

— Thomas Gray

• MINORITIES •

Do minorities have innate
prejudices?

▶ *"How a minority, reaching majority, seizing authority, hates a minority."*

— Leonard H. Robbins

When is the minority always
always wrong?

▶ *"At the beginning!"*

— Herbert V. Prochnow

• MISFORTUNE •

"The man who can withstand misfortune is one with...

▸ *the ability to bear with calmness the misfortunes of others."*

— French proverb

• MISTAKES •

Me make mistakes??

▸ *"I never make MISTEAKS!"*

"That's my biggest turkey...

▸ *since Thanksgiving!"*

The only people who make no mistakes are dead people.

▸ *"King Tut hasn't made a mistake in thousands of years."*

"If you must make a mistake...

▸ *make a new one each time!"*

"A man who never made a mistake...

▸ *never made anything."*

"If you don't learn from your mistakes...

▸ *there's no sense making them."*

— Lawrence J. Peter

Are we able to control the degree to which we allow a mishap to hurt us?

▸ *"Mishaps are like knives, that either serve us or cut us, as we grasp them by the blade or the handle."*

— James Russell Lowell

Always make some allowances for a person confronted with learning new skills!"

▸ *"We are all toddlers at first and often toddlers fall down."*

There's only one right way to slip.

▸ *"Slip with your feet — not with your mouth!"*

"The strategy you're using to rectify that problem is far too extreme like...

▸ *using a guillotine to cure dandruff."*

— Clare Boothe Luce

"Many a man gets to the top of the ladder and then finds out...

▸ *it has been leaning against the wrong wall."*

— Laurence J. Peter

Some people go through life getting results. What about others?

▸ *"Others get consequences!"*

— E. Stanley Jones

"I made only one mistake today.

▶ *I got out of bed."*

How making mistakes the right way can lead to wisdom.

▶ *"The road to wisdom? Well, it's plain*
And simple to express:
Err
And err
And err again
But less
And less
And less."

— Piet Hein

"If you have always done it that way...

▶ *it probably is wrong!"*

— Charles F. Kettering

"Sleep on your plans. Not on your mistakes."

▶ *"It's better to sleep on what you plan to*
do than to be kept awake by what
you've done."

How often do we all make the same mistake?

▶ *"This is the first time I did it again*
today!"

"To err is human, but...

▶ *when the eraser wears out ahead of*
the pencil, you're overdoing it."

How to avoid the same mistake.

▶ *"Listen to your memory!"*

From the egotistical man who never makes mistakes.

▶ *"I haven't been wrong since 1961,*
when I thought I made a mistake."

The degree to which every man hates being caught making a blunder.

▶ *"Most men would rather be charged*
with malice than with making a
blunder."

— Josh Billings

Rectify your mistakes!

▶ *"A man who has made a mistake and*
doesn't correct it, is making another
mistake."

— Confucius

What's a real "PRO" at making errors?

▶ *"To err is human; to really foul things*
up requires a computer."

What's the greatest mistake so many people make?	▶ *"The greatest mistake you can make in life is to be continually fearing you will make one."*
	— Elbert Hubbard

And you think you suffer embarrassment when you make a mistake?	▶ *Comment by a former hockey goalie: "How would you like a job where, if you made a mistake, a big red light goes on and 18,000 people boo?"*
	— Jacques Plante

Don't make the same mistake!	▶ *"To stumble twice against the same stone is the proverbial disgrace."*
	— Cicero

• THE MISTRESS •

Why I took a mistress —	▶ *"Just to relieve the monogamy."*

• MODESTY •

What feeling does modesty give you?	▶ *"The feeling that others will soon discover just how wonderful you are."*

When men are great — modesty often goes out the door.	▶ *"When you're as great as I am, it's hard to be humble."*
	— Muhammad Ali

"With people of only moderate ability modesty is mere honesty but...	▶ *with those who possess great talent it is hypocrisy."*

I must tell you that I'm a modest non boasting man.	▶ *"Modesty prevents me mentioning my many other virtues."*

Sarcastic comment to a braggart lacking modesty.	▶ *"Modesty is a vastly overrated virtue."*
	— John Kenneth Galbraith

"Modesty is the art of encouraging people to find out for themselves...	▶ *how important you are."*

He's insufferably vain!	▶ *"He's the kind of guy who can't look into the mirror without taking a bow."*

• MONEY •

Lend money to a friend and you'll often lose the friend! Borrow unduly and you'll be a poor conserver of your resources.

▶ *"Neither a borrower nor a lender be;*
For loan oft loses both itself and friend,
And borrowing dulls the edge of
    husbandry."
— William Shakespeare

"If a fool and his money are soon parted...

▶ *why are there so many rich fools?"*

"Money is like manure.

▶ *Good only when spread around."*
— Carl Sandburg

Yesterday is a cancelled check; tomorrow is a promissory note...

▶ *today is the only cash you have*
— so spend it wisely."
— Kay Lyons

"Money isn't everything but...

▶ *it's way ahead of whatever's in second place!"*

Should you ask yourself where all your money went?

▶ *"Never ask of money spent*
Where the spender thinks it went.
Nobody was ever meant
To remember or invent
What he did with every cent."
— Robert Frost

"The jingle of coins is music to the proprietor but...

▶ *only clatter to the cashier."*
— Harry Bosley

Why is money like sex?

▶ *"Money, it turned out, was exactly like sex, you thought of nothing else if you didn't have it and thought of other things if you did."*
— James Baldwin

Is money the ultimate key to happiness?

▶ *"The man with $10,000,000 is probably no happier than the man with $9,000,000."*

A sick pun about Dollars and Cents.

▶ *"Dollars buy more when accompanied by sense."*

What are "The two most beautiful words in the English language?"

▶ *"Check enclosed."*
— Dorothy Parker

Does money get you friends?

▶ *"Money can't buy friends, but you can get a better class of enemy."*

"Money doesn't grow on trees."

▶ *"Money doesn't grow on sprees."*

Does having money always make things better?

▶ *"I never been in no situation where havin' money made it any worse."*
— Clinton Jones

Money — indeed — brings many, many things.

▶ *"Money brings honor, friends, conquest, and realms."*
— John Milton

Will a good income assuage or aggravate a misfortune?

▶ *"There are few sorrows, however poignant, in which a good income is of no avail."*
— Logan Smith

What is the similarity of money and a butterfly?

▶ *"A butterfly is the second most beautiful thing with wings. The first is money."*

To those who say "Money isn't everything!"

▶ *"Money is the sixth sense, without which you cannot enjoy the other five."*
— Somerset Maugham

"When I had money...

▶ *everyone called me brother."*
— Polish proverb

"I've got all the money I'll ever need...

▶ *if I die by four o'clock."*
— Henny Youngman

"Money isn't everything but...

▶ *only those who've got it can claim it!"*

Should you marry for money?

▶ *"Don't marry for money — you can borrow it cheaper."*
— Gabe Kaplan

"The best way to attract money is...

▶ *to give the appearance of having it."*
— Gail Sheehy

What else happens when "A fool and his money are soon parted?"

▶ *"A fool and his money are soon popular."*

"There was a time when a fool and his money were soon parted.

▶ *Now it happens to everybody."*

"It's better to have money and not need it than...

▶ *to have money and need it."*

"Money isn't everything but...

▶ *it gets you almost everything."*

Simple rules for saving money —

▶ *"To save half, when you are fired by an eager impulse to contribute to a charity, wait and count forty. To save three-quarters, count sixty. To save it all, count sixty-five."*

— Mark Twain

• MONEY TO BURN! •

Hollywood money philosophy —

▶ *"Try to have lots of The Hell With You money! When you can say to anybody 'The hell with you Buster' — you've got it made."*

"Money with her disappears like...

▶ *a snowflake on a hot stove!"*

"For most, the irony of life is that by the time you have money to burn...

▶ *the fire has gone out."*

• MONEY WON'T BUY! •

Money will buy pretty good acquaintances — but will it buy sincere friendship?

▶ *"Money will buy a pretty good dog but it won't buy the wag of his tail."*

— Josh Billings

"There are a lot of things money won't buy but...

▶ *try and buy anything without it!"*

• MONEY AND EVIL! •

"Love of money is the root of half the evil in the world.

▶ *And lack of money is the root of the other half."*

Money is the root of all evil!

▶ *Correctly worded.*
"The love of money is the root of all evil."

— Bible

• MONEY AND GOD •

"If you want to know what God thinks of money...

▶ *look at the people he gives it to."*

• MONEY AND GREED •

"It is in the nature of man to strive to gain money and to increase it...

▶ *and his great desire to add to his wealth and honor is the chief source of misery for man."*

— Moses Maimonides

How do you reconcile this with "Honesty pays?"

▶ *"He without benefit of scruples His fun and money soon quadruples."*

— Ogden Nash

Does getting lots of money satisfy wants?

▶ *"Riches enlarge, rather than satisfy appetites."*

— Thomas Fuller

• MONEY AND IDEALISM •

Are you one of those idealists who say money isn't important?

▶ *"Better to have the legal tender of the realm than the counterfeit scrip of Idealism."*

"Whenever he says it's not the money but the principle of the thing he cares for...

▶ *just offer him the money and see how quickly the principle vanishes."*

— Ruth Smeltzer

• MONEY AND ITS IMPORTANCE •

How important is money in life?

▶ *"When I was young I thought that money was the most important thing in life; now that I am old I know that it is."*

— Oscar Wilde

• MONEY AND ITS POWER! •

Money has power over all men but to what limits?

▶ *"Whoever has sixpence is sovereign over all men, — to the extent of the sixpence; commands cooks to feed him, philosophers to teach him, kings to mount guard over him, — to the extent of sixpence."*

— Thomas Carlyle

That which enough money lets me do.

▶ *"Money lets me do what I like to do — and NOT do what I dislike doing."*

Does large Quantity of Money automatically endow you with being a person of Quality?

▶ *"Money is one of those rare things where Quantity is Quality."*

• MONEY PUZZLE! •

"One of the greatest money puzzles is...

▶ *how a fool and his money got together in the first place."*

• MONEY AND ITS STATUS •

Money — the symbol of your status and worth in society.

▶ *"Money is the way society shows that it values what you are doing."*

• MONEY TALKS! •

Money talks — but an unfunny joke from a man of money commands laughter.

▶ *"Money is honey, my little sonny, And a rich man's joke is always funny."*

— T.E. Brown

Making money doesn't need good English.

▸ *"When money talks few people criticize its grammar."*

Languages and money.

▸ *"There are hundreds of languages in the world, but the dollar can speak them all."*

It's tough to hang on to money.

▸ *"That money talks
I'll not deny,
I heard it once:
It said, Goodbye."*

— Richard Armour

• MONEY AND ITS VERSATILITY •

The versatility of money.

▸ *"Father earns it,
Students burn it,
Mother lends it,
Coeds spend it,
Forgers fake it,
Taxes take it,
Misers crave it,
Robbers seize it,
Rich increase it,
Gamblers lose it.
I could use it."*

• MONEY AND WORK •

"No bees, no honey...

▸ *No work; no money!"*

Should you save up money for when you're old?

▸ *"Work hard and save your money and when you are old you will be able to buy the things only the YOUNG can enjoy."*

• MONOTONY •

"It was so boring at the seaside resort that...

▸ *one day the tide went out — and never came back."*

"The way not to lead a monotonous life...

▸ *is to live for others."*

— Fulton J. Sheen

"I was bored... ▶ *right down to my cuticles!"*

Which is it? Monotony or Monogamy? ▶ *"Having only one wife at a time."*

"About as exciting as... ▶ *watching grass grow."*

• MORALITY •

How you feel when you're moral and when you're immoral.
▶ *"What is moral is what you feel good after and what is immoral is what you feel bad after."*
— Ernest Hemingway

What is enlightening about accepting the new morality?
▶ *From the World War II war trials — "The so-called new morality is too often the old immorality condoned."*
— Lord Shawcross

"In terms of right and wrong — what we need is a return to the morality that says...
▶ *right is right even though nobody is right; and wrong is wrong even when everybody is wrong."*
— Clement C. O'Sullivan

You've done me wrong!
▶ *"Thou art weighed in the balance and art found wanting."*
— The Bible

"Immorality is the morality of those who...
▶ *are having a better time."*
— H.L. Mencken

What place in Hell should be reserved for those who remain neutral on moral issues?
▶ *"The hottest places in hell are reserved for those who, in time of great moral crisis, maintain their neutrality."*
— Aligheri Dante

Alvin Toffler in his book 'Future Shock' reveals the revolutionary changes in our life styles and attitudes to morality.
▶ *"Right now, I'm beginning to be shocked that I'm not as shocked as I used to be."*
— Lucille Ball

• MOTHERS •

Mother's Day — ▶ *"7 a.m. to midnight."*

"Only a mother would think her daughter has been a good girl when...

▶ *she returns from a date with a Gideon Bible in her hand."*

There is no greater "LOVE" than that of a mother!

▶ *"If I were hanged on the highest hill, Mother o' mine, O mother o' mine! I know whose love would follow me still, Mother o' mine, O mother o' mine!"*
— Rudyard Kipling

Why mothers were invented.

▶ *"God could not be everywhere, so he made mothers."*
— Jewish proverb

"An unwed mother is...

▶ *a misconception."*

Estee Lauder says that a daughter-in-law will never exactly be a daughter.

▶ *"Why should she when she has her own mother? But I found I can be the next best thing. If you open your heart and heritage to a daughter-in-law, she'll love you for it."*
— Estee Lauder

• MOTIVATION •

How many reasons generally impel us to do things?

▶ *"There are two reasons for doing things — a very good reason and the real reason."*

• MOTTO •

Motto of the Duchess of Windsor which she had emblazoned upon her living room wall.

▶ *"I'm not the miller's daughter, but I've been through the mill."*

• THE MOUSETRAP •

Correct this quote.
"If you build a better mousetrap, they'll beat a path to your door."

▶ *"If a man can write a better book, preach a better sermon, or make a better mousetrap than his neighbor — though he builds his house in the woods, the world will make a beaten path to his door."*
— Ralph Emerson

"If a man makes a better mousetrap than his neighbor...

▶ *the chances are he will catch mice!"*

• YOUR MOUTH! •

Your features.

▶ *"God gives you your other features but you make your mouth yourself."*

• THE MOVIES •

How valid is it to label literature and movies as adult?

▶ *Labeling literature and movies as "adult" would be all right if "adult" meant the maturing of judgment instead of just the passage of years.*

Asked of Warner Bros. Pictures —
"Will the public ever go for talking pictures?"

▶ *"Who the hell wants to hear actors talk?"*

— Harry M. Warner

"Photography is truth.

▶ *Cinema is truth 24 times a second."*

What happens to a book when it's made into a film?

▶ *"You can't judge a book by its movie."*

— Hollywood maxim

• MURPHY'S LAW •

"If anything can go wrong...

▶ *it will!"*

O'Toole's Commentary on Murphy's Law —

▶ *"Murphy was an optimist!"*

• MUSIC •

Which language is understood all over the world?

▶ *"Music is the universal language of mankind!"*

— Henry Wadsworth Longfellow

What hurts most about today's music?

▶ *"Today — it isn't facing the music that hurts. It's listening to it!"*

How some people react to musical recitals.

▶ *"Nothing soothes me more after a long and maddening course of pianoforte recitals than to sit and have my teeth drilled."*
— George Bernard Shaw

The invisible power of music.

▶ *"Music hath charms to soothe the savage beast."*
— James Bramston

That which a sophisticated pianist can appreciate in another pianist.

▶ *"The notes I handle no better than many pianists. But the pauses between the notes — ah, that is where the art resides!"*
— Arthur Schnabel

Advice on music which was written before anyone ever envisioned the loudness of Rock Music.

▶ *"If one hears bad music it is one's duty to drown it in conversation."*
— Oscar Wilde

The surprising sensual feature of music.

▶ *"Music is the only sensual pleasure that exists without vice."*

"Music is the one art that works on the feelings directly and not through the medium of thought."
— Arthur Schopenhauer

▶ *"Music is a language without a dictionary whose symbols are interpreted by the listener according to some unspoken Esperanto of the emotions."*
— Aaron Copland

"I could have been a violinist but...

▶ *I was too high strung."*

What Rock Music is to many people.

▶ *"Rock Music is thought destroying noise."*
— Pope John Paul II

A reminder to symphony conductors not to overdo phony histrionics.

▶ *"Conductors must give unmistakable and suggestive signals to the orchestra — not choreography to the audience."*
— George Szell

Sign on Music Shop Door —

▶ *"Out to Lunch. Usually Bach by One. Offenbach Sooner."*

"He sings like a rusty door hinge.

▶ If Van Gogh could hear him he'd cut off his other ear."

"Music is the only language...

▶ in which you cannot say a mean or sarcastic thing."

— John Erskine

The effect of music on your body?

▶ "Psychologists have found that music does things to you whether you like it or not. Fast tempos invariably raise your pulse, respiration, and blood pressure; slow music lowers them."

— Doron K. Antrim

The endless possible combinations of music within the twelve notes of the octave!

▶ "I know that the twelve notes in each octave and the varieties of rhythm offer me opportunities that all of human genius will never exhaust."

— Igor Stravinsky

Q. "What are your views on music?"

▶ A. "I love music especially the notes C and E."

N

• NARROW MINDED •

"He's so narrow minded that...

▶ *he can look through a keyhole with both eyes at the same time."*

• NATIONHOOD •

"The Pilgrim Fathers landed on the shores of America and fell on their knees.

▶ *"Then they fell upon the aborigines."*
— American saying

• NATURE •

A reminder not to take for granted the infinite beauties of nature.

▶ *"I walk in the garden, I look at the flowers and shrubs and trees and discover in them an exquisiteness of contour, a vitality of edge or a vigor of spring as well as an infinite variety of color that no artifact I have seen in the last sixty years can rival... Each day, as I look, I wonder where my eyes were yesterday."*
— Bernard Berenson

Four basic sequential Rules of Nature.

▶ *"Copulation, Procreation, Overpopulation, Starvation."*

• NECESSITY •

The difference between a
Necessity and a Luxury.

▶ *"Necessity": Something you cannot
get along without, but do.
"Luxury": Something you ought to
get along without, but don't.*

"Necessity is the mother of
invention."
What is invention?

▶ *"Invention is the mother of necessity."*
— Thorstein Veblen

Have Necessities and
Luxuries changed roles?

▶ *"Times change. Cars are now
regarded as necessities and children
as luxuries."*

• YOUR NEEDS •

What are the Wants of a
human being and will he ever
achieve them all?

▶ *"Freud said that man wants most of all
to be loved; Adler said that he wants
most of all to be significant; and Jung
said that he wants security."*

"What this country needs is...

▶ *a spot remover to remove the spots left
by other spot removers."*

"I sure don't need that any
more than...

▶ *a moose needs a hatrack!"*

Everybody has to be
somebody to somebody...

▶ *to be anybody!"*
— Malcolm S. Forbes

• NEGOTIATING •

I'd like to solve our differences
but you're putting too many
obstacles in the way!

▶ *"You're the one who's driving nails into
our discussion; then you cut the heads
off and expect me to pull them out with
my teeth."*
— Mikhail Gorbachev

• NEIGHBOURS •

A good neighbour and noise.

▶ *"A good neighbour is one who makes
noise the same time as you do."*

• NERVOUS! •

"I was so nervous...

▶ *you could march an army to the beat of my heart."*

"He's as nervous as...

▶ *a long tailed cat in a room full of rocking chairs."*

• NETWORK •

Samuel Johnson's exquisite definition of Network.

▶ *"Anything reticulated or decussated, at equal distances, with interstices between the intersections."*

• NEUTRALITY •

"To know what is right and not do it...

▶ *is the worst cowardice."*

— Confucius

• THE NEW AND UNUSUAL! •

Your first exposure to anything in nature provides the greatest novelty and pleasure.

▶ *"One sees things for the first time only once."*

— Theodore H. White

• NEWS •

"The kind of bad news you're giving me...

▶ *is like telling an undertaker you've just given birth!"*

Can the media make or break aspiring politicians?

▶ *"In the old days men had the rack. Now they have the press."*

— Oscar Wilde

Newspaper want ad —

▶ *"Lost: Thick-lensed eyeglasses. Finder please advertise in bold face print."*

How to break bad news!

▶ *"If you have anything to tell me of importance, for God's sake begin at the end."*

— Sara Jeannette Duncan

What NEWS is!

▶ *"If a shoe gnaws at a mouse*
— that's news!"

Thomas Jefferson preferred
newspapers without a
government to a government
without newspapers.

▶ *"I disapprove of what you say, but I will*
defend to the death your right to say
it."

— Voltaire

What can the Good News be
about the Bad News?

▶ *"The good news is that the bad news*
wasn't as bad as it could have been."

— Roger Brinner

That which newspaper men
often must do for success.

▶ *"You have to stoop to scoop!"*

"The Law of Chronic
Irrelevance". Junk news hits
the front pages, vital news the
back.

▶ *"This law fastens the public mind on*
the temporary and unimportant, a
sensation of the moment, the vital
news often buried in the back pages."

— Bruce Hutchison

Why you don't have to read
the newspaper.

▶ *"News is the same thing everyday only*
to different people."

• NEW YORK •

"The emigrant's dream of
New York City...

▶ *where the roads are paved with gold*
and the cavities with asphalt."

• NO!! •

"When he gives you a NO...

▶ *it's like a guy driving a rivet!"*

I'm a real soft touch. I can't
say NO!

▶ *"I'm like the girl who could only say NO*
to the question she couldn't hear."

• NOISE •

Definition of Noise:

▶ *"A stench in the ear."*

— Ambrose Bierce

• THE NOSE •

The kind of nose everybody would like to have.

▶ *"A nose that can see is worth two that sniff."*

— Eugene Ionesco

• NOSTALGIA •

In 1885, you could buy a steak for 17 cents a pound and a new suit for five dollars. You could build a house for $550 and buy a gallon of whiskey for 25 cents.

▶ *"A doctor earned $1000 a year; a salaried employee was lucky at $12 a week. Life expectancy was 38 years — and you could seldom save for old age. Were the good old days really that great?"*

Nostalgia about "girls' charms!"

▶ *"Remember the old days when girls had hidden charms and hid them!"*

Four memorable nostalgic words.

▶ *"Once upon a time!"*

"Oh for the good old days when a juvenile deliquent was a kid who...

▶ *owed eight cents on an overdue library book!"*

Have things changed?

▶ *"Even nostalgia isn't what it used to be."*

A prayer for clean air!

▶ *"Oh for the good old days when sex was dirty and the air was clean!"*

Are the so-called golden ages of the past only in our imagination?

▶ *"No man, correctly informed of the past, will be disposed to take a morose or desponding view of the present."*

— Thomas Babington Macauley

Why is there always nostalgia for the past?

▶ *"The past always looks better than it was because it isn't here."*

— Finley Peter Dunne

Will nostalgia for the good old days hold only for the distant past?

▶ *"As lousy as things are now, tomorrow they will be somebody's good old days."*

"The good old days."
Were they really that good?

▶ *"The good old days are neither better nor worse than the ones we're living through right now."*

— Artie Shaw

"In the good old days they also used to speak of...

▶ *the good old days."*

"Some old-fashioned nostalgia! Who can remember...

▶ *— When you had to hand crank a car before it would start?*
— When letters were mailed for three cents?
— And when doctors made house calls?"

• MAKING "NOTES" •

"The habit of making notes contributes to invention and initiative.

▶ *Millions of dollars worth of valuable ideas have been lost because of the want of a stub pencil and a scrap of paper."*

— Alex Osborn

• NOTHINGNESS •

Something to do is infinitely better than nothing to do.

▶ *"Thank God every morning when you get up that you have something to do which must be done, whether you like it or not. Being forced to work, and forced to do your best, will breed in you temperance, self-control, diligence, strength of will, content, and a hundred other virtues which the idle never know."*

— James Russell Lowell

What's great about having lots to do?

▶ *"There is no pleasure in having nothing to do; the fun is in having lots to do and not doing it."*

"How beautiful it is to do nothing...

▶ *and then rest afterward."*

— Spanish proverb

What is worse than having nothing to do in life?

▶ *"Hell is more bearable than nothingness."*

— P.J. Bailey

• NUCLEAR REACTORS •

Slogan of people who are against Nuclear Reactors.

▶ *"Better be active today than radioactive tomorrow!"*

• NUMBER ONE! •

Why everybody would like to be first.

▶ *"Nobody remembers who was second!"*

"If you aspire to the highest place...

▶ *it is no disgrace to stop at the second, or even the third, place."*

— Cicero

"Nice guys don't always finish last.

▶ *Sometimes they finish a nice second."*

Why it pays to be there first.

▶ *"The first man gets the oyster, the second man gets the shell."*

— Andrew Carnegie

O

• OBNOXIOUS! •

"I don't know what makes him ▶ *whatever it is, it sure works!"*
so obnoxious but...

• OBSERVING •

How to observe a lot. ▶ *"You can observe a lot just by watching."*

— Yogi Berra

• OBSTACLES •

Obstacles becloud your objective. ▶ *"When you're up to your arse in alligators — it's hard to remember that your original objective was to drain the swamp."*

Obstacles can often lead to great reward. ▶ *"Troubles and pains are often the chisel and hammer, cutting away the hindering crust, to reveal the diamond."*

— J.R. Miller

You won't get what you want if you don't break down the barriers. ▶ *"You can't have your omelet without breaking the eggs."*

• OBSTINACY •

He's a touchy but obstinate guy.

▶ *"He's one of those guys you have to handle with gloves — boxing gloves."*

• ODDITIES •

The immensity of One Billion Dollars as against One Million!

▶ *"If you had one million dollars and spent $1000 every day, you'd be broke in about 3 years!*

If you had one billion dollars it would take 3000 years."

"Every little bit does count!" A parable.

▶ *A triumphal feast was scheduled in a village. To insure adequate refreshment, each villager agreed to pour one bottle of his very best wine into a great cask.*
    One villager reasoned. "If I filled my bottle with water, the dilution will be so slight, no one will notice." But when the feast commenced and the great cask was tapped, water poured forth.
    Everyone had thought alike: "My bit will not be missed!"

How Type can lend itself to pictorial interpretation.

▶ *Girls who were raised on cod liver oil have legs like this* ! !
Girls who ride horses have legs like this ( )
Girls who sit at bars have legs like) (
But ... little girls who were well brought up cross their legs like this ✖

An automobile serviceman specializing in foreign cars sent out a business card listing these mechanics:

▶ *Charles Nicholas ......for British autos*
Karl Niklaus.... Volkswagen specialist
Carlos Niccoli ....for Italian models
Charles Nicolles ....for French cars
Carl Nikkoles ...... for Swedish makes
The serviceman who sent the card

— Charlie Nicholas

Love and Kisses Roman style.

▶ *"LXXX"*

Never take things for granted.
Make the ROPE TEST.

▶ *"Years ago a coolie stepped
confidently on a rope bridge over a
gorge. The ropes were frayed and
looked dangerous.
"Aren't you afraid the rope will break?"
the missionary said.
"No" said the coolie.
"Why?" insisted the missionary.
"Because it never has,"
replied the coolie.*

Translation:

stand	took	to	taking
I	he	throw	this

▶ *"I understand he undertook to
overthrow this undertaking."*

Love Pact.

▶ *"Two hearts in one heart.
May we love each other as much
at the end as at the beginning!"*

If you were able to fold a piece
of paper over itself 50 times,
how high up would it reach?

▶ *"Right up to the planet Mars."*

The numeral "One" followed
by 100 zeros is called one
"Googol".

▶ *One Googol followed by 100 zeros
called a "Googolplex".
No matter how tiny you wrote all the
numbers of a googolplex, they could
not all be written on a piece of paper as
wide as the universe.*

In Unity, there is strength!

▶ *He gave the bundle to each of his sons,
and instructed each to break the
bundle. None of the sons being able to
break the bundle, Jacob took it apart
and gave each one a single stick,
which they easily broke.
"My sons," he said, "I would have
you learn two lessons. First, what
none of you alone can do, you all
combined can do; second, when you
are all bound together you cannot be
broken."
Such is the essence of unity.*

"Have a

nice day!"

M,ILL,ION

▶ "Have an

ordinary day!"

▶ INTER   RUPTION   DRI
                                          P

FOOT[1]
    [1]NOTE

— Mary Ann Madden

Were the Chinese right in saying: "A picture is worth a thousand words"?

▶ "In a thousand words you could include the Lord's Prayer, the Sermon on the Mount, the Hippocratic Oath, a sonnet by Shakespeare, and the Magna Carta — and no picture on earth can take the place of these."

If all of man's "50,000-year History"...
1. 40 years ago —
2. 35 years ago —
3. 2 years ago —
4. 9 months ago —
5. 20 days ago —
6. 18 days ago —

7. 10 days ago —
8. 5 days ago —
9. 4 minutes ago —
10. The beatles invaded England —
11. And by the time you finish this story —

▶ were squeezed into the last 50 years.

1. "We got out of the caves."
2. "We learned to write with pictures."
3. "Christianity came along."
4. "The printing press was invented."
5. "We got electricity."
6. "The Wright Brothers took off at Kitty Hawk."
7. "Radio."
8. "T.V."
9. "The first jet."
10. "While you were reading about the jet."
11. "A man on the moon!"

An educated person is one who can spell these 10 words.

▶ "Harass — Embarrass
Supersede — Inoculate
Vilify — Desiccate
Peccadillo — Picnicking
Plaguy — Innuendo."

"Merry Christmas"
in 27 languages

▶ *God Jul (Swedish).*
Glacedelig Jul (Danish).
Gledelig Jul (Norwegian).
Froehliche Weihnachten (German).
Hartelijke Kerst Groeten (Dutch).
Hauskaa Joulua (Finnish).
Joyeux Nöel (French).
Buon Natale (Italian).
Felices Navidades (Spanish).
Boas Festas (Portuguese).
Wesolych Swiat (Polish).
S Rozhdestvom Christova (Russian).
Crystas Rozdzajetsia, Slawyte Jeho (Ukrainian).
Befele Vanebhi (Bohemian).
Boldog Karacsonyt (Hungarian).
Sretan Bozic (Croatian).
Sretan Bozic (Serbian).
Linksmu Kaledu (Lithuanian).
Vesele Vanoce (Czech).
Kala Christougenia (Greek).
Nodlaig Nait Cugat (Irish).
Ge Chenorhavorem St. Zenount (Armenian).
Mele Kaliki maga (Hawaiian).
Chuk-syong takn (Korean).
Yasu Suntel Kowa (Chinese).
Shin-nen omedito (Japanese).
Gajan Kristnask (Esperanto).

Help wanted ad for a Baby
Sitter.

▶ *"Teen-ager to baby sit two evenings a
week. $7 per hour — plus fridge
benefits."*

How to teach a Chinese
immigrant to pronounce the
word FISH.

▶ *gh — as in laugh (F)*
  o — as in women (I)
  ti — as in temptation (SH)

How to tell a man's age
by his diet.

▶ *1. Milk.*
  2. Milk and bread.
  3. Milk, bread, eggs and spinach.
  *4. Oatmeal, bread and butter, green
     apples and all-day suckers.*
  5. Ice cream sodas and hot dogs.
  *6. Minute steaks, fried potatoes,
     coffee and apple pie.*

7. Bouillon, roast duck, scalloped potatoes, creamed broccoli, fruit salad, divinity fudge, demi tasse.
8. Pate de foie gras, wiener schnitzel, potato parisienne, eggplant a l'opera, demi tasse and Roquefort cheese.
9. Two soft boiled eggs, toast and milk.
10. Crackers and milk.
11. Milk.

"The 10 most Expressive Words...   ▶ *in the English language."*

The most bitter word	*"Alone"*
The most reverent	*"Mother"*
The most tragic	*"Death"*
The most beautiful	*"Love"*
The most cruel..........................	*"Revenge"*
The most peaceful	*"Tranquil"*
The saddest	*"Forgotten"*
The warmest............................	*"Friendship"*
The coldest	*"No"*
The one bringing the most comfort..............................	*"Faith"*

— Wilfred Funk

Example of a Malapropism — "A Rude Awakening."   ▶ *"A Shrewd Awakening."*

Two examples of Spoonerisms —   ▶ *"A crushing blow. A blushing crow."*
"Let me show you to your seat.
Let me sew you to your sheet."

A five word rectangle, which reads the same horizontally and vertically.

▶
H	E	A	R	T
E	M	B	E	R
A	B	U	S	E
R	E	S	I	N
T	R	E	N	D

"Don't celebrate ushering in the 21st century on January 1st, 2000!

▶ *The completion of two thousand years occurs Jan 1st, 2001."*

Man's make-up.

▶ *TAKE*
"Enough water to fill a ten-gallon barrel. Enough fat for seven bars of soap. Carbon for 9,000 lead pencils. Phosphorus to make 2,200 match-heads. Magnesium for one dose of salts. Iron to make one medium-sized nail. Sufficient lime to whitewash a chicken coop. Sulphur enough to rid one dog of fleas; and you get an Einstein or a village idiot, according as you arrange the ingredients."

— Dr. T.E. Lawson

"The average reader can read an average book at the rate of 300 words a minute. That means 4,500 words in quarter of an hour, or 1,642,500 words in a year.

▶ *If you spend just fifteen minutes a day, you can read twenty average-length books between January 1st and December 31st."*

Example from "OuLiPo", an abbreviation of Ouvroir de Littérature Potentielle (Workshop of Potential Literature), of a "Snowball Sentence" — a pyramid of words each one a letter longer than the one above, which if read carefully, makes sense.

▶

*O
to
see
man's
stern
poetic
thought
publicly
expanding
recklessly
imaginative
mathematical
inventiveness
openmindedness
unconditionally
superfecundating
nonantagonistical
hypersophisticated
interdenominational
interpenetrabilities.*

The Nine Ages of Man
(A poem in one line
to be read aloud)

▶ *Not old enough to know better*
"   "   "   "   "
"   "   "   "   "
"   "   "   "
"   "   "
"   "
"   "
"
"

— F. Emerson Andrews

Instructions in case of a
Nuclear Bomb Attack...

▶ 1. *"Stay clear of windows.*
2. *Keep your hands free of glasses*
   and cigarettes.
3. *Loosen restrictive clothing.*
4. *Remove eyeglasses.*
5. *Empty pockets of all sharp articles.*
6. *As soon as you see the brilliant*
   flare of the explosion, bend over
   and place your head firmly
   between your legs.
7. *Then kiss your rear end goodbye!"*

• OPERA •

Really now! How good is
opera?

▶ *"Opera is better than it sounds."*

— Mark Twain

The uninformed but truthful
opera goer.

▶ *"He goes to the opera whether he has*
to sleep or not."

• OPINIONS •

"It's a difference of opinion...

▶ *that makes horseracing or*
missionaries."

How would you like to know
what people really think of you.

▶ *"If you want to get rid of some of your*
ego, listen at the keyhole just after you
leave the room."

Should you always accept a
majority opinion as being the
wisest one?

▶ *"If fifty million people say a foolish*
thing, it is still a foolish thing."

— Anatole France

"The man who won't take a stand on an issue is...

▶ one who stands firmly on both feet in mid-air on both sides of an issue."

"A wise man changes his mind...

▶ a fool never!"

How to take opinion when it's given to you.

▶ "When I want your opinion I'll give it to you!"

— Laurence J. Peter

Do you really know what people really think of you?

▶ "The best-loved man or maid in the town would perish with anguish could they hear all that their friends say in the course of a day."

— John Hay

"You wouldn't worry about what people think of you if...

▶ if you knew how seldom they do."

What kind of people don't change their minds?

▶ "If you haven't changed your opinions in the last few years, you may be dead."

• OPINIONATED •

Retort to the opinionated guy who's sure he can predict what's going to happen.

▶ "He who lives by the crystal ball will eat ground glass!"

• OPPORTUNISTS •

"An opportunist is one who opens the door...

▶ before opportunity knocks."

"The Pessimist spends all his time worrying about how he can keep the wolf from the door.
The Optimist refuses to see the wolf until he seizes the seat of his pants.

▶ The Opportunist invites the wolf in and appears the next day in a fur coat."

• OPPORTUNITY •

When opportunity knocks, timing and direction is everything.

▶ *"There is a tide in the affairs of men which taken at the flood leads on to fortune.*
Omitted, all the voyage of their life is bound in shallows and miseries."
— William Shakespeare

Why a lot of people don't take advantage when opportunity knocks.

▶ *"When opportunity knocks, a lot of people say it's making a lot of noise."*

"Opportunity never comes...

▶ *It's here!"*

Do too many of us initiate ideas that others capitalize on?

▶ *"How many a thing which we cast to the ground,*
When others pick it up becomes a gem."
— George Meredith

The reason most people don't recognize opportunities.

▶ *"Opportunities are usually disguised as hard work; so most people don't recognize them."*
— Ann Landers

"Most of us never recognize opportunity until...

▶ *it goes to work in our competitor's business."*

• THE OPTIMIST •

Optimist —

▶ *"One who thinks the situation is deteriorating less rapidly than before!"*

The Optimist
The Pessimist
The Realist

▶ *"The Optimist says, "Please pass the cream." The Pessimist says, "Please pass the milk." The Realist says, "Please pass the pitcher."*

The pessimist says, "Cold weather will hit soon"...

▶ *the optimist says, "Summer is lingering."*

"The optimist sees the doughnut...

▶ *the pessimist the hole."*

Optimist —

▶ *A man who calls bull......t fertilizer."*

How to suffer a loss.

▶ *"Look at what you have left — not at what you have lost."*

"Two men look out through the same prison bars.

▶ *One sees mud and one sees the stars."*

— Frederick Langbridge

"Don't count your chickens before they hatch because —

▶ *"It ain't over till it's over!"*

— Yogi Berra

What kind of attitude ignores facts and reality?

▶ *"Mindless optimism."*

What addiction does an optimist have?

▶ *"An optimist is a hope addict."*

"She's the ultimate in optimists.

▶ *Always hoping for the worst."*

"An optimist is a fellow who believes that whatever happens, no matter how bad, is for the best.

▶ *The pessimist is the fellow to whom it happens."*

Optimism and the tea kettle.

▶ *"Optimism allows a tea kettle to sing even though in hot water up to its nose."*

The optimist and the housefly.

▶ *"The optimist is one who believes a housefly is looking for a way to get out."*

— George Jean Nathan

• ORIGINALITY •

How you know when you say something original.

▶ *"If they haven't heard it before, it's original."*

"Most originality is... ▶ *nothing but judicious imitation."*

— Voltaire

"Originality is by no means a matter, as some suppose, of impulse or intuition to be found. ▶ *It must be elaborately sought."*

— Edgar Allan Poe

Is originality always original? ▶ *"Originality is undetected plagiarism!"*

"He who walks in another's tracks... ▶ *leaves no footprints."*

The art of appearing to be original. ▶ *"Originality is the art of concealing your source."*

— Franklin P. Jones

• OSTENTATION •

It's the exception for a wealthy person not to conspicuously display worldly goods. ▶ *"Wealth has never been a sufficient source of honour in itself. It must be advertised, and the normal medium is obtrusively expensive goods."*

— John Kenneth Galbraith

Is it "vulgarity" to ornament what is already beautiful? ▶ *"To gild refined gold, to paint the lily, To throw a perfume on the violet, To smooth the ice, or add another hue Unto the rainbow, or with taper-light To seek the beauteous eye of heaven to garnish, Is wasteful and ridiculous excess."*

— William Shakespeare

• THE OUTLOOK! •

The philosophy that too many of the world's people have adopted. ▶ *"With all its hope, dreams and promises, the world continues to deteriorate. Give up!"*

• OUT OF PLACE! •

"As out of place as... ▶ *a cowbell in a symphony orchestra."*

P

• PRIVATE "OWNERSHIP" •

In the search by philosphers for the best form of society, where does socialism and collective ownership rate?

▶ *"Again, how immeasurably greater is the pleasure, when a man feels a thing to be his own..."*

— Aristotle

• THE PACIFIST •

What kind of citizen is an absolute pacifist?

▶ *"The absolute pacifist is a bad citizen; times come when force must be used to uphold right, justice and ideals."*

— Alfred North Whitehead

• THE PALINDROME •

A Palindrome is a sentence, phrase, or word that reads the same forwards or backwards.

▶ 1. *"Rise to vote sir."*
2. *"Boss is sob."*
3. *"Step on no pets."*
4. *"A man, a plan, a canal, Panama."*
5. *"Sit on a potato pan, Otis."*

From the Bible.
"In the beginning was the word."
Q. What were the first words spoken?

▶ *"Madam I'm Adam."*

| A palindrome in which each word itself is a palindrome. | ▶ *"Anna: Did Otto peep? Otto: Did Anna?"* |

| As Napoleon lamented — | ▶ *"Able was I ere I saw Elba."* |

A palindrome made of a four word rectangle which reads the same horizontally and vertically, as well as forwards and backwards.

▶

S	T	A	R
T	U	B	A
A	B	U	T
R	A	T	S

• PANDEMONIUM •

"Pandemonium did not reign.   ▶ *It poured!"*

— John Kendrick Bangs

• PANIC •

When to go into panic and when to be calm.

▶ *"It is very much better sometimes to have a panic feeling beforehand, and then to be quite calm when things happen, than to be extremely calm beforehand and to get into a panic when things happen."*

— Winston Churchill

• PARACHUTISTS •

"I could have been a parachutist but...

▶ *nothing ever opened up."*

• THE PARANOID •

"Just because you're paranoid...

▶ *doesn't mean everybody isn't out to get you."*

• PARENTING •

A reminder to men. Spend a little more time on your families!

▶ *Nobody ever said on his death bed — "Why didn't I spend more time working on my business."*

From George Bernard Shaw —
"Don't set yourself up as an example for your children to follow but rather as a warning."

▶ From letters of Junius —
"I do not give you to prosterity as a pattern to imitate, but as an example to deter."

"Smack your child every day.

▶ If you don't know why — he does."
— Joey Adams

"If your children haven't hated you in one way or another...

▶ you've failed as a parent."
— Bette Davis

The difference between becoming a father and being a father.

▶ "To become a father is not hard, To be a father is, however."

"Level with your child by being honest.

▶ Nobody spots a phony quicker than a child."

What relationship is Parenting to jail?

▶ "Parenting is a life sentence without parole."

That which parents have to remember.

▶ "You are the 'bows' from which the "arrows' are sent"!

The tragedy of society never having provided compulsory schooling in parenthood.

▶ "Parenthood remains the greatest single preserve of the amateur."

— Alvin Toffler

Two rules for kids!

▶ Rule 1. "Homework comes before recreation."
Rule 2. "There are no exceptions to rule 1!"

A lament about the awe of a child for his father and what often happens when the child becomes a teenager.

▶ "Oh, to be only half as wonderful as my child thought I was when he was small, and only half as stupid as my teenager now thinks I am."
— Rebecca Richards

"When children say they hate their parents, that's OK. In fact that's considered normal."
How about parents?

▶ "But when parents even indicate dislike for their children, they're complete monsters!"

"You cannot teach a child to take care of himself unless you will let him try to take care of himself.

▶ *He will make mistakes and out of these mistakes will come his wisdom."*

— H.W. Beecher

The pluses and minuses of raising a baby.

▶ *"A Baby will make love stronger, days shorter, nights longer, bankroll smaller, home happier, clothes shabbier, the past forgotten, and the future worth living for."*

— Paul Dickson

"The best thing parents can spend on their children is...

▶ *time not money!"*

"Let thy child's first lesson be obedience.

▶ *And the second will be what wilt."*

— Benjamin Franklin

Do some parents suffer frustration in over indulging their children?

▶ *"Americans are like a rich father who wishes he knew how to give his sons the hardships that made him rich."*

— Robert Frost

Fantasy of a mother after her kid has given her a rough day.

▶ *"Mommy, are you sure this is the way to make pizza?"* *"Shut up, Junior, and get back into the oven."*

"There are many ways to abuse a child.

▶ *Doing nothing is one of them!"*

— Foster Parents Plan of Canada (1985)

"The trouble with the family is that children grow out of childhood but...

▶ *parents never grow out of parenthood."*

What will kids remember parents for?

▶ *"Kids won't remember if the house was all neat, but they will remember if you read them stories."*

Which category of people are least qualified to have children?

▶ *"Parents are the last people on earth who ought to have children."*

— Samuel Butler

How much should you give your child?

▶ *"A child, like your stomach, doesn't need all you can afford to give it."*

How many parents are there who are really qualified to be parents?

▶ *"Most of us become parents long before we have stopped being children."*

That which parents would sometimes like to say to themselves when their kids drive them to extraction.

▶ *"Avenge yourself! Live long enough to be a problem to your children."*

How "parents" should handle their kids!

▶ *"Take time out! Don't take it out on your kids"!*

"If you love your son, give him a whack every now and then.

▶ *If you hate him, cram him with dainties!"*

— Chinese proverb

How long does a child remain a parent's concern?

▶ *"The thing about having a baby is that thereafter you have it."*

"Often what a child learns over his father's knee is worth as much as...

▶ *what he learns at his mother's knee."*

What are we forgetting to give our children?

▶ *"We have been so anxious to give our children what we didn't have that we neglected to give them what we did have."*

How much should we spend on children?

▶ *"In bringing up children, spend on them half as much money and twice as much time."*

— Laurence J. Peter

Europeans' disrespect for North American parents in the rearing of children.

▶ *"The thing that impresses me most about North America is the way parents obey their children."*

— Edward, Duke of Windsor

How can a father best set an example of love?

▶ *"The most important thing a father can do for his children is to love their mother."*

— Theodore Hesburgh

"As a child, my family's menu consisted of two choices.

▶ *"Take it, or leave it."*

— Buddy Hackett

What kind of parents believe in heredity?

▶ *"Parents with intelligent children believe in heredity!"*

As the sultan said to his small boy — "Don't bother me.

▶ *Go and ask one of your mothers."!*

The difference between the help from a father and help from a son.

▶ *"When a father helps his son, both smile. But when a son must help his father, both cry."*

— Talmud

Take the initiative. Reduce the influence that clever advertising has upon far too many kids. And on too many adults too!

▶ *1. First teach your kids how to recognize useful and informative advertising. 2. Show how close-up shots exaggerate size.*
3. How come paid actors make out the food they taste is so delicious! 4. Don't literally believe the words "best," "fastest," "sweetest".
5. Watch for small print — "assembly required" — "batteries not included" — "parts sold separately."
6. Explain vague meanless words like "helps prevent tooth decay" — or "part" of a nutritional breakfast.
7. Let them hear you yell out loud and often at commercials with which you disagree. This eliminates "preaching" to kids.
8. Don't feel bad about saying NO "before" you go shopping — but with valid reasons.

• PARKINSON'S LAW •

The more time you have — the longer it takes you to do the job.

▶ *"Work expands so as to fill the time available for its completion."*

— Northcote Parkinson

• PARTNERS •

How your servant decides to become your partner.

▶ *"If you pay your servant badly, he will pay himself."*

"When two partners in a business always agree...

▶ *one of them is unnecessary."*

That which often happens to 50/50 partners when the other partner isn't looking.

▶ *"Forty for you, sixty for me And equal partners we will be."*

— Gerald Barzan

• PASSPORTS •

Your Passport Photo.

▶ *"If you really look like that — you aren't well enough to travel."*

• PATIENCE •

How patience and toil can bring reward.

▶ *"Everything cometh to him who waiteth So long as he who waiteth Worketh like hell While he waiteth!"*

"The quality of a Genius is...

▶ *a greater aptitude for patience."*

The man without patience suffers himself unnecessary stress.

▶ *"How poor are they who have not patience. What wound did ever heal but by degrees!"*

— William Shakespeare

The meaning patience takes when you're in a traffic jam.

▶ *"Patience means being able to idle your motor when you feel like stripping your gears."*

"The secret of patience is...

▶ *to do something else in the meantime."*

What can patience do for a mulberry leaf?

▶ *"With time and patience the mulberry leaf becomes a silk gown."*

— Chinese proverb

How Patience and Impatience can affect your life.

▶ *"One moment of patience may ward off a great disaster; one moment of impatience may ruin a whole life."*

Let nature teach you patience. ▸ *"Great Oaks from little Acorns grow."*

"Be not afraid of growing ▸ *"Be afraid only of standing still."*
slowly.
— Chinese proverb

"Patience is bitter but... ▸ *its fruit is sweet."*
— Henri Rousseau

"Patience is an infinite ▸ *for being bored."*
capacity...

Does everything come to him ▸ *"Everything comes to him who hustles*
who waits? *while he waits."*
— Thomas A. Edison

Prayer of the modern ▸ *"Dear God, I pray for patience. And*
American for patience. *I want it right now!"*

Patience — ▸ *"Being able to wait for the first*
coat of paint to dry before adding the
second."

"A 'watched pot' never boils. ▸ *It 'boils over' the*
minute you stop watching"!

• PATRIOTISM •

"My country, right or wrong ▸ *My mother, drunk or sober."*
is like saying...
— G.K. Chesterton

• PEACE •

Definition of what Peace is in ▸ *"Peace in international affairs is a*
international affairs. *period of cheating between two*
periods of fighting."
— Ambrose Bierce

How the world can achieve ▸ *"We have to make the peace*
peace. *industry more lucrative, more*
interesting, and more exciting
than the war industry. It's a
simple as that and if it's
not then we lose."
— Yoko Ono

• THE PEDESTRIAN •

"A pedestrian is an individual travelling slowly enough...

▶ *to read traffic signs."*

• PEOPLE •

"People who live in glass houses shouldn't throw stones."

▶ *"People who live in grass houses shouldn't get stoned!"*

"People who need people are the unluckiest people in the world.

▶ *People who enjoy people are the lucky ones."*

Are people really that much different from each other?

▶ *"People are much more alike inside than they are on the surface."*
— Verne Burnett

"The ugliest of trades have their moments.

▶ *Were I a grave digger, or perhaps a hangman, there are some people I could work for with a great deal of pleasure."*
— Douglas Jerrold

"People who live in glass houses are always looking for...

▶ *maids who will wash windows."*

"There are only two classes of people relating to character and personality.

▶ *First class and no class."*

Why you generally feel more at ease in the presence of three people than two people.

▶ *"With three or more people there is something bold in the air: direct things get said which would frighten two people alone and conscious of each inch of their nearness to one another. To be three is to be in public — you feel safe."*
— Elizabeth Bowen

There are three kinds of people who participate in events.

▶ *"Those who make things happen, Those who watch things happen, and Those who say 'what happened?'"*

"People who live in glass houses...

▶ shouldn't live within a stone's throw of one another."

The insignificance of most people.

▶ "Most people get public recognition only twice in their lives — their birth notice and their obituary."

What kind of people think they know themselves?

▶ "Only the shallow know themselves."

— Oscar Wilde

What percentage of people can you stand being with?

▶ "Nine-tenths of the people were created so you would want to be with the other tenth."

— Horace Walpole

Do people get into a rut and by-pass the many pleasurable things of life?

▶ "There are people who so arrange their lives that they feed themselves only on side dishes."

— José Ortega Y Gasset

"People who live in glass houses...

▶ shouldn't!"

"Safety First population surveys show...

▶ 90% of all people are caused by accidents!"

Why, when two people meet, do six people really meet?

▶ "Whenever two people meet there are really six people present. There is each man as he sees himself, each man as the other person see him, and each man as he really is."

— William James

• PERCEPTION •

How perception is warped by bias.

▶ "The man with a hammer perceives a world of nails."

"The closest to perfection a person ever comes is...

▶ when he fills out a job application form."

— Stanley J. Randall

• PERFORMANCE •

"People forget how fast you did a job but...

▸ *they remember how well you did it."*

If you want to perform well, remember the 5-P's.

▸ *"Proper; Preparation; Prevents; Poor; Performance."*

• PERSEVERE! •

"Fall seven times.

▸ *Stand up eight!"*

— Japanese proverb

Persevere! Reach for your goal and then you can ease up.

▸ *"Hit the ball over the fence and you can take your time going around the bases."*

— John W. Raper

Motto of Smokenders to quit smoking.

▸ *"Nothing in the world will take the place of perseverance.*
Talent will not: Nothing is more common than unsuccessful men with talent.
Genius will not: Unrewarded genius is almost a proverb.
Education will not: The world is full of educated derelicts.
Persistence and Determination alone are Omnipotent."

— Calvin Coolidge

Don't give up until things are beyond your control.

▸ *"Don't fall before you're pushed!"*

— English proverb

• PERSISTENCE •

Persistence generally gets results.

▸ *"A falling drop will carve a stone."*

— Lucretius

What is the most important thing a man must do to become a champion?

▸ *"Fight one more round!"*

— Jim Corbett

"Never give up.

▶ *The mighty oak was once a little nut that held its ground."*

— B. Barbara

• PERSONALITY •

"He has a split personality.

▶ *I can't stand either one of him!"*

He's a real sour puss!

▶ *"A February face, so full of frost, of storm and cloudiness."*

— William Shakespeare

Your basic personality doesn't change.

▶ *"Vultures don't become vegetarians!"*

"Personality is to man...

▶ *what perfume is to a flower."*

— Chales M. Schwab

The difference between being "Kinky" and being "Perverted".

▶ *"Someone who's Kinky uses a feather and someone who's perverted uses the whole chicken."*

"Consider how hard it is to change yourself...

▶ *and you'll understand what little chance you have trying to change others."*

How much does it cost to live if you have a split personality?

▶ *"A split personality is the only case where two can live as cheaply as one."*

A sour disposition.

▶ *"A sliver of lemon peel!"*

To a sour temperament.

▶ *"You're developing a very even temperament — always miserable!"*

Is our true personality ever truly revealed?

▶ *"All of us are freaks! Some of us are obvious. Some of us are freaks in private."*

• PERSPECTIVE •

Perspective from the standpoint of a mouse.

▶ *"A cat is a lion to a mouse."*

To go forward — what do you have to do to get a better perspective?

▶ *"You have to step backward, the better to jump forward."*

— French proverb

• PERSUADING •

How NOT to influence people.

▶ *"You cannot antagonize and influence at the same time."*

How to persuade in the most effective way.

▶ *"One catches more flies with a spoonful of honey than with 20 casks of vinegar."*

Force will not convince.

▶ *"You have not converted a man because you have silenced him."*

He's so persuasive!

▶ *"He could charm honey out of a hornet's nest"!*

"To be persuasive, we must be believable.

▶ *To be believable, we must be credible. To be credible, we must be truthful."*

— Edward R. Murrow

One fact stands out in bold relief in the history of man's attempts for betterment. That is that when compulsion is used, only resentment is aroused, and the end is not gained.

▶ *Only through moral suasion and appeal to man's reason can a movement succeed."*

—Samuel Gompers

Why Nazi Germany was able to be so persuasive.

▶ *"The object of oratory alone is not truth, but persuasion."*

— Thomas B. Macaulay

Your argument wasn't the least bit convincing!

▶ *"It was like trying to convince an eight-year-old that sexual intercourse is more fun than a chocolate ice cream cone."*

— Howard Gossage

"If you would persuade...

▶ *you must appeal to interest rather than intellect."*

— Benjamin Franklin

Which will persuade people more — Facts or Emotion?

▶ *"People don't ask for facts in making up their minds. They would rather have one good, soul-satisfying emotion than a dozen facts."*
— Robert Keith Leavitt

"It would be easier to endow a fool with intellect than...

▶ *to persuade him that he had none."*

Coerced persuasion won't work.

▶ *"A man convinced against his will Is of the same opinion still."*
— Samuel Buttler

All epoch-making revolutionary events have been produced not by the written but by...

▶ *the spoken word."*
— Adolf Hitler

• THE PESSIMIST •

"A pessimist is...

▶ *a person who not only believes the worst is going to happen — but that it's going to happen to him!"*

Why a pessimist feels good.

▶ *"A pessimist is one who feels good for fear he'll feel worse when he feels better."*

"A pessimist is...

▶ *one, who, of two evils, chooses both."*
— Oscar Wilde

The difference between an Optimist a Pessimist and a Realist.

▶ *"An Optimist looks at the world through rose-colored glasses, a Pessimist through dark sunglasses, and a Realist through bifocals."*

In what way does a Pessimist resemble an optimist?

▶ *"A pessimist is the eternal optimist always hoping for the worst."*

A pessimist's assessment of the state of the world.

▶ *"Worse than last year and better than next."*

"With all the misfortune in the world...

▶ *if the pessimists aren't happy now, they never will be."*

"He's such a pessimist that when he looks at a rainbow...

▶ *all he sees is black and white."*

"An optimist laughs to forget. ▶ *A pessimist forgets to laugh."*

A Calamity Jane. ▶ *"A prophet of Gloom, Doom and Despair."*

Pessimist — ▶ *"A guy who really knows what is going on."*

How a pessimist sees rain. ▶ *"He sees a droplet and imagines a flood."*

— Chinese proverb

Women's morality! ▶ *"A pessimist thinks all women are*
A pessimist's and an optimist's *immoral, and so does an optimist."*
views.

• THE PETER PRINCIPLE •

"In a hierarchy every ▶ *How Edmund Burke said it in 1782 —*
employee tends to rise to his *"All men that are ruined — are ruined*
level of incompetence." *on the side of their natural*
(Laurence J. Peter) *propensities."*

The Peter Principle in practice ▶ *"Socrates", a competent teacher who*
showing historic figures who *became his own lawyer.*
rose to their level of *"Nero", a musician who became an*
incompetence. *emperor.*
"Julius Caesar", a great general who
became a politician.
"Adolf Hitler", a master politician who
became a general.

• PHILOSOPHY •

Definiton of Philosophy — ▶ *"A system for being unhappy intelligently."*

The Hippie and drug ▶ *"You have to go out of your mind to*
philosophy of the 1960's. *use your head."*

— Timothy Leary

"The pursuit of wisdom by ▶ *if all philosophers were put*
intellectual means requires so *together in one room, enough hot*
much analysis and critique *air would be generated to drive*
that... *windmills from now to eternity."*

A reminder of how insignificant man is in trying to figure out what life and this universe is all about.

▶ *"It is good that a philosopher should remind himself, now and then, that he is a particle pontificating on infinity."*
— Will and Ariel Durant

"To be a philosopher is not merely to have subtle thoughts nor even to found a school.

▶ *It is to solve some of the problems of life not only theoretically but practically."*
— Henry David Thoreau

A great philosopher wrote: "I ought, therefore I can."

▶ *His name: "I. Kant"*

Hegel, the philosopher, said that whenever society is in favour of the status quo, (THESIS) other forces will be opposed. (ANTITHESIS)

▶ *As in physics, "For every action, there is an equal and opposite reaction".*
— Isaac Newton

New philosophy for the day.

▶ *"Dread only one day at a time!"*
— Charles M. Schulz

From Stephen W. Hawking's book — A Brief History of Time. "Few of us spend much time wondering why nature is the way it is. Most of us leave these questions to the experts.

▶ *We want to make sense of what we see and to ask: What is the nature of the universe? What is our place in it and where did it and we come from? Why is it the way it is?"*

• THE PHONY •

Guide to exposing the real phony.

▶ *As the saying in Hollywood goes — "Scratch beneath the phony tinsel and you'll find the real tinsel!"*
— Oscar Levant

She's a cold aloof phony.

▶ *"She's got the high-nosed aloofness of the human icicle."*

"If you're going to be a phony...

▶ *be sincere about it!"*
— James H. Boren

She's a real phony!

▶ *Speaking of Dame Edith Sitwell — "She's genuinely bogus."*
— Christopher Hassall

To the phony "holier than thou" accuser.

▶ "He that is without sin among you, let him first cast a stone."

— The Bible

To a phony who is trying to appear virtuous.

▶ "Every man is entitled to the defects of his virtues of which you have so many!"

Beware of the sugary insincere tongue that can also become a sharp sword.

▶ "The bee that has honey in her mouth has a sting in her tail."

— John Lyly

"As phony as...

▶ studio laughter."

Be a phony long enough and you'll become a real phony.

▶ "Wear a mask long enough and it becomes your real face."

Never get taken in by a theatrical display of tears and prayer.

▶ "My grandfather used to tell me that whenever you see a fellow go up to the mourners' bench and begin to pray out loud, you'd better go home and lock your smokehouse."

— President Harry S. Truman

• THE PICTURE •

In what way is a picture similar to and different from a poem?

▶ "A picture is a poem without words."

— Horace

• THE PIKER •

"The piker who knows how to get a free ride is one who has the ability...

▶ to keep talking while the other guy takes the check."

• PLAGIARISM •

"All work and no plagiarism makes...

▶ a dull speech."

The only difference between plagiarism and research is —

▶ "Footnotes."

Plagiarism —

▶ *"The sincerest form of larceny."*

Is plagiarism always
plagiarism?

▶ *"If you steal material from one source,
it's plagiarism. If it's from several
sources, it's research."*

— Wilson Mizner

• PLAN! •

Plan things so that the part
you enjoy most is not at the
beginning — but at the end.

▶ *"'Tis the dessert that graces all the
feast, for an ill end disparages
the rest."*

— William Shakespeare

"You seldom get what you go
after unless you know in
advance what you want.

▶ *"Indecision has often given an
advantage to the other fellow because
he did his thinking beforehand."*

— Maurice Switzer

The way to reach your target.

▶ *"If you aim for nothing — you'll surely
hit it!"*

Always have a backup plan!

▶ *"The mouse that has but one hole is
soon caught."*

— Arabian proverb

If you want to be safe, always
have a backup plan!

▶ *"When a mouse smiles at a cat, you
can be sure there's a hole nearby."*

Without an aim and a plan,
you'll never reach your target
or destination.

▶ *"Our plans miscarry because they
have no aim. When a man does not
know what harbor he is making for, no
wind is the right wind."*

— Seneca

How a realist anticipates.

▶ *"If everything is going well — get ready
to expect the unexpected."*

The flaw in planning for the
future.

▶ *"The future — that's the best thing
ever invented for ruining the present."*

— Brigitte Bardot

As ye sow, so shall you
reap.

▶ *"He that plants thorns
must never expect to gather
roses."*

Better know where you're going or else! ▸ *"If you don't know where you are going, you will probably end up somewhere else."*
— Laurence J. Peter

"Most people don't plan to fail. ▸ *They fail to plan."*

Put something away for a rainy day or else? ▸ *"He who will not economize will have to agonize."*
— Confucius

"Plan ahead. ▸ *It wasn't raining when Noah built the Ark."*

How a smart planner should not lay his plans. ▸ *"PLAN AHEA*
D

Where do the rewards of tomorrow lie? ▸ *"All the flowers of all the tomorrows are in the seeds of today and yesterday."*
— Chinese proverb

"When you don't know where you're going... ▸ *any gust of wind will take you there."*

How many of us really plan ahead? ▸ *"The most decisive actions of our life... are most often unconsidered actions."*
— Andre Gide

• PLASTIC SURGERY •

What you'd like to say to many a "Face Lift". ▸ *"You didn't pay for that plastic surgery, did you?"*
— Johnny Carson

• PLATONIC •

That which platonic is — ▸ *"Platonic is a tonic not associated with gin."*

• PLEASURE •

Too much of a good thing is — ▸ *"Wonderful!"*
— Mae West

"The greatest pleasure in life is... ▶ *doing what people say you cannot do."*

— Walter Bagehot

The true relationship of pleasure and pain in life. ▶ *"Pleasure is nothing else but the intermission of pain."*

— William Scott

"I've had a wonderful night but... ▶ *this is not it!"*

Which produces the more lasting pleasure — the intellect or the heart? ▶ *"The pleasures of the intellect are permanent, the pleasures of the heart are transitory."*

— Henry David Thoreau

• PLUMBERS •

Sign in a plumber's shop — ▶ *"Hope for the best but prepare for the Burst."*

"She was only a plumber's daughter but... ▶ *oh! Those fixtures!"*

"How come the outrageous price of $90.00 for only one tap of the hammer to fix my plumbing? I demand an explanation"! ▶ *"It was $1.00 for the tap — and $89.00 for knowing where to tap."*

As the plumber said during the poker game — ▶ *"In our game a FLUSH beats a FULL HOUSE."*

• POETRY •

A rhyme made of the alphabet and numerals. ▶ *"I often sit and medit8 Upon the scurvy trick of f8 That keeps me still a celib8 Oh, what a f8!"*

"Painting is silent poetry." What is poetry? ▶ *"Poetry is painting that speaks."*

— Simonides

Poetry is the attempt to describe the indescribable.

▶ *"Poetry is the impish attempt to paint the colour of the wind."*

— Maxwell Bodenheim

Poetry is often the fantasy and dream of the impossible.

▶ *"Poetry is the journal of a sea animal living on land, wanting to fly in the air."*

— Carl Sandburg

Is the writing of Free Verse really poetry?

▶ *"Writing free verse is like playing tennis with the net down."*

— Robert Frost

Is poetry a higher art form than prose?

▶ *"Prose": Words in their best order. "Poetry": The best words in the best order.*

— Samuel Taylor Coleridge

"Poetry is the music of thought...

▶ *conveyed to us in music of language."*

• POISE •

Is poise the ability to be at ease?

▶ *"Poise is the ability to be ill at ease inconspicuously!"*

• POLITENESS •

Why is Politeness better than logic?

▶ *"You can often persuade when you cannot convince."*

— H.W. Shaw

If somebody owes you something, make sure you collect it in kind.

▶ *"Do not take payment in politeness."*

• POLITICAL •

"It has been said that politics is the second oldest profession.

▶ *I have learned that it bears a striking resemblance to the first."*

— Ronald Reagan

The difference between a Politician and a Statesman.

▶ *"A politician thinks of the next election, a statesman of the next generation."*

How to hold on to political power.

▶ *"Deceit, hypocrisy, and perjury are necessary and excusable for the sake of holding on to political power."*
— Niccolo Machiavelli

What undesireable characteristic is associated with the profession of politics?

▶ *"You cannot adopt politics as a profession and remain honest."*
— Louis McHenry Howe

An aspiring politician first has to get into office to realize that his doom and gloom allegations of the country's condition turned out to be true.

▶ *"When we got into office, the thing that surprised me most was to find that things were just as bad as we'd been saying they were."*

— John F. Kennedy

The regretful Art that politics truly is in Western democracies.

▶ *"Politics is the art of survival!"*
— Dalton Pearson

What Cicero had to say about Politicians.

▶ *"Politicians are not born, they are excreted."*
— Cicero

"Give a politician some facts and...

▶ *he'll draw his own confusions."*

The tragic absence of truth in our political system.

▶ *"If you ever injected truth into politics you would have no politics."*
— Will Rogers

What an honest politician is.

▶ *"An honest politician is one who when he is bought will stay bought."*
— Simon Cameron

"Many politicians are in the habit of laying it down as a self-evident proposition that no people ought to be free till they are fit to use their freedom.

▶ *The maxim is worthy of the fool in the old story who resolved not to go into the water till he had learned to swim."*
— Thomas B. Macaulay

"Politics is a profession where the paths of glory lead where?

▶ *but to the gravy."*

"The radical invents the views." Later on what follows?

▶ *"When he has worn them out, the conservative adopts them."*
— Mark Twain

How crooked does a public man have to be — to be called crooked?

▶ *"No public man can be just a little crooked."*

— Herbert Hoover

That which people should be called who don't vote.

▶ *The word is IDIOT derived from idiotes, a classical Greek term meaning "citizens who took no part in public voting."*

• POLLUTION •

The fish in today's polluted lakes.

▶ *"It's all I can do these days to keep my head below water."*

The effect of pollution on planet Earth.

▶ *"They're proposing to change the name of the earth to Polluto."*

— Stephen Miller

• POPULATION •

The famous principle illustrating that population growth increases much faster than does the food supply.

▶ *Population 1 2 4 8 16 32 64 128 256*
Food Supply 1 2 3 4   5   6   7   8   9

— Thomas Robert Malthus

• PORNOGRAPHY •

The seven words most commonly used by censors covering pornography.

▶ *"Lecherous,*
Lewd,
Lustful,
Lubricious,
Licentious,
Libidinous,
Lascivious."

Why the law has difficulty deciding what obscenity is.

▶ *"One man's obscenity is another man's lyric."*

• POSSESSIONS •

Possessions mean responsibility. Are they all really worth keeping?

▶ *Philosophic question to ask: "What possessions do I have that cause more trouble and worry than they're worth?"*

There's a big advantage in not having everything!

▶ *"If you had everything, where would you put it"?*

— H.H. Thomson

• THE POSSIBLE AND IMPOSSIBLE •

Nothing is impossible.

▶ *"You can carry water in a fishnet if you wait till it freezes."*

"Nothing is impossible except...

▶ *some people."*

When you're given an impossible assignment —

▶ *"You might as well ask me to shovel smoke into the wind."*

How to tackle a seemingly impossible task.

▶ *"Inch by inch Anything's a cinch."*

A key to the impossible is to know how to avoid the pitfalls.

▶ *"The success of walking on water is to know where the stones are."*

Advice from Confucius to the man who says — "It's impossible!"

▶ *"Man who say it cannot be done should not interrupt man doing it."*

• POSTPONEMENT •

"Most men die at forty but...

▶ *are buried at seventy"!*

"When a man has not a good reason for doing a thing...

▶ *he has one good reason for letting it alone."*

— Walter Scott

"Don't put off till tomorrow what you can do today because...

▶ *if you enjoy it today, you can do it again tomorrow"!*

• THE POSTAGE STAMP •

About sticking a postage stamp onto a letter —

▶ *"Why is it that a stamp won't stick to a letter the way it sticks to another stamp?"*

• POTENTIALITY •

An appraisal of the Possible and the Impossible.

▶ *"If it's possible, it's been done. If it's impossible, it likely will be done."*

• POWER •

If "Power tends to corrupt"
what does absolute power do?

▶ *"Power tends to corrupt and absolute power corrupts absolutely."*
— Lord Acton

Machiavelli on how a
government can gain and keep
Power.

▶ *"Some things which seem to be virtuous would lead, if followed, to one's ruin and some others, which appear to be vices, would result in one's greater security and well-being."*
— Niccolo Machiavelli

Guide to the use of power.

▶ *"O! it is excellent/ To have a giant's strength, but it is tyrannous/ To use it like a giant."*
— William Shakespeare

Has anything else besides
money got power?

▶ *"Knowledge is power."*

— Francis Bacon

• PRAISE •

Praise servants, children and
people for something they
do well.

▶ *"A little sugar is better than a great deal of vinegar."*

The ingredient required when
handing out praise!

▶ *"Whenever you commend, add your reasons for doing so; it is this which distinguishes the approbation of a man of sense from the flattery of sycophants and admiration of fools."*

"Praise, like gold and
diamonds...

▶ *owes its value to its scarcity."*
— Samuel Johnson

Positive reinforcement is the
building up of a child's
confidence in his own abilities.

▶ *"Words of praise, indeed, are almost as necessary to warm a child into a congenial life as acts of kindness and affection."*
— Christian Bovee

On the wall of Joan River's
library —

▶ *"Don't expect praise without envy until you're dead."*

How potent is praise as against the use of other words?

▶ *"There is no verbal vitamin more potent than praise."*

— Frederick B. Harris

Why is praise like champagne?

▶ *"Praise is like champagne; it should be served while it is still bubbling."*

Praise —

▶ *"What you receive when you are no longer alive."*

"Praise not people to their faces, to the end that they may pay thee in the same coin.

▶ *This is so thin a cobweb that it may with little difficulty be seen through; it is rarely strong enough to catch flies of any considerable magnitude."*

"Why are engineers so lamentably cheated of praise? We know our Rembrants, our Wrens, our Henry Moores but...

▶ *who knows who actually erected the buildings and bridges, who cut the streets and installed the pipes and wires that make a city run?"*

• THE PRATTLER •

About the garrulous prattler —

▶ *"She is given to occasional flashes of silence that makes her conversation a pleasure."*

— Sydney Smith

What you'd like to say to the prattler.

▶ *"All the world loves a Leaver."*

It's the empty mind that prattles the loudest.

▶ *"As with narrow-necked bottles: the less in them, the more noise they make in pouring it out."*

— Jonathan Swift

It's over talking that unexpectedly makes trouble for you.

▶ *"It is a good answer which knows when to stop."*

— Italian proverb

"The more you talk...

▶ *the less people remember!"*

How beautiful when the prattler stops talking!

▶ *"That man's silence is wonderful to listen to."*

— Thomas Hardy

To a garrulous woman of beauty.

▶ *"She's a thing of beauty and a JAW forever."*

How to shorten a long winded story.

▶ *"My wife's method is wonderful for making a long story short. She interrupts!"*

"The empty prattler is generally beset with...

▶ *a diarrhea of words and a constipation of thought."*

When somebody's talk is so obnoxious that it makes you billious.

▶ *"Please — Somebody is eating!"*

• PRAYER •

The Serenity Prayer —

▶ *"God grant me the Serenity to accept the things I cannot change, Courage to change the things I can, And Wisdom to know the difference."*

— Reinhold Niebuhr

"The time to pray is not when we are in a tight spot but...

▶ *just as soon as we get out of it."*

— Josh Billings

If you are drowning, will prayer help?

▶ *"No man drowns if he perseveres in praying to God — and can swim."*

— Russian proverb

A Money Prayer —

▶ *"I only ask that Fortune send a little more than I can spend."*

— Oliver Wendell Holmes

Sign on bulletin board of church —

▶ *"If your trouble is deep-seated and of long standing, try kneeling."*

"O Lord help me to keep my big mouth shut until...

▶ *I know what I am talking about."*

Prayer on how to keep up with the Jones's.

▶ *"Stop my neighbors, please, O lord, From buying things I can't afford."*

— Tony Pettito

• PREGNANCY •

Science, Mathematics and Pregnancy.

▶ *"It is now quite lawful for a Catholic woman to avoid pregnancy by a resort to mathematics, though she is still forbidden to resort to physics and chemistry."*

— H.L. Mencken

• PREJUDICE •

"One thing I am NOT — is prejudiced...

▶ *In fact, there are two things I can't stand. One is prejudice. The other is foreigners."*

"There are only two ways to be quite unprejudiced and impartial.

▶ *One is to be completely ignorant. The other is to be completely indifferent. Bias and prejudice are attitudes to be kept in hand, not attitudes to be avoided."*

— Charles P. Curtis

Are there any people on this earth without prejudice?

▶ *"Everyone is a prisoner of his own experiences. No one can eliminate prejudices — just recognize them."*

— Edward R. Murrow

How Benny Goodman, the "King of Swing" explained his decision to break the color line by inviting Lionel Hampton, Teddy Wilson and other blacks into his band:

▶ *"If a guy's got it, let him give it. I'm selling music, not prejudice."*

As civilization advances, does prejudice diminish?

▶ *"Civilization is merely the re-arrangement of prejudices."*

Official Bigotry during the 1960's against Blacks seeking civil liberties.

▶ *"Why would we have different races if God meant us to be alike and associate with each other?"*

— Lester Maddox

Among what kind of individuals may you find least religious prejudice?

▶ *"Individuals having no religious affiliation show on the average less prejudice than do church members."*

— Gordon W. Allport

"I am free of all prejudices." ▸ *"I hate everyone equally!"*
How come?

— W.C. Fields

• BEING PREPARED •

"He's one of those guys who's ▸ *If it ever rains soup, he won't be caught*
always prepared. *off guard with forks."*

• PRESCRIBING •

"You're prescribing the ▸ *like prescribing castor oil to cure*
wrong cure... *diarrhea."*

• PREVENTION •

"An ounce of prevention is ▸ *"When you suspect you're going to be*
worth a pound of cure." *burned at the stake, act swiftly before*
the kindling can be gathered."

— Indian proverb

• THE PRICE! •

Guide to how much you ▸ *"It's unwise to pay too much, but it's*
should pay for something. *worse to pay too little. When you pay*
too much, you lose a little money —
that is all. When you pay too little, you
sometimes lose everything, because
the thing you bought was incapable of
doing the thing it was bought to do."

— John Ruskin

How do you arrive at the ▸ *"Everything is worth what*
true value of a thing? *its purchaser will pay for it."*

— Publilius Syrus

• PRIDE •

"Pride" (definition in the ▸ *"The acid test of whether it is a force*
Oxford Dictionary): *for good or ill in your life is whether you*
"Unduly high opinion of one's *have earned it. If you can honestly say*
own qualities, merits, etc.; *that you have, then you are entitled to*
arrogant bearing or conduct." *all the pride you can hold."*

"I'm so proud. ▸ *If I were a balloon I'd burst."*

• PRINCIPLES •

How do you maintain a lofty principle when it's not expedient to do so?

▸ *"You can't learn too soon that the most useful thing about a principle is that it can always be sacrificed to expediency."*

— Somerset Maugham

• PRIORITIES •

Should we always let first priorities take priority?

▸ *What if Columbus had been told, "Chris, baby, don't go now. Wait until we've solved our No. 1 Priorities — war and famine; poverty and crime; pollution and disease; illiteracy and racial hatred — and Queen Isabella's own brand of 'internal security'."*

— W.I.E. Gates

In what country would you prefer to be a man — a horse — a dog — or a woman?

▸ *"in England I would rather be a man, a horse, a dog or a woman, in that order. In America I think the order would be reversed."*

— Bruce Gould

• PRIVILEGES •

Don't give anybody too much privilege!

▸ *"Give a man an inch and he'll want to become a Ruler."*

• PRIZES •

Time worn contest jocularly insulting your home town.

▸ *"First prize" — one week in your home town.*
"Second prize" — two weeks in the same town.

• PROBABILITY •

There's as much chance of that happening as...

▸ *a fish has of perspiring."*

As improbable as...

▶ *sap from a totem pole."*

"As much chance as...

▶ *a battering ram has of erecting a temple."*

• PROBLEMS •

When you have a problem, first decide if it's worth solving!

▶ *"It takes just as much effort to solve a useless problem as a useful one."*
— C.F. Kettering

"There are no solutions to unknown problems if the problem is not identified.

▶ *The formulation of a problem is often more essential than its solution."*

— Albert Einstein

I can't find the answer to my problem!

▶ *"It's a riddle wrapped up in a mystery, inside an enigma."*

How to get down to the root of a problem.

▶ *"Cutting down a weed is not so good as uprooting it."*
— Selwyn G. Champion

If you want to rectify the problem, first ask the person who knows where the trouble lies.

▶ *"The wearer knows best where the shoe pinches."*
— Spanish proverb

Can anybody measure the degree of worry and stress of one family's problems as against those of another's?

▶ *"All happy families are alike, but unhappy ones are unhappy in their own way."*
— Leo Tolstoy

How to solve a problem.

▶ *"A problem well stated is a problem half solved."*

Does a problem ever get fully solved?

▶ *"Every problem has a solution and every solution creates another problem."*

• PROCRASTINATION •

"Never put off until tomorrow...

▶ *what you can avoid altogether."*

What to usually expect from the person who says — "I'll do it one of these days."

▶ *"One of these days is none of these days."*

"Nothing is so fatiguing as...

▶ *the eternal hanging on of an uncompleted task."*

— William James

"Procrastination is the fertilizer...

▶ *that makes difficulties grow."*

"The sooner you fall behind...

▶ *the more time you have to catch up."*

"Don't put off to tomorrow what you can do today because...

▶ *if you enjoy it today, you can do it again tomorrow."*

To the man who is going to do everything tomorrow.

▶ *"He slept beneath the moon, He basked beneath the sun; He lived a life of going-to-do, And died with nothing done."*

— J. Albery

"People who are habitually behind in their work...

▶ *are habitually behind success."*

— Samuel Smiles

What kind of fault is procrastination?

▶ *"Procrastination is a fault most people put off trying to correct."*

To the procrastinator who won't cross his bridge until he comes to it.

▶ *"You'll cross that bridge when you fall off it."*

"I never put off till tomorrow...

▶ *what I can possibly do — the day after."*

— Oscar Wilde

"He who talks and seldom acts...

▶ *sows the seeds of achievement on barren ground."*

"Study a problem long enough...

▶ *and it may go away."*

— James H. Boren

"Dreading and postponing a task... ▶ *may be more tiring than doing it, and apprehension over delayed unpleasantnesses may so preoccupy us that other things cannot be done effectively."*

"Never put off till tomorrow... ▶ *what you can get someone else to do for you today."*

Why you shouldn't put off a kind act until tomorrow. ▶ *"Defer not till to-morrow to be wise, To-morrow's sun to thee may never rise."*

— William Congreve

• PROFANITY AND CURSING •

"Profanity is... ▶ *the effort of a feeble mind to express itself forcibly."*

Ranting and cursing does serve a soul satisfying purpose. ▶ *"Many a man's profanity has saved him from a nervous breakdown."*

An Arabian curse. ▶ *"May all your teeth fall out except one — so you can have a toothache!"*

To curse and swear! ▶ *"To hurl vituperative epithets!"*

To somebody who has done you an unjustified injury or annoyance. ▶ *"All I can say is you deserve the headache that you just gave me."*

— Billie Martin

• PROMINENT •

"As prominent as... ▶ *a sore thumb on the Venus de Milo."*

• PROMISES •

A justificatoin for breaking your promise. ▶ *"Promises are like pie crusts. They're meant to be broken"*

• PROMOTION •

How to get promoted in an organization.

▶ *"Always remember that the soundest way to progress in any organization is to help the man ahead of you to get promoted."*

— L.S. Hamaker

• PROMPTNESS •

"Better late than never!"

▶ *"Better never late!"*

• PROPAGANDA •

"The secret about propaganda is...

▶ *NOT if it's true but if it works."*

— Adolph Hitler

How to make propaganda work.

▶ *"Simplify the message and repeat it every day — every day — every day!"*

— Joseph Goebbels

• PRUDENCE •

The prudent man knows when to yield.

▶ *"He who fights and runs away May live to fight another day. But he who is in battle slain, Can never rise to fight again."*

— Oliver Goldsmith

Don't court danger when you know the odds are heavily against you!

▶ *"He who has butter on his head should not walk in the sun."*

• PSYCHIATRY •

Today a great number of people go to a psychiatrist needlessly. It's the thing to do. It's fashionable!

▶ *"In California everyone goes to a therapist, is a therapist, or is a therapist going to a therapist."*

—Truman Capote

The question most frequently asked psychiatrists by patients. "Why do you just sit there without saying anything"?

▶ *The psychiatrist's most frequent reply. "What makes you ask"?*

Does a mixed up guy really have to go to a psychiatrist?

▶ *"Anybody who goes to see a psychiatrist ought to have his head examined."*
    — Samuel Goldwyn

Do we really need all that psychiatry?

▶ *"After going to the psychiatrist for a year and spending $20,000 I found out that if I had the $20,000 I spent, I wouldn't have needed all that psychiatry."*

The hysterical patient who kept screaming — "I'm a wigwam, I'm a tent! I'm a wigwam, I'm a tent"!

▶ *Psychiatrist: "Relax, relax. You're two tents."!*

History will reveal that...

▶ *psychiatry was the hoax of the twentieth century.*
    — Vladmir Nabokov

The manner in which many psychiatrists view their profession.

▶ *"If you laid all the psychiatrists end to end around the earth, it would be a good idea to leave them there."*

Psychiatrist to patient —

▶ *"You don't have an inferiority complex. You're simply inferior."*

Two executives meet at the door of their psychiatrist.

▶ *One said to the other. "Are you coming or going?" "If I knew that," said the other, "I wouldn't be here!"*

Psychiatrist to Arab sheik on couch —

▶ *Since when have you been having these recurring dreams about solar energy?"*

Psychiatrist to an incompatible couple —

▶ *"Frankly I don't think either of you would be compatible with anybody!"*

Psychiatrist to patient after examination —

▶ *"You're crazy."*
Patient: "I'd like a second opinion."
Psychiatrist: "You're ugly too."

— Henny Youngman

• PUNCTUALITY •

"The trouble with being punctual is...

▶ *that nobody's there to appreciate it."*

— Franklin P. Jones

• PUNCTUATION •

The importance of a period in a telegram!
"Not getting any better. Come home."

▶ *"Not getting any. Better come home."*

• THE PURITANS •

"The objection to Puritans is not that they try to make us think as they do but...

▶ *that they try to make us do as they think."*

— H.L. Mencken

• LIFE'S "PURPOSE"! •

Is there anything on this earth that hasn't got a use or a purpose?

▶ *"If heaven made him, earth can find some use for him."*

— Chinese proverb

Q

• QUALITY •

The Law of Quality —

▸ *"If it's good, they'll soon stop making it."*

• QUARRELING •

When you argue, speak your mind! Listen to criticism but avoid hasty judgment.

▸ *"Beware of entrance to a quarrel, but, being in,*
Bear 't that the opposed may beware of thee.
Give every man thine ear, but few thy voice;
Take each man's censure, but reserve thy judgement."

Wiliam Shakespeare

"In lovers' quarrels, the party that loves most is...

▸ *always most willing to acknowledge the greater fault."*

— Sir Walter Scott

• QUIETNESS •

"As quiet as...

▸ *a crowded elevator."*

• QUOTATIONS AND PROVERBS •

A Proverb or Saying (the Adage of the ancients) is a terse pithy proposition current among all classes, relating to worldly wisdom as well as moral truth.

▶ *Example:*
"A word to the wise is sufficient."

A Maxim is a brief proposition teaching a moral truth or rule of conduct with practical application.

▶ *Example:*
"Forgiveness is the noblest revenge."

An Aphorism is a speculative rather than practical proposition embodying a doctrine or the principles of a science.

▶ *Example:*
"Originality in Art is the individualizing of the universal."

A Saw is a vulgar proverb.

▶ *Example:*
"A nod is as good as a wink to a blind horse."

An Adage is a proverb of the ancients which has obtained credit by long use.

▶ *Example:*
"Good news doeth good like medicine."

"A proverb is...

▶ *a short sentence based on long experience."*
— Miguel de Cervantes

"Maxims are...

▶ *the condensed cream of wisdom."*

Are all maxims, proverbs and quotations absolute truths?

▶ *"All maxims have their antagonist maxims; proverbs should be sold in pairs, a single one being but a half truth."*
— William Matthews

"The wisdom of the wise and the experience of the ages...

▶ *are perpetuated by quotations."*
— Benjamin Disraeli

"Proverbs are mental gems gathered...

▶ *in the diamond districts of the mind."*
— W.R. Alger

"The study of proverbs may be more instructive and comprehensive than...

▶ *the most elaborate scheme of philosophy."*

— William Motherwell

Which writer gets the final credit for "originating" a proverb?

▶ *"Though old the thought and oft exprest,*
'Tis his at last who says it best."

— James Russell Lowell

Some entries in this book can serve as a refreshing re-discovery.

▶ *"I suppose every scholar has had the experience of reading something in a book which was significant to him, but which he could never find again. Sure he is that he read it there; but no one else ever read it, nor can he find it again."*

— Ralph Waldo Emerson

"By necessity, by proclivity, and by delight, we all quote but...

▶ *most of us misquote"!*

— Ralph Waldo Emerson

"There are many famous, sometimes brilliant and often very great quotations attributed to notable persons,...

▶ *which though false or incorrect, are usually improvements by anonymous requoters."*

— George Seldes

"We never read without profit if with the pen or pencil in our hand,...

▶ *we mark such ideas as strike us by their novelty, or correct those we already possess."*

"Proverbs are in the world of thought what gold coin is in the world of business — Great value in small compass, and equally current among all people. Sometimes the proverb may be false, the coin counterfeit, but in both cases the false proves the value of the true." — D March

▶ *"A country can be judged by the quality of its proverbs."*

— German Proverb

Using an apt quote adds sparkle to what you have to say.

▶ *"I quote others only the better to express myself."*

— Michel de Montaigne

A good way for an uneducated man to become educated.

▶ *"It is a good thing for an uneducated man to read books of quotations."*
— Winston Churchill

Why do we like to quote quotations?

▶ *"By necessity, by proclivity — and by delight, we all quote."*
— Ralph Waldo Emerson

Even if you're not the first who quotes —
"He who quotes will get quoted."

▶ *"Next to the originator of a good sentence is the first quoter of it."*
— Ralph Waldo Emerson

When to use a Quote.

▶ *"When a thing has been said and said well, have no scruple. Take it and copy it."*
— Anatole France

Does it really matter if you can't remember who originated the quotation?

▶ *"If it is the truth what does it matter who said it?"*

The truth that is embodied in most proverbs!

▶ *"I am of opinion that there is no proverb which is not true, because they are all sentences drawn from experience itself, the mother of all the sciences.*
— Cervantes

Do you necessarily have to agree with the meaning of every quotation?

▶ *"Almost every wise saying has an opposite one, no less wise, to balance it."*
— George Santayana

"Next to being witty yourself, the next best thing is...

▶ *being able to quote another's wit."*

When the freshman was asked his opinion of the "bard."

▶ *"I don't see why people make such a fuss over Shakespeare. All he did was bring together a bunch of old well-known quotations"!*

R

• RAGE •

"I feel like Houdini. ▶ *I'm fit to be tied.*"

• RAIN •

"There's been no rain and it's ▶ *the trees are chasing the dogs.*"
so dry that...

How an umbrella defines rain. ▶ *"Something that when you take your umbrella — it doesn't."*

• THE RAT RACE! •

If you've let yourself get ▶ *"A rat race can only be won by a rat."*
sucked into the "Rat-Race"
remember —

"Just when you think you've ▶ *they come up with faster rats.*"
got the rat-race licked...

— David Lee Roth

• READING •

"Reading to the mind is... ▶ *what exercise is to the body.*"

— Addison

Should you believe every-
thing you read?

▶ *"Believe half of what you read
but be brilliant enough to know
which half."*

— Talmud

"The art of reading is...

▶ *to skip judiciously."*

"When it comes to reading,
the man who does not read
good books...

▶ *has no advantage over the man who
can't read them."*

— Mark Twain

"Reading without reflecting
is like...

▶ *eating without digesting."*

"When you have the privilege
of reading trash or good
literature...

▶ *will you go and gossip with your
housemaid or your stableboy, when
you may talk with queens and kings?"*

— John Ruskin

• BEING REALISTIC! •

As Eve said to Adam —

▶ *"Half a leaf is better than none."*

"A bird in the hand is better
than...

▶ *one over head."*

You can't make something
into what it's NOT.

▶ *"Whether you boil snow or pound it,
you will have nothing but water
from it."*

Eskimo's version of "Don't
count your chickens before
they hatch!"

▶ *"Don't sell the bearskin before you
catch the bear!"
"Don't shout Dinner before your Knife
is in the Venison!"*

• REBELLION •

"Rebellion to tyrants is...

▶ *obedience to God."*

— Motto of Thomas Jefferson

• RECOGNITION •

A grateful comment on acceptance of an Honorary Award received from his peers, 1985 Emmy Awards.

▶ *"The only award worth anything is praise from workers who work at the same bench."*

— Alistair Cook

"When things go right...

▶ *nobody notices."*

"The world is divided into people who do things and...

▶ *people who get the credit."*

— Dwight Morrow

People need recognition.

▶ *"The most agreeable recompense we can receive for things which we have done is to see them known, and to have them applauded."*

— Moliére

• RECONSIDERING •

What is — To Reconsider a decision you've already made?

▶ *"To reconsider is to seek a justification for a decision already made."*

— Ambrose Bierce

• RECTIFYING! •

When somebody makes a Mess, somebody else steps in to set it in order.

▶ *"Action expands to fill the void created by human failure!"*

— C. Northcote Parkinson

• REFRESHING! •

"As refreshing as...

▶ *rain to a fading rose."*

• HUMAN "RELATIONS" •

How to make people like you.

▶ *"Those whom you can make like themselves better will, I promise you, like you very well."*

— Lord Chesterfield

"Today the most useful person in the world is the man or woman who knows how to get along with other people.

▶ *Human relations is the most important science in the broad curriculum of living."*
— Stanley C. Allyn

The test of a beautiful relationship is...

▶ *when you reach home, you know that on the other side of the doorstep, somebody is listening."*
— Clark Gable

It is not good that man should live alone.

▶ *"Therefore shall a man leave his father and mother and shall cleave unto his wife, and they shall be one flesh."*
— The Bible

What is woman's greatest sin when a man wants her or doesn't want her?

▶ *"Failing to be there when a man wants her is woman's greatest sin, except to be there when he doesn't want her."*
— Helen Rowland

How to win and nurture a relationship.

▶ *"Promise her the moon. Give her the sun!"*

It's those endless trivial fights that destroy a relationship.

▶ *"It is the fine rain which drenches."*
— French proverb

That which husband and wife — or playmates — should try to practice.

▶ 1. *"Never part for a day without loving words to think of during absence!*
2. *Never meet without a loving welcome!*
3. *Never let the sun go down upon any anger!"*

"A major joy in life is to have...

▶ *a human relationship with another human being — either in love or in friendship."*

Beware of two people becoming one!

▶ *"In any relationship in which two people become one — the end result is two half people."*

How much should two persons in a relationship be together?

▶ *"Let there be spaces in your togetherness."*
— Kahlil Gibran

A relationbship doesn't work for you. Why?

▶ *"You have to work for the relationship."*

A love note after three years of separation.

▶ *"I'm so miserable without you. It's just like having you around."*

• RELATIVES •

"Distant Relatives are the best kind...

▶ *the further the better."*

• RELATIVITY •

What relativity is.

▶ *"When you sit with a nice girl for two hours, you think it's only a minute. But when you sit on a hot stove for a minute, you think it's two hours. That's relativity."*

— Albert Einstein

• RELAXING •

"The time to relax is...

▶ *when you don't have time for it."*

I like relaxing in a bathtub. I stay there for hours.

▶ *Sometimes I even fill it with water."*

• RELIGION •

"True religion is the life we live but...

▶ *is not the creed we profess."*

— J.F. Wright

"All the high religions — — Christianity, Judaism, Buddhism, Islam, Taoism — exalt the same principles."

▶ *"They point to love and brotherhood as the path to the good life, both for individuals and for society."*

— A.P. Davies

A letter sent to the congregation soliciting donations titled — "A Sermon on the Amount".

▶ *"Render unto Caesar that which is Caesar's and unto God that which is God's — but remember that that which you render unto God is deductible."*

Man, by nature, will always give birth to a religion of one kind or another.

▶ *"Men are idolaters, and want something to look at and kiss and hug, or throw themselves down before; they always did, they always will, and if you don't make it of wood, you must make it of words."*

— Oliver Wendell Holmes

The incredible variety of religions that mankind creates.

▶ *"Man is stark mad; he cannot make a flea, and yet he will be making gods by the dozens."*

— Michel de Montaigne

Comments on the Holy Roman Empire.

▶ *"The Holy Roman Empire is neither holy, Roman, nor an empire."*

— Voltaire

"My theology is a simple muddle. I cannot look at the universe as the result of blind chance, yet I can see no evidence of beneficent design, or indeed of design of any kind, in the details.

▶ *As for each variation that has ever occurred having been preordained for a special end, I can no more believe in it than that the spot on which each drop of rain falls has been specially ordained."*

— Charles Darwin

Ambrose Bierce's definition of religion.

▶ *Religion: "A daughter of Hope and Fear, explaining to Ignorance the nature of the Unknowable."*

— Ambrose Bierce

The kind of religion to be deplored.

▶ *"I want nothing to do with any religion concerned with keeping the masses satisfied to live in hunger, filth and ignorance."*

— Jawaharlal Nehru

"Christianity is...

▶ *the highest perfection of humanity."*

— Samuel Johnson

Preacher to visiting preacher!

▶ *"Preach loud because the agnostics in this church are not good."*

"For Shakespeare, in the matter of religion, the choice lay between Christianity and nothing.

▶ *He chose nothing."*

— George Santayana

"If we were as truly religious as we sound, we'd be getting rid of...

▶ *poverty in this nation. There would be no homeless."*

— George Gallup

Is superstition a religion?

▶ *"Superstition is a religion of feeble minds."*

— Edmund Burke

"If men are so wicked with religion...

▶ *What would they be without it?"*

— Benjamin Franklin

Mankind has invented an almost infinite variety of religions.

▶ *"It has been well said that as the prism exhibits the various colors contained in light, so mankind displays the various forms and shades of religion."*

Should science be without religion — and vice versa?

▶ *"Science without religion is lame, religion without science is blind."*

— Albert Einstein

Sign in church —

▶ *"Support your Church — Play Bingo"*

"Men will wrangle for religion; write for it; fight for it; die for it; anything but...

▶ *live it."*

Sign on church bulletin board —

▶ *"Start living to beat hell!"*

"Americans are assenters rather than believers. They assent to faith, to the beliefs in which one is meant to believe, but...

▶ *they don't necessarily believe them."*

— George Gallup

Can the Devil cite scripture in any religion to serve his purpose?

▶ *"There are scores of thousands of sects who are ready at a moment's notice to reveal the will of God on every possible subject."*

— George Bernard Shaw

Thomas Edison's view on religion.

▶ *"So far as religion of the day is concerned, it is a damned fake... Religion is all bunk."*

— Thomas Alva Edison

"When the white man came, we had the land and they had the bibles.

▶ *Now they have the land and we have the bibles."*

— Chief Dan George

Why you can't change one's beliefs! "For those who believe, no explanation is necessary.

▶ *For those who don't believe no explanation is possible."*

"Whatever I could do to make the ministers' job easier, I did.

▶ *They represented God, and I loved God so much."*

— Jessica Hahn

Bob Hope's views on religion.

▶ *"I go to the Catholic Church, the Jewish Synagogue and the Protestant Church! I don't want to miss out getting into Heaven on a technicality."*

• NON "REMEDIABLE"! •

"What can't be cured...

▶ *must be endured!"*

• REPARTEE •

A rhyming definition of repartee.

▶ *"What a person thinks of after he becomes a departee."*

— Dan Bennett

"As an Ad Libber...

▶ *he couldn't even belch after a Hungarian dinner."*

The repartee you wish you had made!

▶ *"The clever reply you think up on your way home."*

Why I'm stuck for a reply.

▶ *"I have a coat hanger stuck in my throat."*

The most admired kind of repartee —

▶ *"Any reply so clever that it makes you wish you had said it yourself."*

— Elbert Hubbard

What's the worst kind of repartee?

▶ *"Silence is the unbearable repartee."*

— G.K. Chesterton

• REPENTING •

What's the best part of asking Forgiveness for past sins?

▸ *"The sinning is the best part of repentance."*

— Arabic proverb

• REPUTATION •

Reputation —

▸ *"What others are NOT thinking of you."*

— Tom Masson

"A man's reputation is not in his own keeping, but lies at the mercy of the profligacy of others. Calumny requires no proof.

▸ *To create an unfavorable impression, it is not necessary that certain things should be true, but that they have been said. The imagination is of so delicate a texture that even words wound it."*

— William Hazlitt

Is it better to be a bum associating with good people — than being a bum among bums?

▸ *"Associate yourself with men of good quality if you esteem your own reputation; for 'tis better to be alone than in bad company."*

— George Washington

That which a man is known by.

▸ *"In our society a man is known by the company he owns."*

— Gerald F. Lieberman

"By the Company you keep, so shall you be known."

▸ *"He who gets into a hole with a skunk comes up stinking!"*
How Arabia says it:
"He who introduces himself between the onion and the peel does not go forth without its strong smell."

"Many men and many women enjoy popular esteem, not because they are known but...

▸ *because they are not!"*

How to enjoy a good reputation.

▸ *"Give publicly, and steal privately!"*

— Josh Billings

It isn't what they say about you.

▶ *It's what they whisper."*

— Errol Flynn

History rewrites the reputation of famous men.

▶ *"All reputations each age revises. Very few immutable men has history to show."*

— Ralph Waldo Emerson

• REPUTATION OR CHARACTER •

"The circumstances amid which you live determine your reputation.

▶ *What you believe determines your character."*

"Reputation is what you are known to be.

▶ *Character is what you are."*

"Reputation is a manufactured thing, rolled and plated and hammered and brazed and bolted.

▶ *Character is a growth."*

"Reputation comes over one from without.

▶ *Character grows up from within."*

"Reputation is what you have when you come to a new community.

▶ *Character is what you have when you go away."*

"Your reputation may be learned in an hour.

▶ *Your character may not come to light for a year."*

"If you want a position, you need a reputation.

▶ *If you want to keep it, you need character."*

"Reputation makes you rich or makes you poor.

▶ *Character makes you happy or makes you miserable."*

"Reputation will get a man to the top of the ladder.

▶ *But only character will keep him from falling off."*

• RESEARCH •

Guide on when NOT to do research.

▶ *"If a research project is not worth doing at all, it is not worth doing well."*

• RESPECT •

To what degree do most men respect themselves?

▶ *"In his private heart no man much respects himself."*
— Mark Twain

"The way to procure insults is to submit to them.

▶ *A man meets with no more respect than he exacts."*
— William Hazlitt

• RESTAURANTS •

Sign in restaurant just before the Xmas season —

▶ *"Eat now and avoid the holiday rush!"*

Impatiently waiting for a table in a restaurant.

▶ *"If they weren't so crowded here all the time, they'd do a lot more business."*

Sign in a restaurant —

▶ *"Please pay IF served!"*

Sign in a Jewish snack bar —

▶ *"Protect your Bagles, put Lox on them."*

Q. What begins with T, ends with T and is full of T?

▶ *A. "A teapot."*

Sign in Italian restaurant —

▶ *"We offer you pizza and quiet."*
— Bennett Cerf

Complaint by customer to waiter!

▶ *"If this is coffee, I want tea; but if this is tea, then I want coffee."*

Sign in a cafeteria —

▶ *"Courteous and efficient self-service."*

Sign in Chinese Restaurant —

▶ *"You ask credit
I no give
You get mad.
I give credit
You no pay
I get mad.
Better you get mad!"*

Telling the waiter you want your food served hot.

▶ *"I want it so hot that if you can carry it to the table, I don't want it!"*

Sign in Shakey's Pizza
Parlor —

▶ *"Shakey made a deal with the bank.
Shakey doesn't cash checks.
The bank doesn't make pizza."*

"Nobody goes to that
restaurant any more.

▶ *There's too many line-ups!"*

— Yogi Berra

• RESULTS •

"The man who gets the most
satisfactory results is not
always the man with the most
brilliant single mind but...

▶ *rather the man who can best
co-ordinate the brains and talents of
his associates."*

— W. Alton Jones

What counts — Reasons or
Results?

▶ *"You can only have two things in life,
Reasons and Results, Reasons don't
count."*

"Men, like bullets, go
farthest when...

▶ *they are smoothest"!*

— Jean Paul Richter

You'll never get results
that way!

▶ *"That's like teaspooning water
out of the ocean!"*

• RETAILING •

Sign on retail shop —

▶ *"Business not going on as usual during
alterations!"*

Sign in shoe store —

▶ *"Wherever you go, wear good shoes.
Remember, they always follow you!"*

Sign on Suburban Shop
door —

▶ *"Out to Lunch. If not back by five,
out to dinner also."*

"Don't be afraid to throw
yourself on the mercy of the
salesclerks. That's why they're
there — if...

▶ *you can find them"!*

Sign in an expensive
boutique —

▶ *"If you can't find it — be grateful!"*

Sign in fruit
store —

▶ *"Don't squeeze me until I am yours!"*

Sign on store window — ▶ *"If we don't have it, you don't need it!"*

• RETALIATION •

"The only people to get even with are... ▶ *those who have helped you."*

• RETIRED •

What's the word "retired" got to do with being tired? ▶ *"Retired is being tired twice, I've thought, First tired of working, Then tired of not."*

— Richard Armour

• RETIREMENT •

"Retirement is... ▶ *the ugliest word in the language."*

— Ernest Hemingway

Which NON merriment does retirement bring? ▶ *"Retirement takes all the fun out of Saturdays!"*

To retire is the beginning of — ▶ *"Death."*

— Pablo Casals

When older people retire, do they ever really do all the things they dream of doing? ▶ *"Retirement is the time when you never do all the things you intended to do when you'd have the time."*

— Laurence J. Peter

• REVENGE •

"If an injury has to be done to a man... ▶ *it should be so severe that his vengeance need not be feared."*

— Niccolo Machiavelli

How to really get even. ▶ *"Success is the best revenge."*

— French proverb

• RHETORIC •

The well turned phrase is what gives a thought its sparkle. ▶ *"All the fun's in how you say a thing."*

— Robert Frost

Speaking of punctuation, remember — "That that is is that that is not is not is that it it is." ▶ *When it is punctuated it becomes: "That that is, is. That that is not, is not. Is that it? It is."*

• THE RICH AND THE POOR •

In the long run — to be rich becomes meaningless! ▶ *"If thou art rich, thou art poor For like an ass whose back with ingots bows Thou bearest thy riches but a journey And death unloads thee."*

— William Shakespeare

"It doesn't matter if you're rich or poor... ▶ *as long as you have money."*

— Joe E. Lewis

"God shows his contempt for wealth by... ▶ *choosing the nouveaux riches to give it to."*

"Not what we have, but what we enjoy... ▶ *constitutes our abundance."*

— J. Petit-Senn

Is a full purse everything? ▶ *"It isn't that a full purse is so good. It's that an empty one is so bad!"*

— Talmud

Do rich men ever have enough money? ▶ *"If all the rich men in the world divided up their money amongst themselves, there wouldn't be enough to go around."*

— Jules Bertillon

"The only thing I like about rich people is... ▶ *their money!"*

— Lady Astor

"The haves have the better food,... ▶ *the have-nots the better appetite."*

The penalty of being rich. ▶ *"It is the wretchedness of being rich that you have to live with rich people."*

— Logan Pearsall Smith

"It is better to live rich than... ▶ *to die rich."*

— Samuel Johnson

The rich are primarily concerned with wasteful expenditures in order to impress others with their material wealth. ▶ *They busy themselves with "conspicuous consumption."*

— Thorstein Veblen

The reason some people are stingy... ▶ *is also the reason they are rich."*

"If the rich could hire other people to die for them... ▶ *the poor could make a wonderful living!"*

"Poverty must have many satisfactions." Why? ▶ *"Else there would not be so many poor people."*

— Don Herold

The unfairness of how society treats the rich and the poor. ▶ *"When the rich falls, it is an accident; when the poor falls, he is called drunk."*

— Turkish proverb

"I've been rich and I've been poor. I've found out that... ▶ *rich is better!"*

— Sophie Tucker

"If you want to know how rich you really are... ▶ *find out what would be left of you tomorrow if you should lose every dollar you own tonight!"*

— William J.H. Boetcker

What's worse than not being rich now? ▶ *"It is more pitiable once to have been rich than not to be rich now."*

— J. Petit-Senn

How NOT to get rich. ▶ *"You can't spend yourself rich any more than you can drink yourself sober."*

— Herman E. Talmadge

What's better than being NOT rich?

▶ *"Nouveau is better than no riche at all."*

— On the wall of Joan River's library

"Many speak the truth when they say that they despise riches, but what kind?

▶ *"They mean the riches possessed by other men."*

— Charles Caleb Colton

Are most people of wealth necessarily happy?

▶ *"Before we set our hearts too much upon anything, let us examine how happy they are, who already possess it."*

— La Rochefoucauld

The hazard of getting too rich.

▶ *"Prosperity makes few friends!"*

— French proverb

• RIDDLES •

"Riddle" (definition)

▶ *"A question or statement intentionally worded in a dark or puzzling manner, and propounded in order that it may be guessed or answered, especially as a form of pastime; an enigma, a dark saying."*

— Oxford English Dictionary

Answers to the following riddles appear on page 347

1. "The beginning of
    eternity,
   The end of time and space,
   The beginning of every end,
   And the end of
    every place."

2. "In marble walls as white
    as milk,
   Lined with a skin as soft as silk;
   Within a fountain crystal clear,
   A golden apple doth appear.
   No doors there are to
    this stronghold
   Yet thieves break in and
    steal the gold."

3. "What has a head like a
   cat, feet like a cat, tail like a
   cat, but is not a cat?"

4. "I died without being born
   And married my father when I
    was only a day old,
   Yet I never had a mother.
   Who am I?"

5. "I am a poor iron knight,
   I have no arms but always
      point right.
   I have no feet but I must
      always go.
   And must stand on duty
      both day and night
      through.
   If ever I rest, all will
      complain."

6. "What is it that goes on four
   legs in the morning, two
   at noon and three legs in
   the evening?"

7. "What goes out but
   never comes back?"

8. "Black I am and much
      admired,
   Men seek me until they're
      tired;
   When they find me, break
      my head,
   And take me from my resting
      bed."

9. "When one does not
   know what it is, then it is
   something; but when one
   knows what it is, then it is
   nothing."

10. "I never was, am always to be,
    None ever saw me, nor ever
       will,
    And yet I am the confidence
       of all
    Who live and breathe on this
    terrestrial ball."

11. "I am sitting above a horse
    which was not born, whose
    mother I hold in my hand."

12. "What has a neck but
    no head?"

13. "What comes once in a
    minute, twice in a moment,
    but not once in a thousand
    years?"

14. "A riddle, a riddle, as
       I suppose;
    A hundred eyes and never
    a nose."

15. "Use me well and I am
       everybody;
    Scratch my back and I am
       nobody."

16. "Lives in winter,
    Dies in summer,
    And grows with its root
       upwards."

17. "What belongs to you,
    But others use it more than
    you do?"

18. "What is it that you can keep
    after giving it to someone
    else?"

19. "There are two splendid horses, one black as pitch, the other of shining crystal; each runs ahead of the other but never catches it."

20. "He who has it doesn't tell it; He who takes it doesn't know it; He who knows it doesn't want it."

21. "What fastens two people yet touches only one?"

22. "A red maiden is sitting in a green summerhouse, If you squeeze her she will cry And her tears they are as red as blood, But yet her heart is made of stone."

Answers to "Riddles" from pages 345 & 346

1. The letter "E"

2. Egg

3. Kitten

4. Eve

5. Clock

6. Life cycle of man. (3 legs mean 2 legs and a cane)

7. Breath

8. Coal

9. Riddle

10. Tomorrow

11. Horse drawn by a pencil

12. Bottle

13. The letter "M"

14. Potato

15. Mirror

16. Icicle

17. Your name

18. Your word

19. Day and night

20. Counterfeit money

21. Wedding ring

22. Cherry

• YOUR RIGHTS •

The guy who speaks up is the guy who gets the attention.

▶ "The baby that does not cry will not get the breast."

— Turkish proverb

| What is one of the greatest rights in the world? | ▶ *"The greatest right in the world is the right to be wrong."* |

• RIGHT AND WRONG •

"When I am right, no one remembers.	▶ *When I am wrong no one forgets!"*
To the fellow who was satisfied with being almost right.	▶ *"You can't be just a little pregnant, dead, or right!"*
Is settling for half right good enough?	▶ *"Half right is always half wrong."*

• RISK! •

Take chances too often and you court disaster!	▶ *How it is said in Arabia: "The pitcher that goes to the well often enough gets broken at last."* *"The camel that travels often to Mecca will return lame at last."*
"Don't be afraid to go out on a limb.	▶ *That's where the fruit is."*
Beware! Great risk doesn't always pay off!	▶ *That's a valiant flea that dares eat his breakfast on the lip of a lion.* — William Shakespeare
"Take calculated risks.	▶ *That is quite different from being rash."* — George S. Patton

• ROYAL COMMISSIONS •

| Do Royal Commissions sometimes serve a purpose? | ▶ *"If Moses had been a Royal Commission, the Israelites would still be in Egypt."* |

• RUMOUR •

"If you haven't heard a good rumour by 10 a.m.... ▶ *start one!"*

• THE RUSH! •

"If they try to rush me, I always say...

▶ *I've only got one other speed — and it's slower."*

— Glenn Ford

What causes the rush — and what causes the delay when you have something to do?

▶ *"The reason for the rush is the delay. And the reason for the delay is the rush."*

• THE RUT! •

A rut versus a grave.

▶ *"The only difference between a rut and a grave is dimensions."*

"A Rut is...

▶ *a small grave."*

• RUTHLESSNESS •

"When you're trying to get something done, don't worry too much about stepping on someone else's toes.

▶ *Nobody gets his toes stepped on unless he is standing still or sitting down on the job."*

S

• SADISTS •

Who are sadists kind to?

▶ *"A sadist is a person who is kind to masochists."*

— Vincent McHugh

• PLAYING IT "SAFE"! •

How people of Turkey would say — "A bird in the hand is worth two in the bush."

▶ *"Better a sparrow today, than a goose tomorrow."*

— Turkish proverb

• THE SALESMAN •

The versatility needed to be a salesman.

▶ *"He who works with his hands is a laborer. He who works with his hands and his head is a craftsman. He who works with his hands, head and heart is an artist. He who works with his hands and his head and his heart and his feet is a salesman."*

"Only a salesman who sells headstones knows that he has a permanent customer.

▶ *The rest of us salesmen have to keep our customers alive."*

"The salesman should not be ashamed of his calling, but...

▶ *rather of his not calling."*

What do mediocre salesmen always overlook?	▶ *"Successful salemanship is 90% preparation and 10% presentation."* — Bertrand R. Canfield
The superficial and tragic facade of an old salesman.	▶ *"He's a man out there in the blue, ridin' on a smile and shoeshine ... a salesman has got to dream, boys."* — Arthur Miller
An important reminder to salesmen.	▶ *"In selling, as in golf, the follow through is important."*
How to be a better salesman.	▶ *"Talk slow, write fast."*
To be a salesman of ideas or anything, you've got to know what you're talking about.	▶ *"Unless you sound certain Your selling is hurtin'!"*
How to become a super salesman.	▶ *"Sell the sizzle not the steak!"* — Elmer Wheeler
"We are all salesmen every day of our lives.	▶ *We are selling our ideas, our plans, our enthusiasms to those with whom we come in contact."* — Charles M. Schwab
Sign in window of vacant shop —	▶ *"We undersold everybody!"*
Don't be so fast to sell things!	▶ *"I would rather be the man who bought the Brooklyn Bridge than the one who sold it."* — Will Rogers

• SALESMANSHIP •

| The sign that didn't work for a wood carver selling birdhouses: "Birdhouses for Sale." | ▶ *The sign that did work: "To let — for a song."* |
| Even though your're not in the commercial sales field, you may be a real pro as a salesman and not know it. | ▶ *"We are all salesmen every day of our lives. We are selling our ideas, our plans, our enthusiasms to those with whome we come in contact."*
— Charles M. Schwab |

Beware of what a super salesman can do to you!

▶ *"I went in to buy a truck and went out with a sports car."*

"The order that stays sold is...

▶ *the order that the buyer has sold himself."*

"Good selling is not merely a way to distribute what has already been produced.

▶ *Competitive selling is more than a way of slicing up the pie; it is a way of increasing the size of it as well."*

"Everything we touch turns to...

▶ *SOLD."*
— Real estate broker's motto

Sign on a little Hollywood bar —

▶ *"Women with Cloth Coats Welcome!"*

If your Selling Pitch is clicking — it's the wrong time to ease up.

▶ *Remember:*
"A rolling stone gathers momentum!"

"In one day, Sampson slew 1,000 Philistines with the jawbone of an ass.

▶ *Every day, ten million sales are killed with the same weapon."*

"Don't talk about your product or idea.

▶ *Talk about the prospect!"*

Sign on a furniture store window —

▶ *"Prefire Sale."*

Whether we know it or not — what are all of us doing all of the time?

▶ *"Everyone lives by selling something."*
— Robert Louis Stevenson

Optometrist teaching his son how to sell eyeglasses.

▶ *1. After fitting the customer with glasses say — "The charge is $35." Then pause and see if he flinches.*
2. If the customer doesn't flinch you then say — "That's for the frames. The lenses will be another $35."
3. Pause and watch for the flinch. If the customer doesn't flinch, you say "Each".

• SALVAGE SOMETHING! •

At least salvage something.

▶ *"Don't throw the baby out with the bath water!"*

Warning about the short-sightedness of society, and the lack of political will by our government, in the handling of education of our children, and in the profligacy of the nation's budget in general.

THREE CHOICES!
1. *"We can let it happen."*
2. *"We can make it happen."*
3. *"We can say — 'what happened' "?*

When you get into a chaotic mess, don't denounce! Instead — Salvage!

▶ *"It is better to light one small candle than to curse the darkness."*
— Confucius

• SAVAGES •

That which Savages are.

▶ *"Tribes of people who don't know that anything is wrong, until missionaries tell them."*

• SCARCE •

"As scarce as —

▶ *fingernails on the Venus de Milo."*

• THE SCHIZOPHRENIC •

As the schizophrenic said —

▶ *"I've half a mind to do it."*

A schizophrenic poem.

▶ *"Roses are red*
Violets are blue
I'm schizophrenic
And so am I!"

• THE SCIENCES •

A layman's interpretation of Einsteins Theory of Relativity.

▶ *"There was a young lady named Bright*
Who could travel much faster than light
She started one day
In the relative way
And came back on the previous night."

Mrs. Isaac Newton also tries to help make a discovery.

▶ *"Another apple just fell off the tree, dear. Why don't you come out and look at it — maybe you'll make another discovery."*

Which scientist generally gets credit for a new idea?

▶ *"In science the credit goes to the man who convinces the world, not to the man to whom the idea first occurs."*
— William Osler

Newton said, "For every action, there is an equal and opposite reaction."

▶ *"If all pulled in one direction the world would keel over."*
— Yiddish proverb

To what degree would science have advanced had scientists not ignored laws and beliefs of their time?

▶ *"Every great advance in natural knowledge has involved the absolute rejection of authority."*
— Thomas Huxley

"There are more comets in the sky than...

▶ *there are fishes in the sea."*
— Johannes Kepler

Knowing about science versus knowing about philosophy.

▶ *"Science is what you know, philosophy is what you don't know."*
— Bertrand Russell

• THE SECRET •

I can keep a secret, but?

▶ *"I can keep confidential what you tell me but the people I tell it to can't."*

"Keeping a secret from some people is like...

▶ *trying to smuggle daylight past a rooster."*

"Three may keep a secret if...

▶ *two of them are dead."*
— Benjamin Franklin

"Nothing is so burdensome as...

▶ *a secret."*
— French proverb

How to test your friend's ability to keep a secret.

▶ *"Tell your friend a lie. If he keeps it secret, then tell him the truth."*
— Portuguese proverb

The one situation where you can't keep a secret.

▶ *"Nothing is harder to do secretly than stub your toe."*

"In marriage, the secret of
happiness is...

▶ *to keep a lot of secrets."*

"Every betrayal of a secret is
the fault of...

▶ *the person who confided it."*
— French proverb

"Be discreet about what
you're going to reveal!

▶ *Your friend has a friend, and your
friend's friend has a friend."*

"If you would keep your secret
from your enemies...

▶ *keep it also from your friends!"*
— Arabian proverb

"To keep your secret is
wisdom but...

▶ *to expect others to keep it is folly."*
— Oliver Wendell Holmes

"A secret is no secret unless...

▶ *it is shared."*

• SEEING •

What to do when you want to
see farther.

▶ *"Go as far as you can see and when
you get there you'll be able to see
farther!"*

As the "carpenter" said...

▶ *"you should see what I saw"!*

• THE SEER •

"A seer is...

▶ *what people think you are when you
guess right."*

"If you think you can see
so well into the future...

what's my next question"?

• SELECTIVITY •

Be discriminate when you
hand out praise!

▶ *"He who praises everybody, praises
nobody."*
— Samuel Johnson

• SELF-ACCEPTANCE •

If you won't be a phony to yourself — you likely won't be a phony to others.

▶ *"This above all — to thine own self be true,*
And it must follow, as the night the day,
Thou canst not then be false to any man."

— William Shakespeare

How to rationalize yourself into accepting yourself.

▶ *"I am as my Creator made me, and since He is satisfied, so am I."*

— Minnie Smith

Who are the really lucky people who can enjoy leisure?

▶ *"Only a person who can live with himself can enjoy the gift of leisure."*

— Henry Greber

"You've got to learn to live with yourself.

▶ *The only problem is —*
wherever I go, I can't get
rid of myself."

How much do you like yourself?

▶ *"If you were someone else, could you stand yourself?"*

Don't downgrade yourself. You're really not that bad.

▶ *"Every man in the world is better than some one else. And not as good as some one else."*

— William Saroyan

• SELF-DEFENSE •

"The best defense is a good offense...

▶ *and the more offensive the better."*

"Self-defense is...

▶ *Nature's oldest law."*

— John Dryden

• SELF-DENIGRATION •

Never downgrade yourself.

▶ *"Never exaggerate your faults; your friends will attend to that."*

— Robert C. Edwards

When you can't remember what the right answer should be

"I have a teflon memory at times. Nothing sticks to it."

"Don't downgrade yourself. ▶ *People will find it out soon enough!*"

• SELF-DESCRIPTION •

"A man always describes himself unconsciously... ▶ *whenever he describes anyone else.*"
— George Bernard Shaw

• SELF-DETERMINATION •

Has government the right to intrude into areas of private behaviour and morality? ▶ *"The only purpose for which power can be rightly exercised over any member of a civilized community, against his will, is to prevent harm to others. His own good, either physical or moral, is not a sufficient warrant... Over himself, over his own mind and body, the individual is sovereign."*
— John Stuart Mill

"To exercise self-determination through secession is... ▶ *to blow apart the union, to pit people against one another and to sow discord, bloodshed and death.*"
— Mikhail Gorbachev

• SELF-ESTEEM •

"He who knows himself best... ▶ *esteems himself least.*"
— H.G. Bohn

"Everybody has to be somebody... ▶ *to somebody to be anybody.*"
— Malcolm S. Forbes

I was so self conscious that... ▶ *every time football players went into a huddle, I thought they were talking about me.*"
— Woody Allen

Some people think their problem is to... ▶ *"Know thyself."*
— Socrates

Maybe it's better for some peole not to know themselves! ▶ *"Know thyself? If I knew myself, I'd run away."*
— Goethe

If you can stand yourself, can life without amenities still be liveable?

▶ *"A man can stand a lot as long as he can stand himself. He can live without hope, without friends, without books, even without music, as long as he can listen to his own thoughts."*

— Axel Munthe

• SELF-EVIDENT •

When is something Self-evident?

▶ *"Self-evident is when it is evident to one's self and to nobody else."*

— Ambrose Bierce

• SELF-IMPORTANCE! •

The egocentric and his self inflated importance.

▶ *"He was like the rooster in Edmond Rostand's play who believed that the sun could not rise without his crowing."*

I'm really something"!

▶ *"I wish I could clone myself."*

"The fly sat upon the axle-tree of the chariot-wheel, and said...

▶ *What a dust do I raise!"*

— Francis Bacon

• SELF-IMPROVEMENT •

How to improve yourself.

▶ *"He who stops being better, stops being good."*

— Oliver Cromwell

• SELF-PITY •

How to be a Pro at self pity.

▶ *"Forget the good things in life and concentrate on the bad. Always be pessimistic. Never forget a grudge. And always feel sorry for yourself!"*

• SELF-POSSESSION •

Self Possession —

▶ *"One of the very best of earthly possessions."*

— George Prentice

• SELF-PRESERVATION •

If you suspect that the seller is a con artist, here's what to say before you sign.

▶ *"Do you mind if I first run this by my lawyer?"*
— Ralph Nader

Self preservation will always prevail.

▶ *"A hungry wolf will attack a lion."*
— Turkish proverb

The annoyance you feel when attacking somebody who defends himself.

▶ *"That's a vicious animal. When one attacks him, he defends himself."*
— French proverb

"Self preservation is...

▶ *the first law of nature."*

Hungry people won't be appeased by mere words.

▶ *"It is a difficult matter to argue with the belly since it has no ears."*
— Cato

• SELF-RESPECT •

"He who allows himself to be a worm...

▶ *must not complain if he is trodden upon."*

"Self-respect" — definition.

▶ *"No one is as yet suspicious."*
— H.L. Menchen

You can discipline your mind to accept insult without hurt.

▶ *"No one can make you feel inferior without your consent."*
— Eleanor Roosevelt

• SELF-RESPONSIBILITY •

We, and we alone, are responsible for tying ourselves up in knots.

▶ *"We ourselves forge the chains that bind us."*
— Charles Dickens

• SELF-REVELATION •

"When you get too big for your breeches...

▶ *you split your pants and reveal yourself for what you are!"*
— Leo Bascaglia

"You can tell more about a person by what he says about others than...

▶ *you can by what others say about him."*

• SELF-WORTH •

If all I'm worth are my possessions, what is my worth?

▶ *"If I am what I have — and if what I have is lost who then am I?"*

— Erich Fromm

• COMMON "SENSE" •

The relationship of common sense to education.

▶ *"Common sense is in spite of, not the result of, education."*

— Victor Hugo

• SERVICE •

"Service to others is...

▶ *the rent we pay for a room in heaven."*

When you want fast service!

▶ *"I want it here so fast that if it's ready by yesterday, I don't want it!"*

When the service is too slow.

▶ *"As Solomon said to his 1000 wives — For Better Service Take A Number!"*

• SEX AND THE SEXES •

How a man can make a woman do anything.

▶ *"If you can make a woman laugh you can do anything with her."*

— Nicol Williamson

"Women need to realize that today's so-called sexual freedom is not freedom at all.

▶ *Promiscuousness is devastating and demoralizing to human character."*

— Sheila Graham

What is the difference in sexual capacity of woman as against man?

▶ *"A woman is a woman until the day she dies, but a man's a man only as long as he can."*

If a woman means NO — she better say NO!

▶ *"She half consents who silently denies."*

— Ovid

I like girls!

▶ *"I like girls in blue I like girls in red. But mostly I like girls when..."*

"If sex is such a natural phenomenon...

▶ *how come there are so many books on how to?"*

— Bette Midler

Why men should never hesitate to try with women!

▶ *"Whether they give or refuse, women are glad to have been asked."*

— Ovid

"If you're over 40, the best antidote against conception is...

▶ *to appear in the nude."*

Kinsey on sex.

▶ *"The only unnatural sex act is that which you can't perform."*

How does an unattractive woman look in the dark?

▶ *"When the candles are out all women are fair."*

— Plutarch

Where is Rape not prevalent?

▶ *"Among the porcupines, rape is unknown."*

— Gregory Clark

Egyptian Queen to Pharoah —

▶ *"Not tonight, dear. I have a Mummy Ache."*

— Shelby Friedman

What has adversely affected the allure of semi-nudity?

▶ *"Nudity has taken all the eroticism out of semi-nudity."*

— Gregory Nunn

"Whoever named it necking was...

▶ *a poor judge of anatomy."*

— Groucho Marx

Do chaste women like being chaste?

▶ *"There are few chaste women who are not tired of their trade."*

— La Rochefoucauld

To what degree should a smart woman show her affecton to a man?

▶ *"In nine cases out of ten, a woman had better show more affection than she feels."*

— Jane Austen

A fantasy many men would like to hear women say.

▶ *"Being your slave what would I do but tend upon the hours and times of your desires."*
— William Shakespeare

Does a man of power create sexual desire in woman?

▶ *"Power is the ultimate aphrodisiac."*
— Henry Kissinger

"Birth Control would be more attractive if...

it were made retroactive."

Name an unusual sexual behaviour!

▶ *"The strangest of all sexual aberrations is celibacy."*

No matter how often husband and wife fight, how come they always find time to have kids.

▶ *"No matter how much cats fight, there always seem to be plenty of kittens."*
— Abraham Lincoln

Is there any man, who during his life, does not cheat at one time or another?

▶ *" 'Tis my opinion every man cheats in his way, and he is only honest who is not discovered."*
— Susannah Centlivre

"Give me an older woman every time.

▶ *They don't yell. They don't tell And they're as grateful as Hell."*

"They're giving answers on sex today that...

▶ *people never knew there were questions for."*

In today's society of sexual freedom and aberrations, may there be people discontent with merely two sexes?

▶ *"Breathes there a man with hide so tough Who says two sexes aren't enought?"*
— Samuel Hoffenstein

Erotic fantasy.

▶ *"Licence my roving hands, and let them go, Before, behind, between, above, below."*
— John Donne

"Help Stamp Out Rape...

▶ *say Yes!"*

A man's fantasy of a lady's bosom.

▶ *"No bosom in nature is so beautiful as what imagination forms."*

"You mustn't force sex to do the work of love or...

▶ *love to do the work of sex."*
— Mary McCarthy

What literary pursuit turns a woman on?

▶ "All a writer has to do to get a woman is to say he's a writer. It's an aphrodisiac."

— Saul Bellow

"Woman, in lovemaking is like...

▶ a lyre which gives up its secret only to him who knows how to play on it."

— Honoré de Balzac

The similarity of the sun's eclipse to a lady's partly unbuttoned blouse.

▶ "You know it's there and you know it's interesting — but you're not supposed to stare at it."

The kind of men Mae West liked.

▶ "I only like two kinds of men: domestic and foreign."

Every She and every He always knows which is which.

▶ "And here's the happy bounding flea —
You can not tell the he from she.
But she can tell and so can he."

— Roland Young

"Between man and woman there is little difference but...

▶ 'vive la difference'."

"Answering questions is a major part of sex education.

▶ First, always give a truthful answer to a question; secondly, regard sex knowledge as exactly like any other knowledge.

—Bertrand Russell

Is there any man who won't turn around for a second look at a pretty ankle?

▶ "Breathes there the man with soul so dead,
Who never has turned round and said,
Hmm, not bad!"

What stage are you at in sex?

▶ "I'm at a stage of life where if she says Yes — it's an offer I can't accept."

"Good morals, like good art begins...

▶ with drawing a line"!

"Where does virgin wool come from?

▶ From sheep that run the fastest."

How to win a woman without using words.

▶ *"Win her with gifts, if she respect not words;*
Dumb jewels often, in their silent kind,
More quick than words, do move a woman's mind."

— William Shakespeare

Where the sex drive begins and ends.

▶ *"The sex drive is a physical craving that begins in adolescence and ends at marriage."*

— Robert Byrne

Definition of a Nymphomaniac —

▶ *"The female counterpart of a normally constituted male."*

"A jerk is one who, when he invites a girl up to see his etchings...

▶ *shows her his etchings."*

"It's boring for a 71-year old broad to sing about how bad she wants it, even if...

▶ *it is true that we frequently want it badly."*

— Lena Horne

"Sex education has been introduced into the sixth-grade curriculum.

▶ *The child concluded that he was related to his mother by birth, but to his dad only by marriage."*

"Two is company.

▶ *Three is terrific!"*

— Frank Dane

What are ladies' unmentionables?

▶ *"Unmentionables — those articles of ladies' apparel that are never discussed in public, except in full-page, illustrated ads."*

"Sex is like politics.

▶ *You don't have to be good at it to enjoy it!"*

— Rich Little

Surprises at a nudist colony.

▶ *"Having spent my entire vacation in a nudist colony, I was somewhat taken aback when a lady shook my hand and said: 'Good-bye, Mr. Nunn, I hope to see more of you.'"*

— Gregory Nunn

In defense of prostitution.

▶ *"My method is basically the same as Masters and Johnson, only they charge thousands of dollars and it's called therapy. I charge fifty dollars and it's called prostitution."*
— Xaviera Hollander

"When you have found the place where a woman loves to be fondled...

▶ *don't you be ashamed to touch it any more than she is."*
— Ovid

Abortion...

▶ *"The issue that began at the dawn of time and it will end when the earth ceases to circle the sun."*

Women of all stations in life look and taste alike to a man except for one thing?

▶ *"Were it not for imagination, a man would be as happy in the arms of a chambermaid as of a duchess."*
— Samuel Johnson

What counts in sexual intercourse?

▶ *"It's quality, not quantity, that counts."*
— Dr. David Reuben

How NOT to get her to say Yes!

▶ *"Faint heart ne'er won fair lady."*
— G. Eliot

There's a new book out on sex titled —

▶ *"All you wanted to know about sex and were afraid to ask your children."*

"There's no saucepan so ugly that it won't find a pot to match."

▶ *"There is no one, no matter their size, shape or accent, who doesn't turn someone else on, somewhere, somehow."*
— Larry Levenson

There is hardly anyone whose sexual life, if it were broadcast...

▶ *would not fill the world at large with surprise and horror."*
— W. Somerset Maugham

What attracts a man more — a lady's mind or her body?

▶ *"Men are more interested in women's minds than their bodies — according to leading anthropologists and other liars."*

"Once upon a time a He and a She started out on a platonic friendship and...

▶ *they ended up in a Bed Heat."*

The sexual revolution for so many Teenagers regrettably omits the spiritual.

▶ *"Sex today is a three letter word with a four letter connotation."*

What to say if you've just brought her in out of the rain.

▶ *"Why don't you get out of your wet clothes and into a dry martini!"*

• SHAKESPEARE—AN APPRAISAL •

Shakespeare's soliloquy in Hamlet — "To be or not to be."

▶ *"It is the most famous speech in modern literature, with an appeal that neither repetition nor parody can destroy.*
It dramatizes for each one of us the baffled individual in the agony of indecision."

— H. Peterson

An appraisal of Shakespeare's Sonnets.

▶ *"In the estimation of the majority of competent judges they constitute the highest achievement of the human mind in the region of pure poetry."*

— Harmsworth Encyclopedia

Shakespeare's works crossed the boundaries of language.

▶ *"A great poem by Shakespeare remains a great poem in whatever language it is printed."*

Why George Bernard Shaw despised Shakespeare.

▶ *"With the single exception of Homer, there is no eminent writer, not even Sir Walter Scott, whom I can despise so entirely as I despise Shakespeare when I measure my mind against his."*

— George Bernard Shaw

• SHARING •

Who are often most eager to share?

▶ *"Those who have nothing are always eager to share it with others."*

• SHUT UP! •

Guard your words!

▶ *"Oh Lord — Help me keep my words gracious and tender because tomorrow I may have to eat them!"*

Five guides on when you should speak.

▶ *"If you your lips would keep from slips,*
Five things observe with care;
To whom you speak, of whom you
speak,
And how, and when, and where."
— W.E. Norris

"Never speak unless...

▶ *you can improve on silence."*

Don't say it — you may be sorry!

▶ *"Words once spoken, can never be recalled."*

Is remaining silent sometimes the right course?"

▶ *"I have noticed that nothing I never said ever did me any harm."*
— Calvin Coolidge

Listen to everybody! But how much should you say?

▶ *"Give every man thy ear, but few thy voice."*
— William Shakespeare

"An ounce of keeping your mouth shut is worth...

▶ *a pound of explanation."*

"If you wouldn't write it and sign it...

▶ *don't say it!"*

— Earl Wilson

Never talk when you don't know what you're talking about!

▶ *"Don't let your tongue cut your throat!"*
— Irish proverb

"If silence be good for the wise" who is it even better for?

▶ *"How much the better for the fools!"*
— Talmud

Guide on when to shut up!

▶ *"Better to be silent and be thought a fool than to speak and remove all doubt."*

Why we haven't got one ear and two tongues.

▶ *"God gave us two ears and one tongue so we should listen twice as much as we talk."*

| How to silence the other fellow. | ▸ "Please be quiet while I'm interrupting!" |
| "Blessed is he who has little to say and... | ▸ abstains from giving wordy evidence of the fact"! |

• SIGNS •

Sign in Chemistry laboratory.	▸ "Caution! Chemist who falls in acid — absorbed in work."
Sign at highway construction site —	▸ "Men working ahead — we hope!"
Sign in Yugoslavia government building elevator —	▸ "Push button of wishing floor. If the cabin should enter more persons, each one should press number of wishing floor. Driving is then going alphabetically by natural order."
Sign in Japanese restaurant	▸ "If the season of our food didn't like you, you are allowed to keep your pay."
Sign on ship captain's door —	▸ "Out to "LAUNCH".
Sign in newspaper office expressing annoyance over misspelled words.	▸ "SPELL IT RIHGT!"
Sign over bench —	▸ "Wet paint. Watch it or wear it!"
Sign on lawn of church:	▸ "Keep off. This Means Thou!"
Sign above mirror at a motel pool!	▸ "Mirror mirror on the wall, Who is 'barest' of them all"?
Sign in Old English Tavern	▸ RULES of this TAVERN

RULES of this TAVERN
4 pence a night for bed
6 pence with potluck
2 pence for housekeeping
No more than five to sleep
   in one bed
No boots to be worn in bed
No razor grinders or tinkers
   taken in
No dogs allowed in the
   kitchen
Organ Grinders to sleep
   in the wash house

— C. Lemuels Inn

Sign in a toy shop:

▶ *"Children of permissive parents admitted only on a leash."*

• "SIGNIFICANCE" OF THE TRIVIAL! •

"For Want of a Nail!"

▶ *"For want of a nail the shoe was lost,*
For want of a shoe the horse was lost,
For the want of a horse the rider was lost,
For the want of a rider the battle was lost,
For want of a battle the kingdom was lost —
And all for the want of a horseshoe nail."

— Benjamin Franklin

• SILENCE •

Can remaining silent sometimes be immoral?

▶ *"Silence is said to be golden but sometimes it is yellow!"*

The immorality of, and the real meaning of Silence.

▶ *"Silence gives consent!"*

— Oliver Goldsmith

Silence —

▶ *"Having nothing to say and saying it."*

Advice to somebody who's talking rubbish.

▶ *"A closed mouth gathers no foot."*

• SIMILES •

Is a thought greatly enhanced by a beautiful simile?

▶ *"A good simile is the sunshine of wisdom."*

— Hosea Ballou

• SIMPLICITY •

In any job, reduce the whole to its parts in simplest terms.

▶ *"Think in simples!"*

— Frank Lloyd Wright

• SIN •

"He who has committed a sin twice...

▶ *does not think it a sin any longer."*

— Talmud

| How would you categorize gluttony and lust? | ▶ *"Gluttony and lust are not sins but very honest pastimes."* |

— José Cela, Spanish novelist

• SINCERITY •

| "As sincere as... | ▶ *an undertaker's get well card."* |

| What's better than being two faced? | ▶ *"Better to be one sided than two faced!"* |

| "He's as phony as... | ▶ *a three dollar bill."* |

• SINGING •

| What's significant about not knowing how to sing? | ▶ *"You don't have to know how to sing; it's feeling as though you want to that makes the day successful."* |

— Monta Crane

• SLAVERY •

| Lincoln's aversion to slavery. | ▶ *"A house divided against itself cannot stand — I believe this government cannot endure permanently half-slave and half-free."* |

— Abraham Lincoln

• SLEEP •

| Four-point program on "How to Sleep." | ▶ *1. "Go to bed.*
2. Close your eyes.
3. Go to sleep and —
4. Wake up — that's very important!" |

— Robert Benchley

| Sleep — the great leveler. | ▶ *"God bless whoever invented sleep, the mantle that embraces the thoughts of all men, food that satisfies all hunger, the weight that balances the scales and makes the shepherd the same as the king, the fool the same as the wise man."* |

— Miguel de Cervantes

The greatness and kindness of Sleep.

▶ *"Nature's most overwhelming generosity!"*

"Man is the only animal that goes to sleep when he is not sleepy, and...

▶ *awakes when he is."*

"If you would like to sleep in every morning...

▶ *Early to bed and early to rise — till you make enough money to do otherwise."*

"Laugh and the world laughs with you...

▶ *Snore and you sleep alone."*

What kind of people sleep like a baby?

▶ *"People who say they sleep like a baby usually don't have one."*

When you want to sleep and you can't!

▶ *"One thought cannot awake without awakening others."*
— Marie Ebner-Eschenbach

• THE SLOP! •

The advantage of being sloppy and disorganized.

▶ *"One of the advantages of being disorderly is that one is constantly making exciting discoveries."*
— A.A. Milne

• SLOW AND SURE! •

"He's so slow...

▶ *that in a race with a pregnant woman, he'd run third!"*

"Spurts don't count.

▶ *"The final score makes no mention of a splendid start if the finish proves that you were an also ran."*
— Herbert Kaufman

• BEING "SMART"! •

The difference between being "Smart" and being "Brilliant".

▶ *"Smart" is when you believe only half of what you hear.*
"Brilliant" is when you know which half to believe.

The difference between being "Industrious" and being "Smart".

▶ *"Industrious": getting to work half an hour before the boss does. "Smart": getting there 30 seconds before he does.*

• SMILES •

How to make a smile become really beautiful.

▶ *"A smile is something that is no earthly good to anybody till it is given away."*

"A smile so big...

▶ *it introduced one ear to the other."*

Who is the fellow most likely able to smile when things are really going wrong?

▶ *"The fellow who can smile when things go wrong is probably just going off shift."*

"The world is like a mirror reflecting what you do...

▶ *And if you face it smiling, it smiles right back at you!"*

Effect of a smile on the Rich and on the Poor.

▶ *"None are so rich that they can get along without it... and none so poor, but are made richer for its benefits!"*

• THE SMELL! •

"He doesn't know he smells any more than...

▶ *an onion knows it smells."*

• SMOKE •

The Law of Smoke —

▶ *"Regardless of where you sit, the wind will always blow the smoke from a barbecue in your face."*

• SMOKING •

"A cigar is like a woman...

▶ *you have to warm her before you assault her."*

— Winston Churchill

"Go on smoking.

▶ *Who needs two lungs!"*

To our customers —
"We have excellent facilities
for smokers...

▶ *outdoors"!*

Sign in an office re Smoking:

▶ *"If you smoke — don't exhale!"*

• SMUGNESS •

To the person who always
interrupts your explanation
because he always thinks he
knows what you're going to say.

▶ *"Some will never learn anything
because they understand everything
too soon."*

• THE S.O.B. •

"An S.O.B. is...

▶ *somebody who never hurts another
person's feelings unintentionally."*

Why there are so many
S.O.B.'s?

▶ *"The bee is such a busy soul,
He has no time for birth control.
And that is why, in times like these,
We have so many sons of bees."*

• SOCIAL ATTITUDE •

How concern for good taste
was exercised during the 1950's
prior to the sexual revolution.

▶ *1. The "New York Times" changed an
advertisement for "naughty but
nice" to "Paris-inspired — but
so nice."*

*2. And a nightclub advertisement of
"50 of the hottest girls this side of
hell" became "50 of the most
alluring maidens this side of
paradise."*

"Let the punishments of
criminals be useful.

▶ *A hanged man is good for nothing, but
a man condemned to public works still
serves the country, and is a living
person."*

— Voltaire

"Today women are respected lawyers, judges, heads of state political leaders, journalists, military officers, and corporate executives.

▶ *Women are no longer ostracized if they choose to marry or not to marry. To have children or not. To work outside the home or inside the home."*

A reply to "How are things?" when they are improving scarcely at all.

▶ *"Things are deteriorating less rapidly than before."*

Social status exists even among those of the lowest classes.

▶ *"There is no being so poor and contemptible, who does not think there is somebody still poorer and still more contemptible."*
— Samuel Johnson

"Today, too many husbands and wives think they're entitled to Life, Liberty and...

▶ *the Happiness of Pursuit."*

• SOCIAL BEHAVIOUR •

What always happens to conduct that is at first condemned?

▶ *"There is no possible line of conduct which has at some time and place been condemned, and which has not at some other time and place been enjoined as a duty."*
— William Lecky

Facetious self-denigration.

▶ *"I can't remember when I had a better time! That's the trouble when you get old. You can't remember."*

Most of the time I can put up with you, but there are times when...

▶ *"I do desire we may be better strangers."*
— William Shakespeare

The pendulum of social behaviour that you detest today will eventually swing the other way later on.

▶ *"What is fanatiscism today is the fashionable creed tomorrow, and trite as the multiplication table a week after."*
— Wendell Phillips

• SOCIAL ETIQUETTE •

Nothing is so deflating in image as a limp handshake.

▶ *"I love a hand that meets my own with a grasp that causes some sensation."*

• SOCIAL LIVING •

"Man can now walk safely in outer space.

▶ *"On the street — not yet!"*

"If you give up smoking, drinking and sex, you don't live longer.

▶ *It just seems like it."*

"We live in a society in which 'letting it all hang out' and being candid are regarded as virtues.

▶ *The climate of openness has had an especially deleterious effect upon courtesy within families and society."*
— David Reisman

• SOCIAL STRATA •

Let no man look down upon the work of another!

▶ *"If all the garbage men and all the preachers quit at the same time, which would you miss first?"*

• SOCIALISM •

"The inherent vice of capitalism is the unequal sharing of blessings." What about socialism?

▶ *"The inherent virtue of socialism is the equal sharing of miseries."*
— Winston Churchill

• SOCIETY •

What is ominous about our advanced technological society?

▶ *"Our lifetime may be the last that will be lived out in a technological society."*
— Isaac Asimov

"My definition of a free society is...

▶ *a society where it is safe to be unpopular."*
— Adlai E. Stevenson

• SOLITUDE •

Definition of Solitude —

▶ *"Solitude is a good place to visit, but a poor place to stay."*

— Josh Billings

When is solitude a pleasure?

▶ *"Solitude is a fine thing; but it's a pleasure to have some one to whom you can say it's a fine thing."*

— Honoré de Balzac

Everybody needs his own private solitude and breathing space.

▶ *"I never found companion that was so companionable as solitude."*

— Henry David Thoreau

"Solitude vivifies.

▶ *Isolation kills!"*

— Joseph Roul

• SOLUTIONS •

Does a good solution really solve the problem?

▶ *"There's no such thing as the perfect solution. Every solution, no matter how good, creates new problems."*

• SPEAK UP! •

What can happen when nobody speaks up against injustice?

▶ *"In Germany they came first for the Communists, and I didn't speak up because I wasn't a Communist. Then they came for the Jews, and I didn't speak up because I wasn't a Jew. Then they came for the trade unionists, and I didn't speak up because I wasn't a trade unionist. Then they came for the Catholics, and I didn't speak up because I was a Protestant. Then they came for me, and by that time no one was left to speak up."*

— Martin Niemoeller

"Are you a man or a mouse?

▶ *Squeak up!"*

Speak up for your rights.
Don't get pushed around!

▶ *"The wheel that squeaks the loudest is the one that gets the grease."*

• SPEAKING AND TALKING •

What's the effect when you speak about yourself?

▶ *"When all is summed up, a man never speaks of himself without loss; his accusations of himself are always believed; his praises never."*
— Michel de Montaigne

When a speaker says "It goes without saying,"...

▶ *it means "He'll say it just the same."*

"He's got a voice like...

▶ *a diesel truck in second gear."*

In a previous generation, most men would have been shocked to think women knew such things as four-letter words.

▶ *"Today, many women use 'toiletmouth' words, not only without shame, but without even a blush."*

What part of the human body grows sharper with use?

▶ *"A sharp tongue is the only edged tool that grows keener with constant use."*
— Washington Irving

"After all is said and done...

▶ *more is said than done."*

A vulgarism for —
"Foolish exaggerated talk sometimes works."

▶ *"Bull .... Baffles Brains!"*

How to say "I told you so."

▶ *"I'm not going to say I told you so."*

What to do when you don't know what you're talking about.

▶ *"When in doubt mumble!"*

Which three "bones" in your body are needed for success in becoming a good speaker?

▶ *"The WISHBONE that gives you the desire to be a good speaker. The JAWBONE that gives you the means of expressing yourself. The BACKBONE that talks you into slugging for success."*

• SPEECHES •

"Your words of introduction paid me such a great tribute that...

▸ *for my next approaching birthday, I'm going to call on you to make the very same speech again."*

Guide to making a speech.

▸ *"If you haven't struck oil in the first three minutes — stop boring!"*
— George Jessel

Advice to a man making a speech.

▸ *"All nice guys finish 'fast'."*

"It is but a poor eloquence which only shows...

▸ *that the orator can talk."*
— Joshua Reynolds

When a man makes a speech — how many speeches does he really make?

▸ *"I really make four addresses. First is the speech I prepare in advance; that is pretty good. Second is the speech I really make. Third is the speech I make on the way home, which is the best of all; and fourth is the speech the newspapers next morning say I made, which bears no relation whatever to the others."*
— William Lyon Phelps

There were three things wrong with your speech.

▸ *"In the first place it was read. In the second place it was read poorly. — And in the third place it was a poor speech in the first place."*

What impresses more — the message — or style of delivery?

▸ *"No speech can make a boring speaker good"!*

Winston Churchill said he could write a two hour speech in ten minutes. But to write a ten minute speech took him two hours.

▸ *"I have only made this letter rather long because I have not had time to make it shorter."*
— Blaise Pascal

Don't always get taken in by the clever impromptu speech!

▸ *"It usually takes me more than three weeks to prepare a good impromptu speech."*
— Mark Twain

Beware when making a speech! ▶ *"Blessed is he who has little to say and abstains from giving wordy evidence of the fact."*

Advice to the after dinner speaker!
"When you speak, don't sound like a big wheel. ▶ *"Remember. The longer the SPOKE the greater the TIRE."*
— G. Carere

"The man who makes a bad thirty-minute speech to two hundred people... ▶ *wastes one hundred hours of the audience's time — which should be a hanging offense."*
— Jonkin Lloyd Jones

"He was such a boring speaker! ▶ *You had to wire the seats to make the audience sit up straight."*

"No speech can be entirely bad if... ▶ *it is short enough."*
— Irvin S. Cobb

Definition of a Boring Speaker — ▶ *"A person who can dilute a 2 minute idea sufficiently to fill a 30 minute speech."*

"The object of oratory is... ▶ *not truth but persuasion."*
— Thomas Babington Macaulay

The kind of speakers who are appreciated. ▶ *There are speakers who please me, To whom I'll allude: They say, "Now, in conclusion" And promptly conclude*

How long should a speech be? ▶ *"A speech, like a bathing suit, should be long enough to cover the subject — and short enought to be interesting."*

• SPEEDY! •

"He really moves so fast that... ▶ *when he slows down, he slows down to a run!"*

"He's so fast that when he goes to bed and turns out the light... ▶ *he's asleep before the light goes out."*

"He's so fast! ▶ *He can play tennis by himself."*

"He's so slow they're naming
a wine after him...

▶ *Dead Duck.*"

He's as fast as...

▶ *a centipede on a treadmill.*"

• THE SPINSTER •

"Spinster's Prayer" —

▶ *"Just give me man*
With a million or two,
Or one that is handsome
Would happily do,
A dashing young fellow
Is swell any day,
Or one that is famous
Would suit me O.K.
But if the man shortage
Should get any worse
Go back to the very
First line of this verse."

• SPORTS •

As the sports announcer
said —

▶ *"That was a complicated play, fans.*
So we're going to run it again for you
fans scoring in bed."

— Bert Randolph Sugar

"You don't get fired for
cheating...

▶ *you get fired for losing.*"

— Darryl Rogers

Above and beyond the call
of physical endurance —
train, train, train!

▶ *"Training has to be like*
water torture — constant"!

Baseball is in the lifeblood
of America. Baseball is hot
dogs and beer, precision and
ballet. The game is a human
work of art.

▶ *"Baseball is an American*
art form"!

— Roger Kahn

• GET "STARTED"! •

Is starting the hardest part of
starting?

▶ *"He who is outside his door already*
has a hard part of his journey
behind him."

— Dutch proverb

Edging your way in as a start
is at least better than what?

▶ *"A foot in the door is worth two on
the desk."*

• STATISTICS •

Why it's dangerous to accept
interpretations of statistics.

▶ *"There are 3 kinds of lies : lies,
damned lies, and statistics."*

— Benjamin Disraeli

Why Disraeli called statistics
"damned lies"!

▶ *The ninety-year-old patient
who assured his doctor that
he was unlikely to die, because
statistics prove that few men
die over ninety."*

When drafting a questionnaire,
avoid ambiguity or here's
the result!

▶ *Born — "Yes"
Education — "Fair"
Business — "Rotten"*

• STATUS •

What is the similarity of a
cynic to that of a status seeking
person whose shopping habits
are guided solely by designer
labels?

▶ *"A cynic is a man who knows the price
of everything and the value of
nothing."*

— Oscar Wilde

How the wealthy measured
social status in the days of
Ancient Rome.

▶ *"Modern nobles measure their rank
and consequences according to the
loftiness of their chariots."*

— Ammianus Marcellinus

• STEALING •

How much should you steal to
get respect?

▶ *"A little stealing is a dangerous part,
But stealing largely is a noble art;
'Tis mean to rob a hen-roost of a hen,
But stealing millions makes us
gentlemen."*

It's nice when somebody says
something nice about me.

▶ *"But he that filches from
me my good name
Robs me of that which
not enriches him
And makes me poor indeed."*

— William Shakespeare

• STINGINESS •

"He's so stingy —
▸ *If he paid you a compliment, it would come collect."*

"He's so stingy —
▸ *"He's the kind of guy who still has the first dollar he ever owed."*
— Walter Winchell

"He's so stingy —
▸ *He's just walking around to save funeral expenses."*

• YOUR STRENGTH •

Do you really know your own strength?
▸ *"He knows not his own strength that hath not met adversity."*
— Francis Bacon

He's so strong...
▸ *he's got muscles in his eyebrows"!*

• STRESS •

Stress is not the pressure(s) from the outside.....Those are 'stressors'. Your response to those situations constitutes 'stress'."
▸ *"Guides to reducing stress."*
1. Avoid 100% "Perfectionism". Nobody is expert at everything.
2. Always expect the "Unexpected."
3. Develop a "Realistic Self-image."
Avoid jobs for which you don't have the skills.
4. "Delegate" some of your work to others — even if not up to your standard.
5. Don't expect excessive "Approval." You'll be disappointed.
6. Avoid "Disorganization". Prioritize your tasks in order of importance.
7. Don't pursue "Happiness" as a goal. Happiness is elusive and unexpected.Amassing wealth or possessions is not the answer.
8. Don't worry about the "Future". Plan for the future.

Which is worse — Mental Stress or Physical?

▶ *"The pain of the mind is worse than the pain of the body."*

— Syrus

When should you relax?

▶ *"The time to relax is when you don't have time for it."*

How to conceal and overcome stress.

▶ *"Always behave like a duck — keep calm and unruffled on the surface but paddle like the devil underneath."*

— Jacob Braude

• STUPIDITY •

Do we ever pity stupidity?

▶ *"You pity a man who is lame or blind, but you never pity him for being a fool, which is often a much greater misfortune."*

— Sydney Smith

I'm not as stupid as you may think I am.

▶ *"I may have been born at night but it wasn't last night"*!

"She's so dumb that...

▶ *when she learned that her boyfriend's car needed a new muffler, she started to knit one for him?"*

Idiots and their influence on human affairs.

▶ *"Idiot, n: a member of a large and powerful tribe whose influence in human affairs has always been dominant and controlling."*

— Ambrose Bierce

Could I have been that stupid?

▶ *"I must have had help. I couldn't have been that stupid by myself."*

In what way does genius differ from stupidity?

▶ *"The difference between genius and stupidity is that genius has its limits."*

"I'll say this for your stupidity.

▶ *It's genuine!"*

"He's so dumb...

▶ *he couldn't pass an aptitude test for lifting up paperweights."*

Is there truth in a paradox?

▶ *"There are more horse's asses than horses."*

"She's so dumb...

▶ *she thinks a finger wave is something that follows an irritating remark."*

"She's so dumb" that when I said Oui Oui...

▶ *she thought I was asking to go to the bathroom."*

"He's so empty-minded.

▶ *they named a street after him — DEAD END."*

"He must have a sixth sense.

▶ *There's no sign of the other five."*

"Don't tell me what I mean.

▶ *Let me figure it out for myself!"*

"He's not a case of mistaken identity.

▶ *"He's a case of mistaken nonentity."*
— Barbara Stanwyck

"He who laughs last...

▶ *needed it explained to him."*

"She's so dumb.

▶ *She thinks a coquette is a small Coca-Cola."*

Definition of a Crackpot —

▶ *"A psycho-ceramic."*

"No one is exempt from talking nonsense.

▶ *The misfortune is to do it solemnly."*
— Michel deMontaigne

"He was born silly...

▶ *and had a relapse."*
— Arthur "Bugs" Baer

"Everybody is born stupid.

▶ *Some just remain so."*

If a guy is stupid, he's even dumber to try to appear smart.

▶ *"Where ignorance is bliss 'Tis folly to be wise."*
— Thomas Gray

"I was born this way.

▶ *What's your excuse?"*

The empty brain prattles the loudest.

▶ *"The empty vessel makes the greatest sound."*
— William Shakespeare

"If stupidity ever goes to $40 a barrel...

▶ *I want drilling rights on his head"!*

• STYLE •

How you say a thought is what gives your thought style.

▶ *"Style is the dress of thoughts."*
— Lord Chesterfield

Advice to somebody trying to affect style.

▶ *"Never wear a hat that has more character than you have"!*

• SUCCESS •

How NOT to succeed.

▶ *"Success is seldom achieved by those who contemplate possibilities of failure."*
— Smitty Adams

"The great pleasure in life is doing...

▶ *what people say you cannot do."*
— Walter Bagehot

"The man who wakes up in the morning a success has not been asleep."

▶ *"The heights by great men reached and kept*
Were not attained by sudden flight,
But they, while their companions slept,
Were toiling upward in the night."
— Henry Wadsworth Longfellow

What your personal success so often becomes to your friends.

▶ *"Success is the world's greatest deodorant"!*

If you want to achieve success, you've got to pay a price.

▶ *"If you want to hit the jackpot, you've got to put a coin in the machine."*

Is there any easy way to start at the top?

▶ *"The only way to start at the top is to dig a hole."*

The ABC's of Success.

▶ *"Success is only the old ABC — ability, breaks and courage."*
— Charles Luckman

"Not only does nothing succeed like success but...

▶ *nothing recedes like success."*
— Walter Winchell

How some least likely to succeed achieved success.

▶ *"The secret of success is largely to happen along when luck breaks."*

"No age or time of life, no position or circumstance, has a monopoly on success.

▶ *Any age is the right age to start doing!"*

Is success luck?

▶ *"Success is only a matter of luck — ask any man who fails."*

"Many a man owes his rise in the world to...

▶ *a good kick in the pants."*

Anyone who things of him- or herself as successful would do well to think of it this way: At what am I a success?

▶ *Am I a success as a family member, a partner, a friend, a citizen? Am I a success, in short, as a human being?"*

Is success really ever reached?

▶ *"The road to success is always under construction."*

When a man moves towards success faster than his companions, what sound does he hear that his companions don't hear?

▶ *"If a man does not keep pace with his companions, perhaps it is because he hears a different drummer. Let him step to the music which he hears, however measured or far away."*
— Henry David Thoreau

"Success is the ability to get along with some people and...

▶ *ahead of others!"*

What do you have to do to make progress?

▶ *"Behold the turtle. He makes progress only when he sticks his neck out."*
— James Bryant Conant

Why many average people succeed way beyond the average.

▶ *"It's not so much What you know, but Who you know."*

A sign on the lawn of a church —

▶ *"We Cannot Spell Success Without U."*

Slow but sure!

▶ *"He who stands on tip-toe does not stand firm; he who takes the longest strides is not the fastest walker; he who boasts of what he will do seldom succeeds in all he promises."*
— Chinese philosopher

"Success is a journey...   ▶ *not a destination"!*

"A successful man is one who   ▶ *"A successful woman is one who can*
can make more money than his   *find such a man!"*
wife can spend."
What is a successful woman?

The path of success in   ▶ *"Notwithstanding all that is said about*
business is invariably the path   *'lucky hits,' the best kind of success*
of common-sense.   *in every man's life is not that which*
comes by accident. The only 'good
time coming' we are justified in hoping
for is that which we are capable of
making ourselves."
— Samuel Smiles

How do you get successful?   ▶ *"The secret of success is a secret*
to most people."

The torment of becoming   ▶ *"Becoming Number One is easier than*
Number One.   *remaining Number One."*
— Bill Bradley

How a first wife and a second   ▶ *"Many a man owes his success to his*
wife each affects a man's   *first wife — and his second wife to his*
success.   *success."*
— Red Buttons

Name the one sin attendant   ▶ *"Success is the one unpardonable sin*
with Success!   *against one's fellows."*
— Ambrose Bierce

"Why many people aren't   ▶ *They aren't mediocre enough to*
successful.   *be successful."*

"Never mind about that   ▶ *"Just seed your lawn and see how*
mousetrap.   *quickly the world will wear a path to*
your door."

How to climb the ladder of   ▶ *"A ladder was never made to rest*
success.   *upon."*
— T.H. Huxley

"Don't be misled into believing that somehow the world owes you a living.

▶ *The boy who believes that his parents, or the government, or any one else owes him his livelihood and that he can collect it without labor will wake up one day and find himself working for another boy who did not have that belief and, therefore, earned the right to have others work for him."*

— David Sarnoff

The guy who decides to work really hard generally wins out.

▶ *"The man who rolls up his sleeves seldom loses his shirt."*

What's the toughest thing about success?

▶ *"The toughest thing about success is that you've got to keep on being a success."*

— Irving Berlin

Every giant achievement must start with a tiny beginning.

▶ *"Large streams from little fountains flow, Tall oaks from little acorns grow."*

— David Everett

• SUFFERING •

Those with the greatest suffering are least able to express their degree of pain.

▶ *"The deeper the sorrow the less tongue it hath."*

— Talmud

Can suffering be measured by outward signs?

▶ *"Some people suffer in silence louder than others."*

• SUPERFICIALITY •

Don't get taken in by superficiality!

▶ *"Examine the contents not the bottle."*

— Talmud

"Some men are very entertaining for a first interview, but after that they are exhausted, and run out.

▶ *On a second meeting we shall find them flat and monotonous; like hand-organs, we have heard all their tunes."*

— Charles Caleb Colton

• SUPERIORITY •

"There is nothing noble in feeling superior to some other person.

▶ *The true nobility is in being superior to your previous self."*

— Hindu proverb

• THE SUPERMARKET •

"Whichever line you choose...

▶ *the other line moves faster."*

• SUPERSTITION •

Superstition about a rabbit's foot.

▶ *"The only one who should put faith in a rabbit's foot is a rabbit."*

"Superstition is...

▶ *the religion of feeble minds."*

— Edmund Burke

• SURPRISES •

When do I love surprises?

▶ *"I love surprises as long as I'm ready for them."*

"Don't scare me so unexpectedly!

▶ *Even Humpty Dumpty died of shell shock."*

• SURVIVAL •

Why the tough survive!

▶ *"Tough times never last But tough people do."*

Do the weak inherit the earth?

▶ *"Throughout all past time, there has been a ceaseless devouring of the weak by the strong."*

— Herbert Spencer

"All forms of government fall when it comes to the question of bread.

▶ *Bread for the family, something to eat. Bread to a man with a hungry family comes first — before his union, before his citizenship, before his church affiliation. Bread!"*

— John L. Lewis

"The world is full of cactus. ▶ *But we don't have to sit on it.*"
— Will Foley

The choices available for survival. ▶ *"In this world; a man must either be be anvil or hammer."*
— Henry Wadsworth Longfellow

• SWIMMING •

Why everybody should learn to swim. ▶ *"Drowning is harmful to your health."*

"The reason I can't swim is... ▶ *because my head is too heavy."*

• SYSTEMS •

"Any system that works perfectly... ▶ *will be revised."*

T

• TACT •

Eight guides to "TACT" — the most worthy, the most prized, the most appreciated attribute in everyday living --- the appreciation of what is fit, proper and right.

▶ 1. "Listen attentively.
2. Control your temper.
3. Remember politeness.
4. Criticize privately.
5. Compliment judiciously.
6. Be empathetic.
7. Avoid a dictatorial voice.
8. Know when to avoid argument."

"Tact is the ability to give a person a shot in the arm without...

▶ letting him feel the needle."

"In the battle of existence, talent is the punch...

▶ tact is the clever footwork."

— Wilson Mizner

Tact when describing others.

▶ "The ability to describe others as they see themselves."

— Abraham Lincoln

"If in the Conduct of Life it is essential To Say No — learn to say it tactfully.

▶ Many a man has owed his outward success in life far more to good manners than any solid merit; while, on the other hand many a worthy man with a good heart and kind intentions makes enemies merely by the roughness of his manner."

— Chinese wisdom

The way to use tact when telling lies to others.

▶ *"Tact is to lie about others as you would have them lie about you."*

"There is no calamity...

▶ *that right words will not begin to redress."*
— Ralph Waldo Emerson

"Use tact...

▶ *you jerk!"*

"Diplomacy is to do and say...

▶ *the nastiest thing in the nicest way."*

"Tact in handling men pays off. Men will not work for wages. For a certain sum per day they will go through movements, but when *only* wages are concerned, men will not really work. Men will work only for men.

▶ *I care not what system of efficiency is employed or what mechanical refinements are used, the labor return will be inadequate so long as the personal equation is neglected."*
— Henry L. Willard

"A tactful and considerate person is one who pretends that he...

▶ *never heard that old joke before."*

• THE TAILGATER •

Bumper sticker to discourage tailgaters —

▶ *"Don't drive too close. Driver asleep!"*

• TALENT •

Talent won't work unless you do.

▶ *"Nothing is more common than unsuccessful men with talent."*
— Calvin Coolidge

• TASTE •

How a man of taste will buy his wardrobe.

▶ *"Costly thy habit as thy purse can buy, But not express'd in fancy; rich, not gaudy; For the apparel oft proclaims the man."*
— William Shakespeare

How about those people who have no taste?

▶ *"Bad taste is better than no taste at all!"*
— Arnold Bennett

"Taste is something quite different from fashion.

▶ *It is superior to fashion!"*
— William Makepeace Thackeray

People of GOOD TASTE.

▶ *"To find the good in a thing is a sign of good taste. Some seek the good in life, others the ill. They have the luckier taste who amongst a thousand defects seize upon a single beauty that they may have hit upon by chance"!*

"Taste is the faculty of the mind to preceive what is beautiful in nature and art."

▶ *"Taste is the faculty of the mind to recognize the most delicate beauties and the most minute imperfections."*

To Over Adorn is to vulgarize as it would be...

▶ *"to gild refined gold, to paint the lily, to throw perfume on the violet."*
— William Shakespeare

What to say when you totally disagree with the other person's taste.

▶ *"Every one to his taste as the woman said when she kissed her sow."*
— François Rabelais

What the Wine Snob has to remember and respect.

▶ *"Tutti i Gusti Son Gusti!"*
("All tastes are tastes!")
— Italy

What's worse than accusing a man of Bad Ethics?

▶ *"It is considered more withering to accuse a man of bad taste than of bad ethics!"*
— G.K. Chesterton

Shakespeare said don't gild refined gold or paint the lily (because they're already the ultimate in beauty.) "Neither should you...

▶ *put a mustache on the 'Mona Lisa' "!*

"If everybody were allowed to say his own taste is the best standard, few of us would know...

▶ *a signboard from a Rembrandt, an odour of a decaying carcas from a perfume, a limerick from a sonnet, a pigmy from a Shakespeare."*

"When a vested interest
salesman meets a gullible
uneducated customer...

▶ *the salesman always prevails
and the customer often wails"!*

"Never equate taste in food
with that of taste in the
appreciation of nature,
literature, and art.

▶ *The former needs taste buds.
The latter, study, reason,
judgment, and the faculty of the
mind to recognize and appreciate."*

"People differ more in taste than
in reason or common sense.

▶ *Standards of taste are not
arbitrary. But taste is
eminently an improveable quality."*

People of bad taste are
more to be pitied than
despised!

▶ *"Many people have such a
scent that amidst a thousand
excellences they fix upon a
single defect as if they
were scavengers of men's
minds and hearts."*

• TAXES •

Is there any relationship
between the income tax and
liars?

▶ *"The income tax has made more liars
out of the American people than golf
has. Even when you make a tax form
out on the level, you don't know when
it's through if you are a crook or
a martyr."*

— Will Rogers

The real meaning of unjust
tax laws.

▶ *"They take from the needy
And give to the greedy."*

— Ed Broadbent

"It's better to pay taxes than...

▶ *learn to speak Russian."*

April! The month you pay your
income tax!

▶ *"When April comes I find I earn more
money than I can afford."*

"The art of taxation consists
in...

▶ *so plucking the goose as to get the
most feathers with the least hissing."*

— Jean Baptiste Colbert

What hurts more than paying
income tax?

▶ *"The only thing that hurts more than
paying an income tax is not having to
pay an income tax."*

— Lord Thomas R. Duwar

Inscription on the Department of Justice Building, Washington, D.C.

▶ *"Taxes are what we pay for civilized society."*

— Oliver Wendell Holmes

• TEACHING •

"The Mediocre teacher tells. The Good teacher explains. The Superior teacher demonstrates.

▶ *The great teacher inspires!"*

— Dr. William Arthur Ward

Sign for more pay by teachers on strike.

▶ *"You shud pay us what weer wurth!"*

The value of a teacher.

▶ *"If you can read this — thank a teacher!"*

Plato on "How to Teach".

▶ *"Knowledge that is acquired under compulsion has no hold on the mind. Therefore do not use compulsion, but let early education be rather a sort of amusement."*

— Plato

Guide for teachers to make learning last.

▶ *"What we learn with pleasure we never forget."*

— Alfred Mercier

"A tongue-lashing which strikes the pupil's heart is more effective than...

▶ *many beatings."*

— Talmud

Guide to becoming a good teacher.

▶ *"What's learned with pleasure Is learned full measure."*

How teaching a child affects the education of an adult.

▶ *"Every adult needs a child to teach; it's the way adults learn."*

— Frank A. Clark

An unjustified derision of teachers.

▶ *"He who can does. He who can't teaches."*

— George Bernard Shaw

What a good teacher is relating to understanding and explaining.

▶ *"A good teacher is someone who can understand those not very good at explaining, and who can explain to those not very good at understanding."*

• THE TELEPHONE •

"Ask not for whom the telephone bell ringeth.

▶ *If thou art in the tub, it ringeth for thee."*

The telephone — which we so much take for granted!

▶ *"The telephone is the most important single technological resource of later life."*

— Alex Comfort

The sheer intimacy of intrusion that nothing like a telephone can do.

▶ *"Complete physical union between two people is the rarest sensation which life can provide — and yet not quite real, for it stops when the telephone rings."*

— Cyril Connolly

Telephone advice!

▶ *"Never judge a woman by the sweetness of her telephone voice."*

• TELEVISION •

Television, with all its deficiencies, fulfils a magnificent role for the masses!

▶ *"Television is the literature of the illiterate, the culture of the low-brow, the wealth of the poor, the privilege of the underpriviliged, the exclusive club of the excluded masses."*

— Lee Loevinger

Should we reconcile ourselves to the fact that television can be nothing other than a variety of excellence and drivel?

▶ *"Television is a gold goose that lays scrambled eggs; and it is futile and probably fatal to beat it for not laying caviar."*

— Frank Lloyd Wright

Rejection of an actor aspiring to get into T.V.

▶ *"You have a great face for radio but not for T.V."*

What purpose does T.V. serve for the eyes?

▶ *"T.V. is chewing gum for the eyes!"*
— Frank Lloyd Wright

Why television is a medium.

▶ *"Its bad stuff is not rare and its good stuff is rarely well done."*
— Fred Allen

What to do if voluntary censorship of T.V. isn't working.

▶ *"The ultimate censorship is the flick of the dial."*
— Tom Smothers

"A T.V. Commercial is...

▶ *the pause that depresses."*

T.V. has made artificially contrived image of people more important than their true character.

▶ *"The medium is the message."*
— Marshall McLuhan

Who are the people who torment you most during T.V. programmes?

▶ *"Those who talk while your favourite programme is on and shut up like clams during the commercial."*

• YOUR TEMPER •

"I have one nerve left and...

▶ *you're getting on it!"*
— Lynda Wilson

Never act so drastically toward your enemy that you get hurt in the process!"

▶ *"Heat not a furnace for your foe so hot That it do singe yourself."*
— William Shakespeare

Your Temper and how to use it.

▶ *"Your temper is the only thing that doesn't get better with use."*

What often provokes people into losing their tempers?

▶ *"Many people lose their tempers merely from seeing you keep yours."*
— Frank Moore Colby

"Temper is a precious possession.

▶ *Don't lose it!"*

A fit of temper will reveal a personality you'd prefer people not to know.

▶ *"He submits himself to be seen through a microscope, who suffers himself to be caught in a fit of passion."*
— J.K. Lavater

"Activity conquers cold."
But what controls the heat of
temper?

▶ *"Stillness conquers heat."*
— Lao-Tze

When you lose your temper,
how is your reason affected?

▶ *"Where violence reigns, reason is weak."*

Never overreact so drastically
that you get hurt in the process.

▶ *"Burn not down thy house To fright away the mouse."*

• TEMPTATION •

"The trouble with resisting
temptation is...

▶ *that it may never come again."*

When temptation beckons,
will virtue overcome
temptation?

▶ *"Virtue is insufficient temptation."*
— George Bernard Shaw

Never place temptation near a
reformed crook!

▶ *"A drunkard who has taken the pledge should never be locked up in a wine-cellar."*
— French proverb

I'd like to but —

▶ *"The spirit indeed is willing, but the flesh is weak."*
— Bible

Is it wicked to be tempted?

▶ *"It is no sin to be tempted; the wickedness lies in being overcome."*
— Honoré de Balzac

How to deal with temptation.

▶ *"The only way to get rid of a temptation is to yield to it."*
— Oscar Wilde

What to say when the flesh
is stronger than the spirit.

▶ *"Get thee behind me, Satan."*
— Bible

• TENSENESS •

"He was so tense that...

▶ *his shoe laces split."*

• THE THEATRE •

How to make a show a flop.

▶ *"Spread two hours of sparkling entertainment out over four hours."*
— Johnny Carson

Sign on Theater billboard —

▶ *"HAMLET" — by the author of Twelfth Night*

Derogatory criticism of a stageplay.

▶ *"It was one of those plays in which the actors unfortunately enunciated very clearly."*
— Robert Benchley

• THEOLOGY •

"Theology is an effort to explain the unknowable in terms of the not worth knowing.

▶ *It is not only opposed to the scientific spirit; it is opposed to every other form of rational thinking."*
— H.L. Mencken

• THIRSTY •

As the camel said —

▶ *"I don't care what people say — I'm thirsty!"*

• THOUGHT AND THINKING •

"The only thing I can keep in my head...

▶ *for longer than an hour is a cold!"*

"Teach the young people how to think...

▶ *not what to think."*
— Sidney Sugarman

People doing menial work will never understand why a job of sitting and thinking can produce fatigue to a point of collapse.

▶ *"Thinking is hard work."*
— Thomas A. Edison

"Thinking is like living and dying.

▶ *Each of us must do it for himself."*
— Josiah Royce

"It is more fun contemplating somebody else's navel than...

▶ *your own."*

Most great writers refine and hone the great thoughts of previous great writers.

▶ *"I gather the flowers by the wayside, by the brooks and in the meadows, and only the string with which I bind them together is my own."*
— Michel de Montaigne

Descartes' famous dictum — "I think therefore I am." (Cogito, ergo sum)

▶ *A revised version — "I think that I think, therefore I think I am."*
— Ambrose Bierce

What Darwin's friend Huxley wanted to inscribe on Darwin's gravestone.

▶ *"Beware when the great God lets loose a thinker on this planet."*
— Ralph Waldo Emerson

How much does man hate to think?

▶ *"There is no expedient to which a man will not resort to avoid the real labour of thinking."*
— Sir Joshua Reynolds

When Newton's apple fell what did Newton do about it that millions of others didn't?

▶ *"Millions say the apple fell but Newton was the one to ask why."*
— Bernard M. Baruch

"Most people would die sooner than...

▶ *think. In fact they do"!*
— Bertrand Russell

Think before you entangle yourself in a mess.

▶ *"Things are easier to get into than out of."*

What would happen if everybody thought before they spoke?

▶ *"The silence would be deafening."*
— Gerald Barzan

What George Orwell meant by the word Doublethink in his book "1984".

▶ *"Doublethink means the power of holding two contradictory beliefs in one's mind simultaneously, and accepting both of them."*
— George Orwell

"When you stop to think...

▶ *don't forget to start again!"*

Thank goodness your friends can't read all the thoughts you have about them!

▶ *"If we were all given by magic the power to read each other's thoughts, I suppose the first effect would be to dissolve all friendships."*
— Bertrand Russell

Are first thoughts the wise ones?

▶ *"Second thoughts are ever wiser."*
— Euripides

The smart thing when wrestling with a problem is to write down all your ideas.

▶ *"Just get it down on paper, and then we'll see what to do with it."*

When does man generally ever indulge in the burdensome task of thought?

▶ *"We only think when we are confronted with a problem."*
— John Dewey

"Use Your Head!

▶ *It's the little things that count."*

Have any new thoughts really been said?

▶ *"All my best thoughts were stolen by the ancients."*
— Ralph Waldo Emerson

How the thought process so often leads to forgotten ideas and memories.

▶ *"All thought is a feat of association; having what's in front of you bring up something in your mind that you almost didn't know you knew."*
— Robert Frost

Too much play, food or drink has killed many a person. Has the process of thought ever done the same?

▶ *"Many people have played themselves to death. Many people have eaten and drunk themselves to death. Nobody ever thought himself to death."*
— Gilbert Highet

"Think.

▶ *There must be a harder way!"*

Don't act impulsively without first thinking about the possible damaging consequences!

▶ *"Don't dive into the swimming pool without first seeing if it holds any water"!*

Think before you speak!

▶ *"Never shift your mouth into high gear until you're sure your brain is turning over."*

• THREATENING! •

"Go after a man's weakness, and never, ever, threaten unless you're going to follow through, because...

▶ *if you don't, the next time you won't be taken seriously."*
— Roy M. Cohn

Don't threaten if you can't back it up!

▶ *"Don't let your will roar when your power only whispers."*

— Thomas Fuller

• TIME •

The eternity of TIME.

▶ *"High up in the North in the land of Svithjod, there stands a rock. It is a hundred miles high and a hundred miles wide. Once every thousand years a little bird comes to this rock to sharpen its beak. When the rock has thus been worn away, then a single day of eternity will have gone by."*

— Hendric van Loon

The irretrieveable loss of Lost Time.

▶ *"Lost, yesterday, somewhere between Sunrise and Sunset, two golden hours, each set with sixty diamond minutes. No reward is offered for they are gone forever."*

— Horace Mann

Now is a good time!

▶ *"The man who waits for just the right time to start never gets anywhere."*

— Roger W. Babson

When not to use the word "Never".

▶ *"Never is a long time! Never say never!"*

The incredible amount of time you spend sleeping and eating.

▶ *"A man of sixty has spent twenty years in bed and over three years in eating."*

— Arnold Bennett

Why did nature invent Time?

▶ *"Time is nature's way of keeping everything from happening at once."*

"Time heals all wounds.

▶ *Time wounds all heels."*

— Jane Ace

"Dost thou love life?

▶ *Then do not squander time, for that is the stuff life is made of."*

— Benjamin Franklin

"When you kill time...

▶ *you murder opportunity."*

You will never find time for anything.

▶ *If you want time, you must make it."*

"Time won't stand still unless...

▶ *you're waiting for someone."*

Desk Motto on the subject of Time —

▶ *"Right now is a good time!"*

Definition of Time —

▶ *"That which man is always trying to kill, but which ends in killing him."*
— Herbert Spencer

Why you should fovever be conscious of Time.

▶ *"Suspect each moment, for it is a thief tiptoeing away with more than it brings."*
— John Updike

How does Time affect our attitude towards art and towards fashion in terms of beauty and ugliness?

▶ *"Art produces ugly things which frequently become beautiful with time. Fashion, on the other hand, produces beautiful things which always become ugly with time."*
— Jean Cocteau

"It has been said that time is what we want most...

▶ *but use worst."*

"Never a tear bedims the eye...

▶ *that time and patience will not dry."*
— Bret Harte

• TOASTS •

A toast you wish you could make to the After Dinner Speaker —

▶ *"I just wish you live as long as this evening seems to be."*

A toast to My Mother —

▶ *"Here's to the happiest hours of my life —*
Spent in the arms of another man's wife:
My mother!"

Two hearts in one —

▶ "To Alfred and Margaret
— two hearts in one.
May you love each other
as much at the end as at
the beginning"!

Old Scottish toast to the
Bride and Bridegroom —

▶ "May the hinges of friendship never
rust
Or the wings of love lose a feather!"

Toast to House Speaker
Thomas P. O'Neill, Jr.
"If I had a ticket to Heaven and
you didn't have one too...

▶ I'd give up my ticket to Heaven, and go
to hell with you!"

— Ronald Reagan

The Timless "TIME" Toast —

▶ "Once again with love —
yesterday — today — and
tomorrow."

To a woman of taste.

▶ "I pay tribute now to a woman
of taste, who displays before
you all, her unspoken but
eloquent great taste in
having chosen me as her mate."

Joys and Troubles —

▶ "May your joys be as deep as the
ocean
And your troubles as light as its foam!"

The Horn of Life —

▶ "May you enjoy the horn of life without
blowing it!"

Champagne and Caviar —

▶ "May you have champagne wishes
and caviar dreams!"

— Robert Leach

May you Live —

▶ "May you live all the days of your life!"

— Jonathan Swift

Toast to The Bride —

▶ "Here's to the health of a lovely bride
May happiness be always at her side
And may each day of married bliss
Be as sweet and as loving as all this!"

A Dinner Toast —

▶ "I drink to the general joy of the
whole table."

— William Shakespeare

1000 Happinesses —

▶ *"A thousand happinesses to you!"*

Toast to Your Wife —

▶ *"My wife is magic
Pure and sweet
For she alone —
Makes life complete."*

The Wind and the Sun —

▶ *"May the Wind be always at your
back.
May the Sun shine warm upon your
face!"*

Wishing Joy —

▶ *"I wish you all the joy that you
can wish."*

— William Shakespeare

I Fill this Cup —

▶ *"I fill this cup to one made
up of loneliness alone."*

To a Man and a Woman —

▶ *"Here's to a man and woman. Before
marriage a King and a Queen. After
marriage — two subjects!"*

A North American Indian
toast —

▶ *"May your horses always be swift —
your buffalo abound — and your
women live long and always look
young!"*

Wrinkles —

▶ *"From here forward — may the
wrinkles on your brow come mainly
from smiles!"*

The Best Years —

▶ *"I have given you the best years of my
life — but it was you who made it
possible."*

The Winds and Waves —

▶ *"May the winds and waves navigate
you to tranquil seas!"*

Days of contentment

▶ *"I wish you as many days of
contentment as you can count."*

More than Yesterday —

▶ *I Love You more than yesterday; less
than tomorrow."*

May the Happiest Days —

▶ *"May the happiest days of your past
Be the saddest days of your future!"*

A beautiful toast and
expression of Love —

▶ *"Drink to me only with thine eyes,*
And I will pledge with mine;
Or leave a kiss but in the cup,
And I'll not look for wine."

— Ben Jonson

Indebted —

▶ *"To whom I'm indebted for making life*
worth living."

The Scissors Toast.
"Here's to marriage, that happy
estate that resembles a pair of
scissors...

▶ *So joined that they cannot be*
separated; often moving in opposite
directions, yet punishing anyone who
comes between them."

— Sydney Smith

Toast to a Dinner Guest —

▶ *"Sit down and feed and welcome to*
our table."

— William Shakespeare

Never Above You —

▶ *"Never above you*
Never below you
Always beside you."

As You Slide Down —

▶ *"As you slide down the banister of life,*
may the splinters never point your
way!"

An Alcoholic Toast —

▶ *"Smile and the whole world smiles*
with you. Swear off, and you drink
alone."

Dame Fortune —

▶ *"May Dame Fortune ever smile*
on you;
But never her step-daughter —
Miss Fortune!"

The four "L's."

▶ *"May the fates inspire you to*
Live - Laugh - Learn and Love"!

Roses and Thorns —

▶ *"May those who enter the rosy paths*
of matrimony never meet with thorns!"

An Eskimo Toast —

▶ *"May you have warmth in your igloo*
— oil in your lamp — and peace in
your heart!"

A toast to Friendship —

▶ *"May the hinges of friendship never grow rusty!"*

Many Tomorrows —

▶ *"May you have many more tomorrows!"*

To My Wife —

▶ *"My pleasure and my torment. But the Empress of my Heart."*

Facetious Toast —

▶ *"May you live forever and may the last voice you hear be mine!"*

Toast to a Second Marriage —

▶ *"Here's to a second marriage — the triumph of hope over experience."*
— Samuel Johnson

New Year's Toast —

▶ *"May all your troubles in the coming year be as short lived as your New Year's resolutions!"*

May the Wind —

▶ *"May the wind at your back always be your own!"*

• TOLERANCE •

When my friends have a limited I.Q. should I try to make allowances for them?

▶ *"When my friends are blind of one eye, I look at them in profile."*

"The responsibility of tolerance lies with...

▶ *those who have the wider vision."*
— George Eliot

"Be tolerant towards people.

▶ *Remember adults are only tall children."*

• TOTALITARIANISM •

Is history moving on the side of totalitarianism?

▶ *"Almost certainly we are moving into an age of totalitarian dictatorships. An age in which freedom of thought will be at first a deadly sin and later on a meaningless abstraction. The autonomous individual is going to be stamped out of existence."*
— George Orwell

• DON'T "TOUCH" •

Sign in a Las Vegas antique auto museum.

▶ *"An antique auto is like another man's wife. Look and admire but — DON'T TOUCH!"*

• TRADITION •

When do people generally do things the traditional way?

▶ *"Tradition is what you resort to when you don't have the imagination to do it the right way."*

"There is no sadder or more frequent obituary on the pages of time than...

▶ *we have always done it this way."*

• TRAGEDY •

When tragedy strikes — time can bring relief.

▶ *"The darkest hour has only 60 minutes."*

• TRANSCENDENTAL MEDITATION •

"Transcendal Meditation is the effort to think of nothing.

▶ *That's easy for you! You've been doing it for most of your life."*

• TRAVEL •

There is always educational value to travel.

▶ *"How much a dunce that has been sent to roam/Excels the dunce that stays at home".*
— William Cowper

Sometimes, travelling abroad is more burden and fatigue than pleasure. Is it always worth it?

▶ *"It is not worthwhile to go around the world to count the cats in Zanzibar."*
— Henry David Thoreau

"As the man on the Titanic said to the bartender...

▶ *how about some more ice!"*

Is travel a trade-off? You replace the daily demands of your job with line-ups, legwork at the airport, the bank, and your luggage.

▶ *"A sweet landscape must sometimes atone for an indifferent supper, and an interesting ruin charm away the remembrance of a hard bed."*

— H.H. Tuckerman

Instructions in a Japanese auto rental agreement.

▶ *"When passenger of foot heave in sight, tootle the horn. Trumpet him melodiously at first, but if he still obstacles your passage then tootle him with vigor."*

"Who travels fastest travels alone." — Rudyard Kipling But...

▶ *"Who travels alone, without lover or friend/But hurries from nothing to nought in the end."*

— Ella Wheeler Wilcox

Guide to returning from a foreign country, disgruntled and without cultural gain.

▶ *"Apply the standard of your own culture to that of the country you are visiting"!*

Sign on the door of a hotel room in Hong Kong —

▶ *"Let us know about any unficiency as well as leaking on the service. Our utmost will improve."*

As in reading road maps, when we try to read which path in life to take — the signs become obscured.

▶ *"No matter where we travel, be It North, or South or East, Our highway takes its crucial jog Just where the map is creased.*

— Betty Isler

How to make air travel less dangerous.

▶ *"Air travel will be much safer when they eliminate the automobile ride between the city and the airport."*

How to fully appreciate travel.

▶ *A traveller without observation is a bird without wings.*

Wherever you travel, is there a basic sameness in all of nature?

▶ *"See one promontory, one mountain, one sea, one river, and see all."*

— Socrates

The easiest way to refold a road map is...

▶ *"Differently!"*

People travel for pleasurable relaxation — for an experience — or to enrich their minds.

▶ *"I travel not to go anywhere, but to go. I travel for travel's sake. The great affair is to move."*

— Robert Louis Stevenson

Airlines! Beware of this becoming a slogan!

▶ *"Got time to spare? Go by air"!*

Have you ever been caught off guard answering the door in your hotel room?

▶ *"Do Not Disturb signs should be written in the language of the hotel maids."*

Sign on Mexican tourist bus at door as you are getting off.

▶ *"Don't you forget anything"??*

• A TRIBUTE •

"He was a shooting star.

▶ *We'll long live in his afterglow."*

• TROUBLE •

"Don't look for trouble. It'll be like...

▶ *popping a cork in a champagne bottle. Once it's out, you won't get it back in"!*

While you still have time, should you not look back and philosophize on all the troubles in life that came your way?

▶ *"When I look back on all these worries I remember the story of the old man who said on his deathbed that he had had a lot of trouble in his life, most of which had never happened."*

— Winston Churchill

"If you want to forget your troubles...

▶ *wear tight shoes"!*

If your system works for you, don't look for trouble. Don't try to improve it.

▶ *"If it ain't broke don't fix it."*

"I have never met a man who has given me as much trouble as...

▶ *myself."*

"Never bear more than one trouble at a time.

▶ *Some people bear three kinds — all they have had, all they have now, and all they expect to have."*

— Edward Everett Hale

"Whether you're looking for trouble or for success, remember...

▶ what goes around, comes around."

"If everything seems to be going well...

▶ you have obviously overlooked something!"

Who does you the most mischief — enemies or friends?

▶ "In life it is difficult to say who do you the most mischief, enemies with the worst intentions, or friends with the best."
— Edward Bulwer-Lytton

Would you trade "your" misfortunes for the average other guy's misfortunes?

▶ "If all our misfortunes were laid in one common heap, whence every one must take an equal portion, most people would be content to take their own and depart."
— Solon

"I'm always saying things that get me into a mess.

▶ I'm one of those guys who's going to die of throat trouble. They're going to hang me."
— Harold Ballard

"Troubles are like babies.

▶ They only grow by nursing."

"He that seeks trouble...

▶ always finds it!"

"Once you open a can of worms...

▶ they'll multiply and you'll need a bigger can to recan them."

Guide to keeping out of trouble.

▶ "It is easier to stay out than get out."
— Mark Twain

"Don't look for trouble! Once the toothpaste is out of the tube...

▶ it's going to be hard to get it back in."

How to avoid making trouble for yourself.

▶ "A closed mouth gathers no foot."

Who does trouble generally rain on?

▶ "Trouble will rain on those who are already wet."

My Troubles are tripping all over each other.

▶ "One woe doth tread upon another's heel, so fast they follow."
— William Shakespeare

Which people drive us up the wall most?

▶ *"The people we care for the most give us the most trouble."*
— George Santayana

Why you should never tell your Troubles to others.

▶ *"Half of them aren't the least bit interested, and the rest are delighted that you're getting what they think is coming to you."*

• TRUST •

When should you stop trusting a person?

▶ *"Trust not him that hath once broken faith."*
— William Shakespeare

Should you trust money?

▶ *"Put not your trust in money. Put your money in trust!"*
— Oliver Wendell Holmes

Guide to whom you should trust least.

▶ *"He who mistrusts most should be trusted least."*
— Theognis

Never trust an agreement with anybody untrustworthy — unless you've got some clout to follow up with as protection!

▶ Mr. Fox says to Mr. Cock, *"All the animals have agreed to live in peace with one another."* Then the cunning Mr. Fox tries to persuade Mr. Cock to come down from his perch.
— Aesop

Should you always trust the handwriting on the wall?

▶ *"The handwriting on the wall may be a forgery."*
— Ralph Hodgson

The guiding principle by which the U.S.A. and Russia trust each other.

▶ *"Trust but verify"*!

"There's only one person more foolish than the man who trusts nobody.

▶ It's the man who trusts everybody."

• TRUTH •

"The best part about the truth is...

▶ *that you don't have to remember what you said."*

Is a man smart to tell his wife about his unfaithful misadventures?

▶ *"He knows little who will tell his wife all he knows."*
— Samuel Johnson

When should I prefer to please one person in preference to the multitude?

▶ *"When I have a difficult subject before me — when I find the road narrow, and can see no other way of teaching a well-established truth except by pleasing one intelligent man and displeasing ten thousand fools — I prefer to address myself to the one man and to take no notice whatever of the condemnation of the multitude."*
— Moses Maimonides

In what age group will you find most truthtelling?

▶ *"Pretty much all the honest truthtelling there is in the world is done by children."*

"The best way to keep one's word is...

▶ *not to give it."*
— Napoleon

Does anybody in court ever tell the whole truth?

▶ *"No witnesses except God could tell the truth, the whole truth and nothing but the truth, and up to now He has not appeared in any court as a witness."*

"The girl who lays all her cards on the table is...

▶ *usually left playing solitaire."*

"Every truth passes through three stages before it is recognized.

▶ *In the first it is ridiculed, in the second it is opposed, in the third it is regarded as self-evident."*
— Arthur Schopenhauer

"I want everyone to tell me the truth...

▶ *even if it costs him his job."*
— Sam Goldwyn

"The truth of a thing does not become greater by its frequent repetition.

▶ *Nor is it lessened by lack of repetition."*
— Moses Maimonides

Truth will prevail.

▶ *"No army can stop an idea whose time has come!"*

— Victor Hugo

How truthful should you be to your friends?

▶ *"Why upset your friends by lying to them. Tell them the truth and lose them completely!"*

"Let the truth and right by which you are apparently the loser be preferable to you...

▶ *to the falsehood and wrong by which you are apparently the gainer."*

— Moses Maimonides

Do things said in anger often reveal the truth?

▶ *"Never forget what a man has said to you when he was angry."*

— Henry Ward Beecher

"What is a lie?

▶ *" 'Tis but
The truth in masquerade."*

— Lord Byron

Is it sometimes too damaging to tell the truth?

▶ *"The truth is often so dangerous it needs a bodyguard of lies."*

— Sir Winston Churchill

• TRY! •

Try enough times and one of them may work!

▶ *"I think and think for months and years. Ninety-nine times, the conclusion is false. The hundredth time I am right."*

— Albert Einstein

"Trying times are...

▶ *no time to quit trying."*

Despite repeated failure, if you keep trying, one of them will ultimately pay off.

▶ *"If you plow the land long enough, you have to be able to harvest sometime."*

— Chinese proverb

"If at first you don't succeed...

▶ *Cry, Cry again!"*

Try — even if you can't achieve perfection!

▶ *"Better to do something imperfectly than do nothing perfectly."*

"Fanaticism consists in redoubling your efforts when...

▶ *you have forgotten your aim."*

— George Santayana

That last tiny effort may make the difference.

▶ *"Water boils at 212 Fahrenheit. At 213 (one degree higher) it makes steam."*

• TWICE •

Definition of Twice —

▶ *"Twice is once too often!"*

— Ambrose Bierce

• TYRANNY •

Which tyranny has harmed mankind most throughout history?

▶ *"And of all plagues with which mankind are curst, Ecclesiastic tyranny's the worst."*

— Daniel Defoe

U

• SO UGLY! •

"He's so ugly that...

▶ *when snakes see things they see him."*

"Better an ugly face than...

▶ *an ugly mind."*

"He's so ugly that...

▶ *when you look up the word Ugly in the dictionary — his picture is there."*

"She's not pretty! She's not ugly but...

▶ *she's pretty ugly!"*

"She's so ugly...

▶ *when she goes on a trip — her makeup kit weighs more than she does."*

Need any woman ever appear unattractive?

▶ *"There are no ugly women. There are only women who do not know how to look pretty."*
— La Bruyère

"She's so ugly that...

▶ *when she takes off her makeup her dog throws up."*

• ULCERS •

"If you haven't developed ulcers...

▶ *you're not carrying your share of the load."*

To what extent does your food cause ulcers?

▶ *"You don't get ulcers from what you eat, but from what's eating you."*

• THE ULTIMATUM •

What is an Ultimatum in international affairs?

▶ *"An ultimatum in diplomacy is a last demand before resorting to concessions."*
— Ambrose Bierce

• THE UMPIRE •

Remark after a rookie baseball player threw his bat into the air to protest a called strike.

▶ *"Son, if that bat comes down, you're out of the game."*
— Bill Guthrie

• UNDERSTANDING •

"It's not easy to make yourself really understandable but...

▶ *it's easy to be hard to understand."*

I understand. But do you?

▶ *"I know that you believe you understand what you think I said, but, I am not sure you realize that what you heard is not what I meant."*

• THE UNITED NATIONS •

Despite its defects, the United Nations still serves a valuable function.

▶ *"This organization (the United Nations) is created to prevent you from going to hell. It isn't created to take you to heaven."*
— Henry Cabot Lodge

Is the United Nations, with all its flaws, still worth nurturing?

▶ *"To write off the United Nations' achievements in keeping the peace because of its inability to be effective in Czechoslovakia or Vietnam, would be like writing off medical science because it has not yet found a cure for cancer."*
— George Bush

• UNITY •

What to do when discord threatens the unity of a group.

▶ *"Let us all hang together, or we shall most assuredly all hang separately."*
— Ben Franklin

• THE UNIVERSE •

How many stars are there in space?

▶ *"Put three grains of sand inside a vast cathedral, and the cathedral will be more closely packed with sand than space is with stars."*

— Sir James Jeans

Did the universe just evolve by sheer chance?

▶ *"That the universe was formed by a fortuitous concourse of atoms, I will no more believe than that the accidental jumbling of the alphabet would fall into a most ingenious treatise of philosophy."*

— Jonathan Swift

Is life decided by a master plan?

▶ *"I can't believe that God plays dice with the universe."*

— Albert Einstein

Why we can't find the answer to the mystery of the universe.

▶ *"The universe is like a safe to which there is a combination, but the combination is locked up in the safe."*

— Peter de Vries

• UN-PLANNED! •

How to announce an impromptu rap session.

▶ *"The following discussion is going to be random, unstructured, and discursive."*

— David Brinkley

• THE U.S.A. •

The gigantic ethnic mix of non whites in the U.S.A. gives new reality to the Latin slogan engraved on U.S. coins.

▶ *"E PLURIBUS UNUM",
one formed from many.*

The nobility of the American Constitution.

▶ *"The American constitution is the most wonderful work ever struck off at a given time by the brain and purpose of man."*

— William Gladstone

"It's the responsibility of the media to look at the president with a microscope, but...

▶ *they go too far when they use a proctoscope."*
— Richard M. Nixon

A statement President Nixon would prefer not to have said.

▶ *"In all my years of public life I have never obstructed justice."*
— Richard M. Nixon

That which might have been beneficial for some other USA presidents to have said.

▶ *"If nominated I will not accept; if elected I will not serve."*
— William Tecumseh Sherman

What is more exciting than the American presidential campaign?

▶ *"There is no excitement anywhere in the world, short of war, to match the excitement of the American presidential campaign."*
— Theodore White

"Years ago, North America was a melting pot.

▶ *Today it's a pressure cooker."*

The obsequious attitude the office of the USA presidency commands.

▶ *When the President says "Jump!" they only ask, "How high?"*
— John Ehrlichman

Is it true that when America sneezes, the whole world catches a cold?

▶ *"America is a large friendly dog in a small room. Every time it wags its tail it knocks over a chair."*
— Arnold Toynbee

"The motto of the U.S. Postal Service.

▶ *Neither snow nor rain nor heat nor gloom of night stays these couriers from the swift completion of their appointed rounds."*
— Herodotus

After the Bay of Pigs disaster, the popularity of President Kennedy miraculously rose in the polls. He commented to his press secretary...

▶ *"Do you think I have to keep doing stupid things to be popular?"*

Motto of the prestigious New York Times — ▶ *"All the news that's fit to print."*
— Adolph Ochs

"The government of the United States is not in any sense founded upon... ▶ *the Christian religion."*
— John Adams

From John Nance Garner — "The Vice-Presidency of the United States isn't worth a pitcher of warm spit." ▶ *"Once there were two brothers: one ran away to sea, the other was elected Vice-President — and nothing was ever heard from either of them again."*
— Thomas Marshall

A remark he'll always regret. ▶ *"I am not a crook."*
— Richard M. Nixon

The economic injustice of the American Negro. ▶ *"Last hired — first fired."*

"The size of the U.S. National Debt is... ▶ *equivalent to a stack of $1000 bills 67 miles high."*
— Ronald Reagan

White America is fast becoming a minority group tracing its source — not from Europe — but from the Hispanic world, Africa, the Pacific Islands, Asia, and Arabia. ▶ *"Once America was a microcosm of European nationalities. Today America is a microcosm of the world."*
— Molefi Asante

"The President cannot adequately handle his responsibilities and is overworked. It is humanly impossible under the system we have... ▶ *for him fully to carry out his constitutional duty as Chief Executive. I can testify to this."*
— Franklin D. Roosevelt

"No duty the President has to perform is so trying as... ▶ *to put the right man in the right place."*
— Thomas Jefferson

• USELESS •

He's utterly useless to me. ▶ *"He's the hole in the doughnut."*

"He needs it like... ▶ *a moose needs a hatrack!"*

V

• VACATIONS •

Effects of a vacation.

▶ *"No man needs a vacation so much as the person who has just had one."*

While on vacation, does it sometimes seem that others are having such a wonderful time?

▶ *"Your friends don't have any better times on their vacations than you do on yours."*
— William Feather

"If you really look like your passport photo...

▶ *you're not well enough to travel."*

"Those who visit foreign nations, but associate only with their own countrymen, change their climate, but not their customs.

▶ *They return home with travelled bodies, but untravelled minds."*
— Charles Caleb Colton

"Wouldn't it be nice if two weeks on a vacation...

▶ *would seems as long as two weeks on a diet!"*

"The haves can afford vacations.

▶ *The have-nots can't even afford to stay home."*

"My idea of a vacation is...

▶ *to rest quietly in the shade of a blonde."*

Travel is recreation, sampling local food, and observng new cultures — even though attendant stress.

▶ *"The bee, though it finds every rose has a thorn, comes back loaded with honey from his rambles, and why should not other tourists do the same"?*

— Thomas Haliburton

Sign offering a tour of Zurich —

▶ *"Take One Of Our Horse-Driven City Tours — We Guarantee No Miscarriages."*

Is there any place like "Home Sweet Home?"

▶ *"Never any weary traveller complained that he came too soon to his journey's end."*

— Thomas Fuller

"Recreation and vacation are important.

▶ *People who cannot find time for recreation are obliged sooner or later to find time for illness."*

— John Wanamaker

About your trip —

▶ *"I'm getting jet lag just listening to you!"*

"When my luggage and I go on vacations...

▶ *my luggage often goes to more places than I do!"*

Where not to take vacations.

▶ *"Never take vacations To visit relations."*

— Gerald Barzan

A Resort —

▶ *"A hotel where nobody knows how unimportant you are at home."*

"He who will not read up on his destination will...

▶ *get the least out of his visitation."*

Discussing our next vacation.

▶ *"We're not going to go around the world this year. We did that last year. Let's go somewhere else."*

• VARIETY •

"Variety is the spice of life...

▶ *that gives it all its flavour."*

— William Cowper

• THE VEGETARIAN •

How to make more people become vegetarians.

▶ *"If modern civilized man had to kill the animals he eats, the number of vegetarians would rise astronomically."*

— Christian Morgenstern

• VENGEANCE •

How you should handle vengeance.

▶ *"Vengeance is a dish that should be eaten cold."*

• VENTUROUSNESS •

What will a gal respond more to? Timidity — or Venturousness?

▶ *"He who begs timidly courts a refusal."*

— Seneca

• THE VETERINARIAN •

Sign in veterinarian's office —

▶ *"Doctor will be back shortly. SIT. STAY!"*

• VICTORY! •

A Pyrrhic Victory is a victory won at staggering losses.

▶ *Comment by Pyrrhus king of Epirus, after "defeating" the Romans at Asculum: "Another such victory and we are ruined."*

• VIRTUE •

What is the parent of all the other virtues?

▶ *"A thankful Heart is not only the greatest virtue, but the parent of all the other virtues."*

— Cicero

"Some virtue is needed.

▶ *But not too much. Excess in anything is a defect."*

All robber barons first made money. Then followed virtue and respect.

▶ *"First secure an independent income; then practice virtue."*

— Greek saying

Machiavelli on how a government leader should practice virtue.

▶ *"Assume a virtue if you have it not, for everyone sees what you appear to be, but few feel it."*

— Niccolo Machiavelli

Will being virtuous and not having vices necessarily win admiration?

▶ *"He has all the virtues I dislike and none of the vices I admire."*

— Winston Churchill

"The soldier's virtue is...

▶ *Ambition."*

— William Shakespeare

• VISION •

Three men's opinions over a span of 30 centuries on "What is Vision"?

▶ 1. *"Where there is no vision the people perish."*

— Bible

▶ 2. *"Some people see things as they are and ask why. I dream dreams that never were and ask why not."*

— George Bernard Shaw

▶ 3. *"Scientific management and computers will never reduce the importance of the effective dreamer."*

— Herman C. Krannert

The attitude of two stone-cutters when asked by a bystander: "What are you doing"?

—*Stonecutter number one:* "I'm cutting this massive stone into a block."
—*Stonecutter number two:* "I'm part of a team that's building this cathedral."

• VISITING •

In what two ways do visits always give pleasure?

▶ *"Visits always give pleasure — if not the arrival, the departure!"*

— Portuguese proverb

When somebody is visiting too long —

▶ *"I'd like to help you out. Which way did you come in?"*

"The ideal guest is...

▶ *the one who stays at home."*
— Edgar Howe

If you want to keep visitors away —

▶ *"Visit, that ye be not visited."*
— Don Herold

How often should we be with our friends?

▶ *"If we are long absent from our friends, we forget them; if we are constantly with them, we despise them."*
— William Hazlitt

To someone staying too long.

▶ *"Come back when you have a little less time to spare!"*

• MAN'S "VULNERABILITY" •

"Men are much more unwilling to have their weaknesses and their imperfections known than their crimes.

▶ *And if you hint to a man that you think him silly, ignorant, or even illbred or awkward, he will hate you more and longer than if you tell him plainly that you think him a rogue."*
— Lord Chesterfield

Are people in positions of high visibility the ones most vulnerable?

▶ *"The highest and most lofty trees have the most reason to dread the thunder."*
— Charles Rollin

The difference between a coward and a brave man.

▶ *"A coward dies a thousand deaths. A brave man only once"!*

W

• WAFFLING! •

What happens to Middle of the Roaders?

▶ *"We know what happens to people who stay in the middle of the road. They get run over."*

— Aneurin Bevan

• WAITING! •

"All things come to him who waits.

▶ *But not all things wait for him to come."*

• WAR AND PEACE •

The utopia of world peace that the world yearns for.

▶ *"They shall beat their swords into ploughshares, and their spears into pruning-hooks; nation shall not lift up sword against nation, neither shall they learn war any more."*

— Bible

"The great questions of our day cannot be solved by speeches and majority votes but by...

▶ *blood and iron."*

— Otto von Bismarck

Winston Churchill nearing the end of World War II.

▶ *"It's not the beginning of the end — but the end of the beginning."*

"War does not determine who is right...

▶ *only who is left."*

A heroic attitude to war.

▶ *"I have already given two cousins to the war and I stand ready to sacrifice my wife's brother."*
— Artemus Ward

How does war and peace affect sons and fathers?

▶ *"In peace, sons bury their fathers; in war, fathers bury their sons."*
— Herodotus

Sufficient military strength for a country's protection will generally not have God's disapproval.

▶ *"God is always on the side of the big battalions."*
— Voltaire

Do wars ever settle anything?

▶ *"It simply is not true that war never settles anything."*
— Felix Frankfurter

During war should you over-kill your enemy and will he always remain your enemy?

▶ *"We should ever conduct ourselves towards our enemy as if her were one day to be our friend."*
— Cardinal Newman

The good and bad of War and Peace.

▶ *"There never was a good war or a bad peace."*
— Benjamin Franklin

Philosophy during the Spanish civil war fighting against fascism.

▶ *"Better to die on our feet than beg on our hands."*

What is the goal of War and the goal of Business?

▶ *"The goal of war is peace; of business, leisure."*
— Aristotle

"If Christian nations were nations of Christians...

▶ *there would be no wars."*
— Soame Jenyns

Who cause wars?

▶ *"There are no warlike peoples — just warlike leaders."*
— Ralph J. Bunche

How too many nation states of
the world view war and piece.

▶ *"War ought to be the only study of a
prince; and, by a prince, he means
every sort of state, however
constituted. He ought to consider
peace only as a breathing-time, which
gives him leisure to contrive, and
furnishes ability to execute military
plans."*

— Niccolo Machiavelli

Is mankind basically inclined to
wage war?

▶ *"In the last 3,421 years of recorded
history only 268 have seen no war."*

— Will and Ariel Durant

How to preserve peace.

▶ *"To be prepared for war is one of the
most effectual means of preserving
peace."*

— George Washington

How to win an atomic war.

▶ *"The way to win an atomic war is to
make certain it never starts."*

— Omar Bradley

How can man abolish war?

▶ *"War can only be abolished through
war."*

— Mao Tse-tung

• WARNING! •

Before we malign the fur
industry (craftsmen as well
as trappers) should we not
consider the needs of tens
of thousands of native people...

▶ *whose sole source of
livelihood is trapping"?*

Money borrowed at high rates
for leveraged situations
can be unexpectedly hazardous.

▶ *"Borrowed money never forgets
that the interest rate keeps
ticking"!*

How to perplex the "Break
and Enter" artist.

▶ *"Never mind the dog.
Beware of Owner!"*

"It's better to have your
enemy inside the tent
'spitting' out than...

▶ *outside the tent 'spitting'
in!"*

— Lyndon Johnson

• WEALTH AND POWER •

The man of wealth generally gets his demands!

▶ *"Whoever pays the piper, also calls the tune!"*

"You're really rich if...

▶ *you're not thinking of money."*

• THE WEATHER •

"Don't knock the weather.

▶ *Without it, 9 out of 10 people couldn't start a conversation."*

Is there such a thing as bad weather?

▶ *"Sunshine is delicious, rain is refreshing, wind braces up, snow is exhilarating; there is really no such thing as bad weather, only different kinds of good weather."*
— John Ruskin

The miracle of Spring when the weather smiles and life renews itself.

▶ *"It is March 21. Spring has sprung."*

• THE WEDDING RING •

"A wedding ring is intended to be a circle of love...

▶ *which has no beginning and no ending. It symbolizes the endlessness of love."*

What else besides joy lies inside the wedding ring?

▶ *"Oh! How many torments lie in the small circle of a wedding ring."*
— Colley Cibber

• WELCOME! •

How Australians say — "Welcome and good luck to you!"

▶ *"Good on you, mate — and welcome aboard!"*

How to say "WELCOME."

▶ *French — Bienvenue*
Italian — Benvenuti
Czechoslovak — subte vitani
Portuguese — Benvindo
German — Willkommen!
Polish — Witamy
Spanish — Bienvenida

"He's about as welcome right now as...   ▶ *a broken elbow!"*

• WILLS •

Not to have written a will is the unforegiveable procrastination!

▶ *"A contest between relatives is usually conducted with more acrimony than a dispute with strangers."*

— Latin Proverb

Lawyer reading the will —

▶ *"To be brief — none of you will have to worry about inheritance taxes."*

"Where there's a will there's a way."

▶ *"Where there's a will there's a lawsuit."*

The rich uncle who wrote in his will —

▶ *"Being of sound mind, I spent all my money when I was alive."*

• WILL POWER! •

I have very strong will power.   ▶ *"I can resist everything but temptation."*

— Oscar Wilde

• WINNING •

"It's not whether you win or lose that counts.

▶ *It's how you place the blame."*

"The race is not always to the swift, nor the battle to the strong.

▶ *But that's the way to bet."*

— Damon Runyon

Is it easy to be gracious when you're losing?

▶ *"It's easier to be a gracious winner than a gracious loser."*

Show me a good loser and I'll show you...

▶ *an idiot."*

— Leo Durocher

Which of two players attains victory?

▶ *"Victory goes to the player who makes the next to last mistake."*

— S. Tartakower

Is winning everything?

▶ *"Winning isn't everything — it's the only thing."*

— Vince Lombardi

"Win any way you can as long as you can get away with it.

▶ *Nice guys finish last."*

— Leo Durocher

How so many of us don't become Number One?

▶ *"The world is made of people who never quite get into the first team and who just miss the prizes at the flower show."*

— J. Bronowski

Winners versus quitters.

▶ *"A winner never quits
A quitter never wins."*

How do most of us react to losers and winners?

▶ *"Most of us hate to see a poor loser — or a rich winner."*

— Harold Coffin

"Don't look back.

▶ *Something may be gaining on you."*

— Satchel Paige

An oft used guote by former British Prime Minister Harold Macmillan.

▶ *"There's nothing worth the
wear of winning,
But laughter and the love of
friends."*

— Hilaire Belloc

Which sensation is more intense — Winning or Losing?

▶ *"Losing hurts worse than winning feels good!"*

• WISDOM •

Is common sense the result of education?

▶ *"Common sense is in spite of, not the result of, education."*

— Victor Hugo

Insult to or about somebody feigning wisdom.

▶ *"Don't mistake the ferment of an empty brain for the germination of an idea!"*

Is a silent man often thought to be a deep thinking man?

▶ *"Silence does not always mean wisdom."*

— Samuel Taylor Coleridge

The limits of wisdom
relating to your teeth!

▶ *"For there was never yet
philosopher that could endure
the toothache patiently."*
— William Shakespeare

"It is easier to be wise for
others than...

▶ *for oneself."*
— French proverb

Respect age but should you
necessarily endow age with
wisdom?

▶ *"The older I get, the more
I distrust the familiar doctrine
that age brings wisdom."*
— H.L. Mencken

How prevalent is the
existence of common sense?

▶ *"Common sense is very uncommon."*
— Horace Greeley

"Wisdom is meaningless until
your own experience has given
it meaning...

▶ *and there is wisdom in the selection
of wisdom."*
— Bergen Evans

"Wisdom comes from doing
battle with life's problems...

▶ *not from simply reading about them."*

The relationship of gray hair
and age.

▶ *"Gray hair is a sign of age — not
wisdom."*

• WISHING! •

"Many of us spend half
our time wishing for things
we could have if...

▶ *we didn't spend half our
time wishing."*
— Alexander Woollcott

Stop sitting and wishing!

▶ *"Sitting and wishing
Doesn't make one great;
The Lord made good fishing
But you've got to dig the bait."*

Merely wishing won't get
results.

▶ *"If wishes were horses, beggars would
be riders."*

"Some people wish they were
dead.

▶ *I wish I was alive."*

• WIT •

Definition of wit:
"The ability to perceive
in an ingeniously humorous
manner the relationship
or similarity between...

▶ *seemingly incongruous or
disparate things."*

The true meaning of Wit as
against Humour.

▶ *"Wit consists in knowing the
resemblance of things which differ —
and the difference of things which are
alike."*
— Madame de Stael

That which true wit is
intended to do.

▶ *"Wit is a sword; it is meant to make
people feel the point as well as see it."*
— G. K. Chesterton

"Wit is the salt of
conversation...

▶ *not the food."*
— William Hazlitt

To be witty, you need
keenness of perception, or
discernment, ingenuity and
resourcefulness.

▶ *"Wit is the product of art
and fancy."*
— William Hazlitt

Wit is only wit when used
in the context of the subject
being discussed at that
moment, and must have the
element of surprise.

▶ *"The original electrical feeling
produced by any piece of wit
can never be renewed.*
— Sydney Smith

• WOMEN •

Women's beauty and men's
wealth are both transient.

▶ *"There should be as little merit in loving
a woman for her beauty, as a man for
his prosperity, both being equally
subject to change."*
— Alexander Pope

"It is easier for a woman to
defend her virtue against men
than...

▶ *her reputation against women."*

How naked women look best.

▶ "Naked women always look better
with something on."
— W.S. Gladstone

"There was once a girl who
didn't have much upstairs.

▶ But, Oh! What a stairway!"

What Biblical reference
proves that woman can be a
temptress and a villain at the
same time?

▶ "Woman is at once apple and
serpent!"
— Henrich Heine

Women's LIB has put women
in positions of high profile,
and to the astonishment of
the male world, has revealed
that women's brains are the
same size as men's.

▶ "If you would reform the
world from its errors and vices,
begin by enlisting the mothers."
— Charles Simmons

Where does woman rate on
the scale of evolution?

▶ "Woman is nature's most
exasperating but beautiful accident."
— Carey Stephen

I shouldn't have left her.

▶ "Left Right — Left Right —
The girl that I left
Is the girl that was right."

Why many intellectuals love
dumb women.

▶ "I love thee for a heart that's kind
Not for the knowledge in thy mind."
— W.H. Davies

How do men react to a girl
who has too much I.Q.?

▶ "Men seldom makes passes at a girl
who surpasses."
— Franklin P. Jones

She has a beautiful figure.

▶ "She is a symphony of curves — all
sharps and no flats."
— B. Michèle

"It's the warm girls who get
the fur coats...

▶ not the cold ones."

"A woman's place is...

▶ in a home."

The stages of a woman's life.

▶ *"In various stages of her life, a woman resembles the continents of the world. From 13 to 18, she's like Africa — virgin territory, unexplored; from 18 to 30, she's like Asia — hot and exotic; from 30 to 45, she's like America — fully explored free with her resources; from 45 to 55, she's like Europe — exhausted, but not without places of interest; after 55, she's like Australia — everybody knows it's down there but nobody much cares."*

— Al Boliska

A philosophy for "girls" to ponder.

▶ *"Good girls go to Heaven, Bad girls go Everywhere!"*

To what degree should any woman ever hate a man?

▶ *"I never hated a man enough to give him his diamonds back."*

— Zsa Zsa Gabor

"The problem of looking for the perfect woman is...

▶ *that she's probably looking for the perfect man."*

"It is true that women live longer than men...

▶ *especially widows."*

Women can aspire to the same lofty positions as men without practicing male macho masculinity!

▶ *"Men are inspired by the kindness, the tenderness, the nurturing qualities of women. A soft female voice can draw as much attention and have as much effect as a masculine shout."*

— Sheila Graham

"Where did she develop that personality of hers...

▶ *in a car crash?"*

Female Curve —

▶ *"The loveliest distance between two points."*

The woman who doesn't want her virtue taken advantage of had better speak up.

▶ *"She who is silent consents."*

— French proverb

A double entendre about
ladies.

▶ *"If all the young ladies who attended
the Yale promenade dance were laid
end to end, no one would be the least
surprised."*

— Alexander Woollcott

How to win a woman.

▶ *"Don't tell a woman she's pretty.
Tell her there's no other woman like
her, and all roads will open to you."*

— Jules Renard

• WORDS •

It's not what you name it. It's
what it is that counts.

▶ *"What's in a name? That which we call
a rose
By any other name would smell as
sweet."*

— William Shakespeare

You may never get the chance
to say it again.

▶ *"Value your words. Each one may be
the last."*

There's no greater sign of
an uneducated man than the
the wrong use of a big word!

▶ *"Before employing a fine
word, find a place for it."*

— Joseph Joubert

Famous last words —
"Toulousse Lautrec's tailor
once said...

▶ *"Is your belt too tight Toulousse?"*

"The difference between the
right word and the almost right
word is...

▶ *the difference between lightning and
the lightning bug."*

— Mark Twain

Nobody should ever forget
simplicity in writing business
letters.

▶ *Say "Haste makes waste!" not
"Precipitation entails negation of
economy."*

"For it comes to pass oft
that a terrible oath, with
a swaggering accent sharply
twanged off, gives manhood...

▶ *more approbaton than ever
proof itself would have
earned him."*

— William Shakespeare

The right word at the right
time is beautiful.

▶ *"One good word is worth a thousand
pictures."*

The power of words.

▶ "I am by calling a dealer in words, and words are, of course, the most powerful drug used by mankind."
— Rudyard Kipling

Teach children vocabulary at an early age.

▶ To speak well supposes a habit of attention which shows itself in the thought; by language we learn to think and above all to develop thought.
— Carl Victor de Bonstetten

"If you would be pungent, be brief...

▶ for it is with words as with sunbeams — the more they are condensed the deeper they burn."
— Robert Southey

Surprise!
There are actually some good four letter words.

▶ "Help,
Give,
Care,
Feel,
and Love."

Say what you mean and don't use Big Words.

▶ The same thought using big words —

"In promulgating your esoteric cogitations or articulating your superficial sentimentalities and amicable, philosophical or psychological observations, beware of platitudinous ponderosity. Let your conversational communications demonstrate a clarified conciseness, a compact comprehensibleness, no coalescent conglomerations of precocious garrulity, jejune bafflement or asinine affectation. Let your extemporaneous verbal evaporations and expatiations have lucidity, intelligibility and veracious vivacity without rodomontade or Thespian bombast. Sedulously avoid all polysyllabic profundity, pompous propensity, psittaceous vacuity, ventriloquial verbosity and vaniloquent vapidity. Shun double-entendre, obnoxious jocosity and pestiferous profanity, observable or apparent."

How good it is to find a
beautiful word correctly used!

▸ *"Nothing is rarer than the use of a
word in its exact meaning."*

The difference between
Loneliness and Solitude.

▸ *"Language has created the word
loneliness to express the pain of being
alone, and the word solitude to
express the glory of being alone."*
— Paul Tillich

"Kind words are never
lost...

▸ *they keep gong from one person
to another — until they finally
come back to you."*
— Douglas Perry

"The reason the Chinese say
One picture is worth a
thousand words is...

▸ *it's so tough to write a thousand words
in Chinese."*

"Swallowing angry words is
much easier than...

▸ *having to eat them."*

The right word can make
a world of difference.

▸ *"A word fitly spoken is
like apples of gold in
pictures of silver."*
— The Bible

"A book on grammar is...

▸ *a book about the way people talk
in books."*

The beauty and unaffected
dynamism of slang.

▸ *"Slang is a language that rolls up its
sleeves, spits on its hands and goes
to work."*
— Carl Sandburg

A new word is introduced
into the American
vocabulary after...

▸ *the first successful mission
into space. "Everything is
'A.O.K.'"*

"One picture is worth a
thousand words, but only if...

▸ *it's the right picture and the wrong
words."*

"There is a great difference
between the right word and the
word that is almost right.

▸ *You can call a woman a kitten, but not
a cat; a mouse, but not a rat; a chicken
but not a hen; a duck, but not a goose;
a vision but not a sight."*

The case against the sloppy use of words.	▶ *"Words are the dress of our thoughts which should no more be presented in rags, tatters and dirt than your person should."* — Lord Chesterfield

• WORK •

"It takes just as much effort to escape work...	▶ *as to do it."*
Revised version of the Peter Principle. "Every loyal employee has his own way of loafing on the job."	▶ *"Work is a nightmare. You want to quit but you need the sleep"!*
"If you want a place in the sun...	▶ *you have to expect some blisters."*
Was it a myth that the Protestant Work Ethic brought dignity?	▶ *"They talk of the dignity of work. Bosh. The dignity is in leisure."* — Herman Melville
The more time you have — the longer it takes you to do the job.	▶ *"Work expands to fill the time available for its completion."* — C. Northcote Parkinson
"The only thing that works...	▶ *is hard work."*
How to work.	▶ *"Work smarter not harder!"*
Until what level does an employee continue to do good work?	▶ *"Work is accomplished by those employees who have not yet reached their level of incompetence."* — Laurence J. Peter
What is the reward of plain hard work versus working with your brain?	▶ *"You can earn bread by the sweat of your brow, but it takes brains to get the cake."*
"Work fascinates me.	▶ *I can look at it for hours."*
What to do if you don't want to work.	▶ *"You have to work to earn enough money so that you won't have to work."* — Ogden Nash

From the "Theory of the Leisure Class" — "The activities of the moneyed class are given society's stamp of approval.

▶ *Labor, by contrast, is regarded as undignified, even by the people who perform it."*
— Thorsten Veblen

No genius knows for sure where his work is leading him.

▶ *"How do I work? I grope."*
— Albert Einstein

Many of the rich don't believe in the Protestant Work Ethic.

▶ *"If hard work were such a wonderful thing, surely the rich would have kept it all to themselves."*
— Lane Kirkland

There is a kind of grease that doesn't soil.

▶ *"Elbow grease; the kind that won't soil a shirt."*
— Gary Moore

When do people like hard work?

▶ *"Most people like hard work, particularly when they're paying for it."*
— Franklin P. Jones

Guide on how to work.

▶ *"Keep your eye on the ball, Your shoulder to the wheel, Your ear to the ground" — Now — try to work in that position!*

Why you can't get hurt with hard work and sweat.

▶ *"Hard work will never kill you, 'Tis said all over town; Sweat is the only liquid In which you cannot drown."*

Has the distaste for work anything to do with the origin and development of civilization?

▶ *"The origin of civilization is man's determination to do nothing for himself which he can get done for him."*
— H.C. Bailey

To a lazy worker —

▶ *"I'd like to compliment you on your work. When will you start?"*

Do women have to work harder than men to earn the same reward?

▶ *"Whatever women do they must do twice as well as men to be thought half as good. Luckily, this is not difficult."*
— Charlotte Whitton

"It is better to have loafed and lost...

▶ *than never to have loafed at all."*
— James Thurber

Philosophy of dodging work
for those who can afford it.

▶ *"Life is too short to do anything for
oneself that one can pay others to do
for one."*

— Somerset Maugham

• OUR WORLD! •

Is our world a nightmare?

▶ *"The more I see of this world in its
present state of ferment, the more
convinced I am, that the Almighty has
set out this sphere of ours as a
madhouse for all the rest of the
universe!"*

— George Bernard Shaw

The difference between
people who think and people
who feel.

▶ *"The world is a comedy to those who
think; a tragedy to those who feel."*

— Horace Walpole

Philosophy of an eight
year old yearning for a
dream world.

▶ *"All the people and me would not
probably want mosquitoes.
Let there be no jerks in
the world."*

— Emily Klassen, Gr. 2

With dictatorships moving
towards democracy, remember...

▶ *——When the ice breaks up,
it can be very dangerous"!*

Maybe we can hope for
peace on earth some day
in this world of ours!

▶ *"Maybe the horse will
learn to fly"!*

• WORRY •

There are two days in every
week about which we should
not worry.

▶ *"It is remorse or bitterness for
something which happened yesterday
and the dread of what tomorrow may
bring, that give us a nervous
breakdown. So forget yesterday and
tomorrow. Battle today only — and
you'll survive!"*

Policy of the ultra
rich in delegating their
financial problems to
hired experts.

▶ *"We deal only with solutions
here — not problems"!*

A good memory test on whether worrying is worth it.

▶ *"What were you worrying about this time last year?"*

For the greatest happiness — what should you stop worrying about?

▶ *"There is only one way to happiness and that is to cease worrying about things which are beyond the power of our will."*
— Epictetus

Which kind of worry affects the brain and which the gut?

▶ *"Little worries are mental, great worries intestinal."*

Worry for the future versus Planning for the future are often confused.

▶ *"He is a wise man who plans for his future — for the plan itself is that which will diminish worry."*
— J. Edward Breslin

What today is in relation to worry.

▶ *"Today is the tomorrow you worried about yesterday.*

Worry and its relationship to bank interest.

▶ *"Worry is the compound interest we pay on trouble before it comes due."*

"She's such a worrier that when she sees the tide go out...

▶ *she wonders if it will ever come back."*

Which worries in life are hardest to bear?

▶ *"Let us be of cheer remembering that the misfortunes hardest to bear are those which never come."*
— James Russell Lowell

What's the reality of most troubles you worry about?

▶ *"If you see ten troubles coming down the road, you can be sure that nine will run into the ditch before they reach you."*
— Calvin Coolidge

"Don't worry about missing the Boat.

▶ *Remember the Titanic?"*

Worry about what your enemy may do to you isn't always imaginary.

▶ *"Even paranoids have real enemies"!*

The futility of worrying.

▶ *"If you think worrying will change a past or future event — you are residing on another planet with a different reality system."*

"She's such a worry wart... ▶ *when she has nothing to worry about — she begins to worry about that.*"

"I've got so many worries that... ▶ *if another problem happened today I wouldn't have time to worry about it for at least 2 weeks.*"

Is there any sense in worrying about things as much as we do? ▶ *"Three out of four things you worry about happening don't happen and three out of four things you don't worry about happening do. Which all goes to prove that even if you're worrying about the wrong things, you're doing just about the right amount of worrying!*"

• WORRY AND STRESS •

How to avoid it! ▶ *"If you can't fight it — Or flee it — Then flow with it!*"

• WRINKLES •

If you're starting to get wrinkles. ▶ *"There is always a lot to be thankful for if you take time to look for it. Right now, I am sitting here thinking how nice it is that wrinkles don't hurt.*"
— James Holt McGavran

"The only pleasant wrinkle is... ▶ *a smile.*"

What, other than age, causes wrinkles? ▶ *"Wrinkles are hereditary. Parents get them from their children.*"

"If you don't have wrinkles... ▶ *you haven't laughed enough.*"

• THE ART OF "WRITING" •

There's no easy path to good writing even by gifted geniuses. ▶ *"Thomas Jefferson spent eighteen days writing and rewriting the Declaration of Independence; Victor Hugo made eleven revisions of one novel; Voltaire was known to spend a whole night toiling over one sentence.*"

How to write clearly — with punch and accuracy.

▶ *"Put it before them briefly, so they will read it; clearly, so they will appreciate it; picturesquely, so they will remember it; and, above all, accurately, so they will be guided by its light."*

— Joseph Pulitzer

Every great writer re-reads, edits, deletes and re-writes.

▶ *"When I re-read I blush, for even I perceive enough that ought to be erased, though it was I who wrote the stuff."*

— Ovid, Roman poet

When should you plagiarize?

▶ *"When a thing has been said and well said, have no scruple; take it and copy it."*

— Anatole France

"What no wife of a writer can ever understand is...

▶ *that a writer is working when he's staring out the window."*

— Burton Rascoe

The difference between Literature and Journalism.

▶ *"Literature is the art of writing something that will be read twice; journalism what will be grasped at once."*

— Cyril Connolly

From "Politics and the English Language" — Five guidelines on how to write:

▶ 1. *"Never use a long word where a short one will do.*
2. *If it is possible to cut out a word, always cut it out.*
3. *Never use the passive where you can use the active.*
4. *Never use a foreign phrase, a scientific word or a jargon word if you can think of an everyday English equivalent.*
5. *Break any of these rules sooner than say anything barbarous."*

— George Orwell

How to be an effective writer.

▶ *"Write something to suit yourself and many people will like it; write something to suit everybody and scarcely anyone will care for it."*

— Jesse Stuart

On the mental drudgery involved in reading long reports —

▶ *"It is sheer laziness not compressing thought into a reasonable space."*
— Winston Chuchill

The significance of a comma in self-evaluation.

▶ *"We are not what we think we are, but what we think, we are."*

It's not by accident that great writers are great.

▶ *"In first-rate writing there is a reason not only for every word but for the position of every word."*

"The tested formula for becoming rich as an author is...

▶ *to write regularly to an uncle who is dying of a surfeit of oil wells."*

"Of all sad words of the writer's pen,

▶ *the saddest are these... I didn't jot it when!"*

Luck can make a man a fortune — but it will never make him a writer.

▶ *"To be a well-favoured man is the gift of fortune; but to write and read comes by nature."*
— William Shakespeare

What's a really tough part of writing?

▶ *"It is often harder to boil down than to write."*
— Sir William Osler

"The obscurity of a writer...

▶ *is generally in proportion to his incapacity."*
— Quintilian

"Your manuscript is both good and original but...

▶ *the parts that are good are not original, and the parts that are original are not good."*
— Samuel Johnson

Michael Caine, playing a writer in the movie *The Romantic Englishwoman* reveals how easy it is to write a book.

▶ *"I've found all the words in the dictionary; now all I have to do is put them in the right order."*

• WRONG! •

Are you sure this is the way to do it?

▶ *"Yes and No — but I could be Wrong!"*
— Steve Allen

"Right is right and...

▶ *wrong is nobody's right"!*

Y

• THE YAWN! •

Does a yawn send a loud message of boredom?

▶ *"A yawn is a silent shout."*

• YEARNING! •

Yearning for a second chance.

▶ *"I wish I were what I was when I wanted to be what I am now."*

"Don't itch for something unless...

▶ *you're willing to scratch for it."*

Z

• THE ZOO •

The Zoo and its relation to people.

▶ *"A zoo is a place where animals study the behaviour of people."*

• THE END •

And now this book ends — "All's Well That Ends Well!"

▶ *"All's Well That Ends!"*

— William Shakespeare

Index of Subjects

A

B

Index of Subjects Continued

Index of Subjects Continued

Index of Subjects Continued

Index of Subjects Continued

Index of Subjects Continued

Index of Subjects Continued

Printed in Canada